COMMUNITIES AND CONNECTIONS
FOR ANCIENT NEAR EAST

In the same series from Bloomsbury:

CLASSICS TEACHING IN EUROPE
edited by John Bulwer

FORWARD WITH CLASSICS
edited by Arlene Holmes-Henderson, Steven Hunt and Mai Musié

STARTING TO TEACH LATIN
by Steven Hunt

TEACHING CLASSICS WITH TECHNOLOGY
edited by Bartolo Natoli and Steven Hunt

COMMUNICATIVE APPROACHES FOR ANCIENT LANGUAGES

Edited by Mair E. Lloyd and Steven Hunt

BLOOMSBURY ACADEMIC
LONDON • NEW YORK • OXFORD • NEW DELHI • SYDNEY

Bloomsbury Publishing Plc
50 Bedford Square, London, WC1B 3DP, UK
1385 Broadway, New York, NY 10018, USA
29 Earlsfort Terrace, Dublin 2, Ireland

BLOOMSBURY, BLOOMSBURY ACADEMIC and the Diana logo are trademarks of
Bloomsbury Publishing Plc

First published in Great Britain 2021

Copyright © Mair E. Lloyd, Steven Hunt and the several contributors, 2021

Mair E. Lloyd, Steven Hunt and the several contributors have asserted their right under the Copyright, Designs and Patents Act, 1988, to be identified as Authors of this work.

For legal purposes the Acknowledgements on p. xi–xii constitute an extension of this copyright page.

Cover design: Terry Woodley
Cover image: Pallas Athene Statue in Vienna, Austria © traveler1116/Getty

All rights reserved. No part of this publication may be reproduced or transmitted in any form or by any means, electronic or mechanical, including photocopying, recording, or any information storage or retrieval system, without prior permission in writing from the publishers.

Bloomsbury Publishing Plc does not have any control over, or responsibility for, any third-party websites referred to or in this book. All internet addresses given in this book were correct at the time of going to press. The author and publisher regret any inconvenience caused if addresses have changed or sites have ceased to exist, but can accept no responsibility for any such changes.

A catalogue record for this book is available from the British Library.

A catalog record for this book is available from the Library of Congress.

ISBN: HB: 978-1-3501-5734-7
PB: 978-1-3501-5733-0
ePDF: 978-1-3501-5736-1
eBook: 978-1-3501-5735-4

Typeset by RefineCatch Ltd, Bungay, Suffolk, NR35 1EF
Printed and bound in Great Britain

To find out more about our authors and books, visit www.bloomsbury.com and sign up for our newsletters.

CONTENTS

List of Figures vii
Notes on Contributors viii
Acknowledgements xi

Introduction Mair E. Lloyd and Steven Hunt 1

Part 1 Introducing Communicative Approaches in School Settings

1 Active Latin in the Classroom: Past, Present and Future *Laura Manning* 9
2 Active Latin Promotes Open-mindedness in Language-learning *David Urbanski* 17
3 Live Latin: Global Experiments in Shakespeare's Classroom *Judith Affleck* 25
4 Communication in All Modes as Efficient Preparation for Reading a Text *Justin Slocum Bailey* 33
5 From Reading to World-Building: Collaborative Content Creation and Classical Language Learning *Justin M. Schwamm, Jr. and Nancy A. Vander Veer* 47
6 Active Latin Teaching for the Inclusive Classroom *Steven Hunt* 55

Part 2 Introducing Communicative Approaches in University Settings

7 Exploring Communicative Approaches for Beginners *Mair E. Lloyd* 67
8 Communicative Latin for All in a UK University *Clive Letchford* 81
9 Active Latin in the Tropics: An Experience with Neo-Latin in Brazil *Leni Ribeiro Leite* 91
10 The Use of *Ludi Domestici* in Communicative Latin *Daniel B. Gallagher* 101
11 Teaching Latin Communicatively to Postgraduate Students *Cressida Ryan* 113

Part 3 Total Immersion in Formal and Informal Settings

12 Global Latin, Active Latin: Kentucky and Beyond *Milena Minkova and Terence Tunberg* 125
13 A Conventiculum for Speakers of Ancient Greek: The Lexington Σύνοδος Ἑλληνική *R. Stephen Hill* 133
14 Teaching Ancient Greek by the Polis Method *Christophe Rico and Michael Kopf* 141

15	Goals and Methods in Teaching Biblical Languages and Exegesis: A View from the Seminary *Daniel R. Streett*	151
16	Latin Teaching in Poland: A New Renaissance with Communicative Approaches? *Sebastian Domagała, Marcin Loch and Katarzyna Ochman*	161
17	Student-led Initiatives at Oxford and Cambridge *Iván Parga Ornelas and Josey Parker*	179

Part 4   Varied Approaches in Unusual Settings

18	New Approaches to Ancient Languages: The Paideia Institute's Pedagogy *Marco Romani Mistretta and Jason Pedicone*	189
19	The *Latinitium* Project *Daniel Pettersson and Amelie Rosengren*	195
20	Primary Language Acquisition of Latin in Bilingual Children: A Case Study *Mallory Ann Hayes and Patrick M. Owens*	203

References	211
List of Abbreviations	223
Index	225

FIGURES

16.1	Plan of the Roman villa. Copyright © Marcin Loch.	166
16.2	Latin and modern languages in state-run schools in Poland. Copyright © Sebastian Domagała, Marcin Loch and Katarzyna Ochman.	173
16.3	Comparison of languages teaching. Copyright © Sebastian Domagała, Marcin Loch and Katarzyna Ochman.	175
20.1	Nominal case acquisition order. Copyright © Mallory Ann Hayes and Patrick M. Owens.	206
20.2	Verb tense acquisition order. Copyright © Mallory Ann Hayes and Patrick. M. Owens.	207
20.3	Mood acquisition order. Copyright © Mallory Ann Hayes and Patrick M. Owens.	207

CONTRIBUTORS

Judith Affleck has taught Classics since 1987 in the UK at Eton College, Harrow School and King Edward VI, Stratford-upon-Avon, respectively. She is a published author for Bloomsbury and other education specialists.

Justin Slocum Bailey is a language teacher, teacher-trainer and curriculum designer based in Michigan, USA. He serves on the board of the North American Institute for Living Latin Studies.

Sebastian Domagała graduated from the University of Warsaw, Poland, with a degree in Applied Linguistics. He teaches English, French and Latin. He is a passionate polyglot, eager to share his enthusiasm for foreign languages. His greatest wish is to make classical literature more accessible by means of the communicative approach.

Daniel B. Gallagher has been the Ralph and Jeanne Kanders Senior Lecturer in Latin at Cornell University, USA, since his retirement from the Vatican's Office of Latin Letters in 2016.

Mallory Ann Hayes teaches Latin at Chesterfield Montessori School outside St. Louis, Missouri, USA. A former Rhodes Scholar, Hayes has taught Latin to students from kindergarten through to high school.

R. Stephen Hill is a PhD student in Classics at the University of Virginia, USA. He earned an MA in Teaching English as a Second Language at the University of Illinois Urbana-Champaign.

Steven Hunt is the Subject Lecturer for the PGCE in Latin (with Classics) at the Faculty of Education, University of Cambridge, UK. He is Editor of the *Journal of Classics Teaching* and a consultant for the charity Classics for All. He has published three books on Classics Education with Bloomsbury Academic.

Michael Kopf has been teaching classical languages through various methodologies at high-school and graduate level since receiving his MA in Ancient Philology from the Polis Institute, Jerusalem, in 2015.

Clive Letchford is a senior teaching fellow in the Department of Classics and Ancient History at the University of Warwick, UK, where he teaches Latin and Greek.

Mair E. Lloyd is a research associate in Latin pedagogy at the Open University, UK, and creates Latin teaching resources at the Cambridge School Classics Project. Publications include her doctoral thesis, *Living Latin: Exploring Communicative Approaches to Latin Teaching* (2017), and *A Survey of Beginner's Language Teaching in UK Classics Departments: Latin* (2018).

Marcin Loch (better known as Martinus) is a lecturer in Adam Mickiewicz University in Poznań, Poland, and leader of the *Schola Aestiva Posnaniensis* (Poznań Summer School). His research interests focus on Latin didactics and Latin sexual vocabulary.

Contributors

Laura Manning researches active Latin language pedagogy at the University of Kentucky, USA, adapting successful teaching practices from the sixteenth and seventeenth centuries for use in present-day classrooms.

Milena Minkova is Professor of Classics at the University of Kentucky, USA. Her most recent publication is a critical anthology of Neo-Latin *Florilegium recentioris Latinitatis* (2018).

Katarzyna Ochman is Assistant Professor of Latin at the University of Wrocław, Poland, and President of the *Societas Philologa Polonorum*. Her research interests include Antonine literature, history of the Latin language and Latin pedagogy.

Patrick M. Owens teaches in the Classics department at Hillsdale College, Michigan, USA. Owens specializes in Neo-Latin literature, language pedagogy and Latin lexicography. He is the editor of the *Morgan-Owens Neo-Latin Lexicon*.

Iván Parga Ornelas is pursuing a PhD in Renaissance Studies at the University of Warwick, UK. He is vice-president of the Oxford Latinitas Project, and a former student and collaborator of the *Accademia Vivarium Novum*.

Josey Parker has just finished her BA in Classics at the University of Cambridge, UK, and will be returning to take an MPhil in the next academic year. Her research interests include Indo-European linguistics, Ciceronian reception, and Renaissance Neo-Latin.

Jason Pedicone is a co-founder and President of the Paideia Institute in New York. He has a PhD in Classics from Princeton University, USA. He teaches Roman History at Fordham University and lives in Manhattan.

Daniel Pettersson is a co-founder of Latinitium.com and is currently writing his doctoral dissertation on language pedagogy in the sixteenth-century *colloquia*. He has taught spoken Latin at universities and schools in Europe and the United States.

Leni Ribeiro Leite is an associate professor of Latin Language and Literature at the Federal University of Espírito Santo, Brazil. Her research interests include Flavian poetry, Neo-Latin in the Americas and Latin teaching.

Christophe Rico is Professor of Greek semantics at the EBAF and Dean of Polis, the Jerusalem Institute of Languages and Humanities. He is the author of *Polis: Speaking Greek as a Living Language* (2015).

Marco Romani Mistretta is Director of European Operations at the Paideia Institute in Rome. He holds a PhD in Classics from Harvard University, USA, and has published widely on ancient intellectual history and its early-modern reception. His research interests focus on science in Graeco-Roman antiquity.

Amelie Rosengren is a co-founder of Latinitium.com, an historian, a published author and a museum educator. Her research has focused on everyday life from antiquity to the early modern era.

Cressida Ryan is Instructor in New Testament Greek at the University of Oxford, UK. Cressida also teaches Latin, with research interests in language pedagogy, the reception of Greek drama and Neo-Latin.

Contributors

Justin M. Schwamm, Jr. taught high-school Latin in North Carolina, USA, from 1992 to 2014. Since 2014 he has worked online with homeschooling families, adult learners and language teachers.

Daniel R. Streett is Associate Professor of Biblical Studies at Houston Baptist University, USA. His research interests focus on Judaism and Christianity in Antiquity. He is the author of *'They Went Out From Us': The Identity of the Opponents in First John* (2011) and *Heavenly Holidays: The Reception of the Jewish Festivals in Early Judaism* (2021).

Terence Tunberg, the founder of the *Conventiculum Latinum Lexintoniense*, a proponent of 'active' Latin for four decades, writes about Latin prose style from antiquity to the present.

David Urbanski is a Latin teacher and Chair of Languages at Brookfield Academy in Wisconsin, USA.

Nancy A. Vander Veer is the co-founder of the Three Column Learning Corporation. She is the programme manager at the Paideia Institute and a former classroom teacher in independent schools. She graduated from Samford University, USA, in 2012 with a BA in Classics.

ACKNOWLEDGEMENTS

This volume had its origins in two Classical Association conferences at the University of Edinburgh in 2016 and then at Leicester in 2018 in which the editors and a small group of friends and colleagues (Terence Tunberg, Laura Manning, Jason Harris, Aislinn McCabe, Alma O'Donnell, Clive Letchford, Rachel Plummer and Fergus Walsh) presented panels on the topic of 'Living Latin' to university academics and school teachers. The idea of speaking Latin to learn Latin had been an important and noticeable trend in some US classrooms for many years previously, but it had not yet entered into the consciousness of the school classroom in the UK. From this point we decided that a concerted effort needed to be made to introduce for wider consideration, not just the practice, but also the theory behind communicative approaches to teaching and learning ancient languages. The result is this book.

An edited volume of this size is a mighty task to complete and there have very many people who have been involved in its production. The biggest thanks must clearly go to our contributors. Their chapters contain carefully thought-through descriptions of practice and the theories behind them and often include word-by-word demonstrations of activities – exemplars for the reader to try out in their own teaching. We wanted this book to demonstrate real-life examples for people to see exactly what goes on in a communicative activity. It is clear from our contributors' stories that adding communicative approaches to the repertoire of teaching methodologies is not a step taken lightly. For some it's a great adventure; for some a shot in the dark; for others, a moment which creeps up on them or is arrived at after months, maybe years, of consideration. Once taken, all feel that the effort was worthwhile both for themselves as teachers and, more particularly, for the learners. Thus, the contributors display a welcome humility in sharing their thoughts and anxieties with us and make the book, we think, the stronger for it. They have gone before and will help to lead the way.

Thanks are also due to the institutional support which we were able to use in completing this volume. For Mair, the Latin pedagogy adventures that have culminated in this book could not have happened without the opportunities offered by the Open University, first to complete a BA Classical Studies and later doctoral research in communicative approaches to Latin teaching. Mair is particularly grateful to her ever-supportive supervisors, Prof Regine Hampel, Dr Ursula Stickler, Dr Linda Murphy and Dr Eleanor Betts, and to Prof James Robson, a marvellous friend and collaborator with whom she has continued to explore ancient language pedagogy as an Open University Research Associate. Mair is also very grateful to King's College London for giving her the chance to put her communicative approaches research into practice at the Modern Languages Centre in 2017.

Steven would like to thank his many friends and colleagues in the Classics teaching world: the University of Cambridge for giving him the privileged position that enables him to research in schools up and down the UK and a band of teacher trainees on the Cambridge PGCE to practise with; the charity Classics for All, which affords him a different perspective on Classics teaching (most notably when exchanging ideas with teachers of modern foreign languages who are training to teach Latin); his UK PGCE companions Rowlie Darby at the University of

Acknowledgements

Sussex and Dr Aisha Khan-Evans at King's College, London; and Prof Emma Stafford at the University of Leeds, whose ear he has bent on far too many occasions about the state of classical languages teaching.

We should both like to extend our gratitude to the team at Bloomsbury Academic for their support in bringing this volume into being. A publication of this size and complexity required the support of an excellent team and we were admirably supported by Bloomsbury: Alice Wright, the commissioning editor, was persuaded over tea and cupcakes at Leicester that the book was a 'good idea' and gave the green light the following year; Lily Mac Mahon continued the excellent service while Alice took leave and she has been a delight to work with. We must also thank the readers of the original proposal, whose thoughtful and encouraging advice helped us to shape the book as a whole.

Finally, we would like to thank our families. Individually, Steven would like to thank his daughter Olivia for bearing so patiently the amount of time he spent tapping away on the computer in the study at home during the long days of lockdown when she could have been using it for editing music videos. Olivia – the computer's yours now!

At the centre of Mair's life always are her sons Ivor and Matthew, whose frank opinions and encouragement sustained and entertained her through all the trials and tribulations of her mature student adventures. Their interest, love and support have added to the fun and eased the pain of completing this volume too.

INTRODUCTION
Mair E. Lloyd and Steven Hunt

This volume brings together accounts of a selection of current communicative practices that we hope will inspire wider exploration of their effects and subsequently enliven ancient language teaching. Although the skill of reading remains firmly at the forefront of our own pedagogical aims, we perceive the need to go beyond approaches that limit language development to this skill alone. We want to help students to experience reading ancient languages without having to painstakingly transpose texts into their own language in order to achieve comprehension. We want to escape the image of ancient languages as codes to be deciphered and to move towards students experiencing them as a normal means of communication in spoken as well as written form. In short, we hope to make ancient languages recognizable as languages and to make them lively and attractive to as wide a range of modern learners as possible.

We hope too that this volume can instigate the creation of a body of scholarly works on communicative approaches to ancient language pedagogy so that our community better understands the possibilities and effects of choices we make in how we teach. We therefore encouraged our authors to draw on research from Modern Foreign Languages (MFL), with its abundance of language-learning theories, to cast light on their experiences of teaching and learning ancient languages. We hope the resulting chapters will begin to develop a specialist branch of language-learning theories and practices that builds on what has been learnt from our MFL cousins, but which acknowledge the different aims and circumstances that ancient languages require.

A final aspiration for this book is that it will promote collaboration around communicative approaches between ancient language practitioners across different organisations, student age groups and countries. The eclectic mix of material collected here, we hope, bears witness to that aim.

What do we mean by communicative approaches?

In shaping this volume, we were aware of a variety of labels used for the kind of practices we felt could be subsumed under our 'communicative approaches' banner. We were ourselves influenced by modern language definitions and by looking back on the brief flourishing of the 'Direct Method' of Latin teaching developed by W. H. D. Rouse and his followers in the first half of the twentieth century in the United Kingdom. We were also aware of the various labels used in ancient language institutions in the US and Europe including 'active' and 'living' as descriptors of teaching approaches. Though none of these various concepts constrained what we included in this volume, each provided a springboard from which to work towards a broad definition.

In MFL, the advent of Communicative Language Teaching (CLT) moved the focus of language development away from accuracy of form and towards successful transfer of meaning, with an emphasis 'on communicative proficiency rather than mastery of structures' (Richards and Rodgers 2014: 84). Howatt (working in the field of English as a Foreign Language (EFL)) described a 'weak' and 'strong' form of 'communicative approach' (1984: 279). The first, 'weak', form comprised instruction about the target language leading to practice in using it to communicate. The second, 'strong', type rested on the premise that language is acquired through communication using the target language itself, which 'stimulates the development of the language system' (Howatt 1984: 279). Howatt described these two different forms of the approach as 'learning to use' and 'using [...] to learn' (1984: 279). In studying ancient languages, where our ultimate intent is the development of reading skills rather than broader communicative competence, the 'using to learn' version of CLT seems closer to our needs, though some element of 'learning to use' may be desirable as a prelude or accompaniment to the stronger form (Lloyd 2017: 123). In MFL, the 'communicating to learn' environment requires native-like competence in the teacher (Celce-Murcia 1991), while for 'learning to communicate', teachers more often use students' native language to explain target language elements that can then be practised by interacting with others (Hall and Cook 2012). Examples of both forms of communicative language teaching are evident in the chapters of this book.

An important characteristic of communicative approaches is their emphasis on the goal of communicative competence across all four language skills: the receptive skills of reading and listening, and the productive skills of speaking and writing (Richards and Rodgers 2014: 107). It might be claimed that students of ancient languages only really need reading skills and that sufficient 'input' to promote them is all that is required. However, that suggests that learning a language through just one receptive mode is possible and desirable, a claim that the authors in this book and many modern language scholars would refute (Swain 1993: 159–60; Mitchell et al. 2013: 41). The importance of including all four skills is acknowledged too in definitions of 'active' or 'living' languages in use among proponents of ancient language immersion events where participants use ancient languages as the means of everyday communication over a prolonged period (Coffee 2012; Lloyd 2017). Implementing 'active' or 'living' definitions in the classroom would imply introducing speaking, listening and self-expression in the target language, alongside the more usual emphasis on reading and explicit instruction in linguistic features. It is the inclusion of these additional oral/aural and productive skills that differentiates communicative approaches from others.

Communicative approaches can be identified through their aims and their practices, but there is no consensus on a single definition, as the plural 'approaches' in the title of this volume acknowledges. It is perhaps more straightforward to explain what we as editors did not consider as 'communicative approaches' when gathering chapters for inclusion. This does not in any way indicate a judgement of these exclusions as of lesser importance in the field of ancient language pedagogy. We hope that they will be given prominence in other future publications.

For the purposes of this volume, we did not consider the grammar-translation method in itself to have a place among 'communicative approaches', focussing as it does on the analysis and translation of language, rather than its use across all four skills. Potential chapters focussing only on the 'reading approach', whereby learners acquire language through meeting it in texts, were also excluded on the grounds of narrow focus on one language skill, albeit the most important skill in terms of the study of classics (Hunt 2016: 7; Rogers 2011: 1; Wilkins 1969:

175). For similar reasons the editors did not seek chapters dedicated to 'comprehensible input' (CI) and the theories of Krashen (1982) because, although the uptake of CI has clearly been extremely influential in Latin teaching in the US and beyond, its initial emphasis on reception might have occluded the productive aspect of 'communicative', 'active' and 'living' approaches that we particularly wanted to capture. However, all three of the approaches excluded here do make appearances in chapters where contributors included them alongside oral/aural or productive approaches. Indeed, all of the chapters from schools and universities in Parts 1 and 2 of this volume mention elements of grammar instruction or provision of 'input' through reading. There are a number of descriptions in Part 3 of full immersion where interaction using all four skills takes place in the target language, and these clearly fit under the 'communicative approaches' umbrella and the 'strong' MFL definition. Other chapters cover situations where some skills have more prominence than others. We initially tried to make sure that all chapters contained some element of extemporized oral production from students (and teachers), because speaking as a means of self-expression is frequently absent in ancient language classrooms and therefore a prominent distinguishing feature of 'communicative approaches'. However, we have also elected to give space to chapters that foreground other productive language skills or even explicit grammar instruction where the authors themselves strongly believe this to be part of a 'communicative approach'. We hope this allows us to present a broad view of the field and its conceptualisation across the Classics community.

What will you find about communicative approaches in this book?

This volume is divided into four parts. The first two describe the introduction of communicative approaches as part of a broader mix of pedagogies in formal teaching settings. Part 1 covers teaching in schools (ages approximately 11–18) and Part 2 universities (18+). Part 3 brings together institutions where learners experience total immersion in the target language. Finally, Part 4 comprises three chapters covering a variety of approaches in unusual settings.

Part 1

Chapter 1: Laura Manning presents a view of past and present 'active' Latin teaching, looking back to Europe in the sixteenth and seventeenth centuries and at current practices in US schools. She identifies promising trends for the future inspired by earlier successful models.

Chapter 2: David Urbanski describes how he set fear aside to pursue active Latin fluency at the Lexington Conventiculum and subsequently encouraged his students to take similar risks with communicative Latin.

Chapter 3: Judith Affleck uses her experience at the *Accademia Vivarium Novum* to transform her classes in Stratford-upon-Avon by introducing the use of oral Latin to enhance students' language development.

Chapter 4: Justin Slocum Bailey gives a detailed account of communicative strategies he uses to lead up to reading authentic Latin texts, his example here being taken from Cicero's *in Catilinam I*.

Chapter 5: Justin Schwamm and Nancy Vander Veer describe classroom communities using Latin texts as springboards to collaborative creation of new story-worlds.

Chapter 6: The first part of the book concludes with Steven Hunt's call to use communicative approaches as part of a teacher-led (rather than government-led) reform of teaching practices to secure the future of Latin in schools and colleges.

Part 2

Chapter 7: Mair Lloyd opens the universities section of the book with a detailed look at Latin interactions recorded in a class for postgraduate beginners. She demonstrates how reflection on MFL and ancient language pedagogical research can help refine teaching practices.

Chapter 8: Clive Letchford describes how his dissatisfaction with the speed at which his students could translate Latin led him to revolutionize his *ab initio* language teaching at the University of Warwick.

Chapter 9: Leni Ribeiro Leite explains how using active Latin along with texts originating in local culture brings the language to life for her students at the Federal University of Espírito Santo, Brazil.

Chapter 10: Daniel B. Gallagher explains the importance of *ludi domestici* (home games), a variety of exercises that build on and contribute to spoken Latin fluency in class leading to enhanced reading skills.

Chapter 11: Cressida Ryan brings us again to Latin teaching for *ab initio* postgraduate students and highlights some of the challenges and points of interest of working with communicative approaches.

Part 3

Chapter 12: This two-part chapter opens with Terence Tunberg describing total immersion at the *Conventiculum Latinum Lexintoniense* at the University of Kentucky. He provides insight into its origins, practices and benefits. Milena Minkova follows this by explaining how the conventiculum led to the establishment of the *Institutum Studiis Latinis Provehendis* (Institute for Promotion of Latin Studies) and its Graduate Certificate and Masters level courses, some of which are taught entirely through the medium of Latin.

Chapter 13: Stephen Hill covers the annual σύνοδος ἑλληνική (Ancient Greek conventiculum) at Lexington, which was inspired by the Lexington Latin Conventiculum and follows many of its practices.

Chapter 14: Christophe Rico and Michael Kopf describe the evolving teaching methodology for Ancient Greek total immersion events at the Polis Institute in Jerusalem.

Chapter 15: Daniel Streett argues for the introduction of immersion environments in *Koine* Greek and other biblical languages in seminary classrooms.

Chapter 16: Sebastian Domagała, Marcin Loch and Katarzyna Ochman aim to reduce the gap between ancient and modern language pedagogies and describe the re-emergence of the Natural Method at the University of Wrocław and at the *Schola Aestiva* in Poznań.

Chapter 17: Ivan Parga Ornelas and Josey Parker close this part of the volume by covering the emergence of student-led Latin-speaking circles at the Universities of Oxford and Cambridge, in which participants develop communicative language skills to complement formal university teaching.

Part 4

Chapter 17: The final part of the volume opens with Marco Romani Mistretta and Jason Pedicone's account of teaching at the Paideia Institute. This encompasses diverse teaching methods, worldwide locations (face to face and online) and learners who range from beginners to trainee teachers.

Chapter 18: Daniel Pettersson and Amelie Rosengren describe the *Latinitium* website that is designed to support communicative approaches through the use of technology.

Chapter 20: The volume concludes with a unique contemporary case study by Mallory Ann Hayes and Patrick Owens, exploring the order of language acquisition and development milestones in two children brought up to be bilingual in Latin and English.

What next?

We consider this book to be the opening gambit of what we hope will be a productive conversation between ancient language teachers, learners, researchers and education influencers in different institutions and parts of the world. We look forward to seeing many more publications exploring communicative approaches in all ancient language teaching and learning settings. We hope that this volume will inspire teachers and learners to experiment with using ancient languages as active, living vehicles for communication in their own learning and teaching, and to broadcast their findings to the Classics community. The practice of publishing reflections on, and evidence of, the effects of our pedagogical choices is long overdue in our field (with a few notable exceptions). We hope that this book will contribute to the Classics community building its own understanding of how ancient languages can be learned successfully so that their study can be enjoyed by future generations across the world.

PART 1
INTRODUCING COMMUNICATIVE APPROACHES IN SCHOOL SETTINGS

CHAPTER 1
ACTIVE LATIN IN THE CLASSROOM: PAST, PRESENT AND FUTURE
Laura Manning

Teachers of classical languages find themselves at a pedagogical crossroads. Latin has been taught as a second language in an unbroken tradition for centuries. Yet now foreign language class enrolments at all levels in the US, including those of the Latin language, are falling at an alarming rate (Looney and Lusin 2018). This chapter presents a brief look at the state of twenty-first-century Latin teaching in the US, an overview of active methods of teaching Latin that were practised in Europe in the sixteenth and seventeenth centuries, and a glimpse at how some of these same teaching methods are being adopted today in US schools, with a view to increasing enrolments and improving student engagement and motivation in Latin classes at the elementary, middle, high-school and college levels.

At the 2019 American Classical League Institute, an annual meeting during which classics teachers discuss issues related to teaching and learning classics, some teachers suggested to me in conversation that the cause of lower enrolments could be teaching practices, especially those that rely heavily on grammar rules being memorized and sentences being translated, with a focus on rarely seen vocabulary taken completely out of real-world context. Students learning Latin using these methods may rearrange English substitutes for the Latin words into an English-like word order in an attempt to understand the meaning of the sentences. This practice of rearranging words to ascertain meaning is met with mixed success, as students are often not quite sure whether they have met the mark. Students may not have the vocabulary or cultural experience to address the content of the sentences, especially when sentences are presented without enough context to assist the student. The result is a situation where students read out their English translations with a questioning lilt at the end of each declarative sentence. This unconscious change in pitch betrays the reality that the material has no clear meaning for the students until the teacher has verified the correct rendering. Students may believe that the meaning of a given Latin sentence is so obscure that only the teacher knows for sure what the sentence really means. That obscurity indicates a lack of emphasis on real communicative purpose for learning and using the language. Chilingaryan and Gorbatenko (2016) made a strong case for the relationship between student motivation and student success in language classrooms. Finocchiaro and Brumfit (1983) in Richards and Rodgers (2014) demonstrated that student motivation is one result of active, communicative approaches to language-learning. A return to that communicative emphasis in Latin classes will enhance student motivation.

Why have I characterized this as a return to communicative emphasis? Because when discussing traditions in Latin pedagogy, Latin teachers with whom I was speaking were often surprised to learn of the rich and successful history of active, communicative pedagogy in Latin classes 500 years ago. Tunberg (2012) described the essential role of active, communicative teaching and learning practices in reading, writing, listening and speaking in the sixteenth and seventeenth centuries. This communicative emphasis in the classroom was a natural outgrowth of societal expectations. While Latin was not the mother tongue of any regional group of people during the Renaissance and afterwards, Latin was used for communicative purposes throughout European society, especially in schools and academic work in the sciences, government and the Church, where official communication regularly took place in the Latin language. Learning to communicate in Latin was useful in terms of preparation for careers and public life. In fact, the argument that Latin is useful surfaces again and again in primary and secondary education and in the academy even today, particularly in discussions about which courses have a place in the curriculum (Wringe 2016). If utility is accepted as a key reason for learning any subject, including Classics, why are we seeing falling enrolments in Modern Foreign Languages in today's global-minded world?

And beyond utility, what good is an ability to read Latin? Two thousand years ago, the Roman orator Cicero famously upheld the value and importance of literature in his defence of his client, the poet Archias. Cicero defended the value of literature and the value of the poets and poetry to the nation, saying that poetry restores the spirit, is inspiring and is filled with morally worthwhile examples to which citizens should aspire. That same kind of defence of literature happened during the Renaissance. Marc Antoine Muret (1526–85), known as Marcus Antonius Muretus, a French humanist considered to be the foremost Latin stylist of his day, frequently presented powerful speeches on the defence of classical literature and its value in the school curriculum (Manning 2016). Learning Latin during the sixteenth and seventeenth centuries, particularly for the educated classes, was more than being able to get by, even at a high level, in the language. The personal correspondence and public orations of speakers, including Erasmus and Thomas More, are filled with classical literary allusions, and this emphasis on Latin literature made its way into the curriculum (Tunberg 2012).

Educators today also offer reasons for keeping classical literature in the curriculum, and their reasons are as valid as those presented by Cicero and Muretus. That perception of the inherent value of original literature continues to have an impact on educational views and practices today. For example, students read Latin literature in courses and exams given under the International Baccalaureate programme (Hertberg-Davis and Callahan 2008; Callahan and Hertberg-Davis 2017). While Latin is clearly not the native spoken language of any people alive today, it is unique in that it has been a *lingua franca* for centuries with the result that a great deal of literature has been written in Latin and that Latin literature addresses the ideas of centuries of authors who grappled with human problems in engineering, civics, medicine, law, mathematics, moral philosophy and more. This abundance of literature offers students opportunities to engage in critical thought about innumerable ideas, and to consider the legacy of these ideas both for now and for the future. As students take their place as adults in the world and seek to improve the societies in which they live, some of the impact of classical culture takes place in the form of reaction against values and practices that are seen to have emanated from the ideas and customs such as slavery, racism and sexism discussed in classical literature (Cox 2018). A view of history that is sometimes painful, particularly when it discusses exploitation, violence, subjugation, and cruelty, can result in a backlash against Latin and Greek languages, literatures and cultures by students and by colleagues who teach in the discipline. Backlash or not, the essential role of literature in Latin classes must not be underestimated.

To think critically about the ideas presented in classical literature and about their consequences requires an ability to engage fully in the language and the cultural mindset in which they were originally written and formed. Such engagement requires that people learn to understand the language deeply. Engagement leads to increased motivation, as noted previously. But how has that teaching and learning been accomplished in past eras? The scope of this chapter allows only a very brief overview of the study's historical context.

Dickey (2016) presented research on how Latin was taught as a foreign language in Rome, drawn from the study of ancient *colloquia* used as teaching texts in the second century BCE onwards. According to her, the students' motivation for learning the Latin language in the eastern Roman empire, where Greek was the primary spoken language, included preparation for careers in the army and in law. By contrast, according to Dickey, people who lived in the western Roman empire learned Greek in order to understand Greek literature. Dickey's textbook (2016) includes some of the *colloquia* that students in the eastern Roman empire used in their study of Latin, offering a glimpse into life in the classroom during this period. Students seem to have spent time learning the alphabet first, sometimes at the direction of older students, and then progressed to read and write syllables, words, phrases and longer passages, eventually working directly with the teacher.

By the sixth century BCE, the way students were taught had changed dramatically. The focus of education itself also shifted, so that *ars grammatica*, the study of grammar, took a central role. This led to the teaching of the *trivium*, which included dialectic (logical argumentation) and rhetoric (persuasive speaking), along with the study of grammatical elements. Soon, with the rise of the university in Europe in the eleventh century, dialectic had the most emphasis in education. During this time, Latin remained the primary language of education.

In my forthcoming doctoral dissertation, I asked how teaching and learning Latin is accomplished in today's communicative classrooms. The context of this study is a review of pedagogical practices from the Renaissance, which included analysis of an oration by Johannes Posselius the Elder (1528–91), an educator whose Greek textbook was used throughout Europe for centuries. In 1589, Posselius set out his plan for educating students in an oration delivered at the University of Rostock. Modern language teachers recognize four communicative competencies: reading, writing, speaking and listening. Posselius addressed all of these, but emphasized the role of speaking both for teachers and for students. Posselius expected the students to speak Latin outside class too, and recommended that schools use spies to watch and report any lapses to the teacher. Students were forbidden to speak German or to speak Latin that was not Ciceronian in style, and they were not to make general errors in speaking Latin. Tunberg (2012) has shown that these spies were actually employed in schools.

Posselius wanted his students to start their study of Latin at age six or seven. They would learn to read right away. He felt that young students could be taught to read Latin before learning to read German. Eventually the teacher would make sure that students would be able to read both languages. As soon as they could read, students would learn vocabulary from a German and Latin bilingual vocabulary book. It was important to Posselius that students understand the meanings of the words in both languages. During this phase, students would learn the parts of speech from a book written for young children, and then they would learn how to decline nouns and conjugate verbs. At this young age, students would learn some statements from the Bible rendered in good Latin, and some of the Roman author Cato's sayings. The teacher was expected to repeat the Latin sentences carefully, so that students would understand all of the words and their endings. This whole process was supposed to take a year or two at the most. Posselius expected that the teacher would then explain Latin grammar briefly and energetically. He stated that it would take an 'industrious and energetic teacher' six months to teach grammar. Students were supposed to know grammar thoroughly, but its study was not meant to drag on for a long time. Posselius stated that five years, for example, would be an extreme amount of time to devote to grammar.

A major difference between the traditional teaching which was actually practised during the Renaissance and modern perceptions of traditional teaching can be seen in a comparative examination of intentional memorization of paradigms. Posselius expected students to memorize the paradigms of declensions and conjugations after they had plenty of practice in using these forms in reading, writing, speaking and listening. This indicates that the method recommended by Posselius was an inductive study of these grammatical forms. Some current textbooks, such as the Jenney Latin programme (1990) and Wheelock's Latin (2011), rely on the deductive study of grammar in which students memorize paradigms and forms and then use the grammatical rules to guide written translation from Latin into English.

Once the students could read and had mastered the grammatical underpinnings of the language, Posselius recommended that students begin to read Cicero's letters. If part of the class was not ready, the class could be split so as to give the students who were not yet ready more experience in the earlier material, while not holding back the students who had demonstrated mastery. When reading Cicero's letters, the teacher was expected to explain the similarities and differences between the way Cicero wrote and the students' first language. Posselius prescribed that students be given a few great books that they would come to know well and love, and that the ultimate goal was for students to love Cicero, who was the model for Latin style throughout Europe during this time.

Posselius also paid attention to the place of writing in the curriculum. There were several types of exercises that the students were expected to complete. The first was the translation of phrases, sentences and continuous passages from German into Ciceronian Latin. The teacher would prepare these German exercises based on a passage from Cicero that students had already read. After submitting their work, the students would see the original passage from Cicero on which the sentences had been based, and then they would make their corrections. Posselius stressed that Cicero's style should be the rubric for corrections, rather than the teacher's opinion of the quality of the writing. The next type of exercise was similar and based on unseen passages of Latin. The teacher would translate one of Cicero's letters, which students had not yet seen, into German; the students would translate these into Ciceronian Latin. Corrections would be made by the students as above. For the final type of exercise, the students would paraphrase a passage from Latin into Ciceronian Latin. It is noteworthy to recall that the only language used in the school was Latin, including all discussion of the work and corrections between teacher and students.

Posselius discussed not only the students and the curriculum, but also described his ideal teachers. These teachers were expected to use entertaining and effective means of getting their point across. They were supposed to be kind to the students and friendly in a parental way. Posselius stated that the teachers should not be cruel or harsh. Above all, the teachers would know Latin and Greek very well, and be able to speak and write in Ciceronian Latin without errors.

This type of pedagogy was followed successfully for a number of years. And then, between the Renaissance and the nineteenth century, there was a gradual shift in the use of languages taking place in the world. During the seventeenth century, vernacular languages were coming to be used increasingly in literature and even in the elite public sphere. By the end of the eighteenth century, the use of Latin in schools was in rapid decline, as the continued rise of nationalism led to increased use of vernacular languages in schools and even in international politics. Finally, the Second Vatican Council of 1962 saw the end of Latin as the language used for teaching in Catholic seminaries. All of these developments contributed to the decline of Latin in schools. Alongside this decline in the use of Latin in public and in schools came a sharp decline in the number of teachers trained in the active use of Latin. This paved the way for the creation of textbooks that could be used in classrooms where there was no teacher who could speak Latin. Speaking Latin came to be seen as an impractical use of educational resources, and the emphasis in Latin classes turned wholly to the study of literature and grammar. During this time, vernacular language textbooks were created that mirrored the new textbooks used for Latin in classrooms where the language was no longer being spoken. Perhaps this was to demonstrate the rigour of foreign language study (Richards and Rodgers 2014). However, throughout the twentieth century in the US and the UK, there was a gradual shift in methods of vernacular language teaching towards more spoken use of the target languages, particularly because of the need for trained speakers who could speak critical languages during times of war. Latin was left behind in this trend, since the army had no need for speakers of Latin. In the last half-century or so, however, there has been renewed interest in communicative approaches to teaching Latin.

Within this context, and with an understanding of this historical background, I observed about fifty students and three teachers in three high schools in Kentucky, USA, in a comparative case study. The students in these schools reflect the demographic diversity of their local communities in terms of race, ethnicity, economic and social class, and gender. Students were between twelve and eighteen years old. In these active communicative classrooms, teachers are well prepared to teach and employ various techniques to help their students to learn. For example, teachers in the study were observed teaching in the following ways. The teachers:

- speak;
- draw;
- act;
- demonstrate;
- read;
- use humour;
- ask questions;
- listen;
- sing;
- use technology;
- chant;
- play;
- show pictures;
- modulate their voices;
- make crafts.

These highly creative teachers continued to use different techniques and practices frequently, and if something is not listed here, it is very likely to be my omission, or perhaps it just did not happen during an observation. In short, the fact that a technique does not appear on this list does not indicate that the teachers were not doing it in their classes.

The teachers observed were kind, friendly in a parental way, and able to entertain their students and foster enthusiasm. In fact, on only one point of Posselius's rubric do the teachers that were observed consistently mark themselves as needing improvement, and that is in their self-evaluation of their ability to speak and write in Latin free from mistakes. All of the teachers in the study expressed their desire to improve their Latin and described their efforts to do so. These efforts include a variety of professional development tasks, including personal engagement in reading Latin literature, previous or future enrolment in college courses, professional development through their schools, and participation in the *Conventiculum Latinum Lexintoniense, Conventiculum Latinum Dickinsoniense* and other similar gatherings. Since Latin is not the first language of any country today, the opportunities to use the language available to teachers and students are much more infrequent than similar opportunities for students and teachers of modern languages and often have to be created by the community of Latin educators. Educators who wish to improve their competency in the Latin language are limited to immersion workshops and weekends, and the workshop format itself dictates the amount and degree of immersion provided. The teachers in my study mentioned their desire to provide as many examples of correct, idiomatic Latin as possible for their students as an important reason for seeking such professional growth opportunities.

The students in these schools were regularly asked to use the Latin language to the extent that they were willing and ready. In none of the schools observed was use of Latin by the students compulsory, in contrast to the recommendations made by Posselius. The teachers held high expectations for their students' success in using the language via the four competencies of reading, writing, speaking and listening and consistently communicated these expectations to their students in a positive and student-friendly manner. Moreover, the teachers built students' competency to higher and higher levels of mastery in order to assist their students in meeting and exceeding these expectations for language-learning. As an example of this work toward mastery, a group of students was expected to communicate orally and in writing with each other and with the teacher about topics of their choosing, using simple sentences with a grammatically singular direct object, then using plural direct objects, and then modifying direct objects with adjectives in a spiralling process.

In the classes observed, all students were able to use the language at least at the word and phrase level (Novice Mid) in speaking and writing in order to communicate ideas and to make requests. Students were sometimes offered the choice of language to respond to questions. An analysis of the observation data showed that when students were offered a choice of language, students chose to speak in Latin 85 per cent of the time. A high level of student comprehension was observed: students in the first four months of the first year of study were all able to understand Latin at least at the Novice Mid level in listening and reading, and frequently at the Novice High level. The American Council on the Teaching of Foreign Languages (ACTFL) describes readers at the Novice High level as 'able to derive meaning from short, non-complex texts that convey basic information for which there is contextual or extralinguistic support' (ACTFL 2012). Students demonstrated this understanding in a variety of ways, including by:

- answering questions about their comprehension;
- explaining their metacognitive techniques;
- answering comprehension questions about a text;
- engaging in simple conversations on a variety of topics;
- drawing pictures;
- translating;
- acting out the story;
- laughing at jokes or humorous parts of stories;
- turning to the correct page or line of a text;
- groaning when a test or assignment was announced;
- asking questions about the grammatical aspects of what they said and heard;
- playing games that ask them to perform some task;
- behaving appropriately in response to a request or other conversational statement;
- restating phrases and sentences in different ways or using different grammar;
- asking questions about cultural practices that are discussed in their reading and in class conversations.

There are some important similarities between today's schools in my study and Posselius's schools:

- the student is encouraged to speak the language;
- reading, writing, speaking and listening are all part of the curriculum;
- grammar is important for learning a language;
- love of literature is an essential goal of language study.

Analysis of the data showed some key differences between what is expected in today's communicative Latin classes and in the pedagogy described by Posselius. The most obvious difference is that today's students are not living in an immersion second-language Latin environment. Instead, they are speaking and hearing Latin as a foreign language for perhaps an hour a day or ninety minutes on alternate school days. Students are not surrounded by many speakers of varying degrees of experience and ability. Instead, their teacher may be the only person at their school or in their life who is a reader and experienced speaker of Latin. Posselius was very clear that in six years of immersive study, all students were capable of learning Latin to a high degree of ability. In only one school in my study did students have the opportunity to study Latin for more than four years at the pre-collegiate level. One other positive outcome was noted, however: there were no spies – speaking Latin, while encouraged in the schools, was not compulsory. Morgan (2001) demonstrated that avoiding negative reinforcement (for example, avoiding spies in Posselius's example) can lead to greater student motivation.

In the light of this brief explanation of Latin teaching and learning in the past and the present, where is the discipline going in the future? In the last ten years at gatherings of Classics educators at the secondary level, there has been a noticeable increase in the number of papers and poster sessions that address active, communicative approaches to teaching Latin. At the

2019 American Classical League Institute, there were no fewer than sixteen papers, panels and workshops devoted to this theme, as well as a pre-Institute excursion that was conducted in Latin. This trend shows that, at least among attendees at this conference, the field is moving in the direction of greater use of active and communicative approaches in the classroom, particularly at the secondary level. Secondary teachers and graduate students have increased their attendance in spoken Latin classes and at active Latin seminars such as the *Conventiculum Lexintoniense* and the *Conventiculum Dickinsoniense* and have expressed their intent to use more active approaches in their classrooms. Further action research in classrooms will drive this discussion forward. The universities have been much slower to adopt these approaches, however. At the joint meeting of the Archaeological Institute of America and the Society for Classical Studies in January 2020, there were no sessions or panels dedicated to this topic of active Latin or communicative approaches. At a roundtable lunch discussion of pedagogy by graduate students, the focus of the conversation was the culture and history classes which these students were teaching, and not on language-learning. This meeting and its roundtable discussions might offer, however, a promising avenue for increased discussion about the future of Classics and active, communicative pedagogy.

The education theorist Michael Apple (2003) offered the suggestion that: 'Sometimes we can go forward by looking back, by recapturing what the criticisms of past iterations of current rhetorical "reforms" have been, and by rediscovering a valued set of traditions of educational criticism and educational action that have always tried to keep the vast river of democracy flowing.' Latin teaching enjoys a long history and as such, has been taught and learned via numerous approaches. By returning to our earlier successful emphasis on active, communicative pedagogy, educators can improve student engagement, which, it is hoped, will have a positive effect on student enjoyment, enrolments and outcomes at all levels.

CHAPTER 2
ACTIVE LATIN PROMOTES OPEN-MINDEDNESS IN LANGUAGE-LEARNING
David Urbanski

One of the things I have noticed as a teacher, in my students and in myself, is just how often the fear of humiliation prevents learning. I have also noticed the opposite of that: how joy can pave its way. My own experience in these respects confirms Krashen's affective filter hypothesis (Krashen 1982: 29–31). I know quite a number of Latin language people (teachers and students) who are intrigued by the world of active Latin (by which I mean listening, speaking and reading in Latin at a decent pace) and want to be able to be part of it, but have been deterred by fear from making the leap. It certainly takes some kind of uncomfortable change. It requires that those who have already worked very hard to become proficient as Latinists suddenly become novices again. In my experience, the change is worth every bit of discomfort, because the joy to be discovered on the other side is just so good. Isn't this how real learning always feels? Genuine learning is adventurous and risky, rather than comfortable.

I am now in my sixth year of pursuing fluency in active Latin. I mark the official beginning of this pursuit with my first week-long Latin total immersion experience at the Lexington *Conventiculum*. There is a full description of this event in Chapter 12 of this volume and some accounts of the student experience in one of our editors' doctoral thesis (Lloyd 2016: 204–31). Attending the *Conventiculum* meant relinquishing use of English and communicating with other participants only in Latin. I felt the adjustment strongly during that first week; it was not subtle. My mind would not let me sleep more than a few hours each night throughout that week for its churning of Latin idioms. My brain kept demanding to know how to say anything and everything in Latin. It suddenly became important and good to know how to say 'Chinese food', and 'on the second floor of the other building', and my mind was entirely overcome by the pure joy of learning.

My view of Latin has never been quite the same since. I came out on the other side with a clear understanding that anything and everything actually can be communicated in Latin, and that I was on a path to discovering as much of the Latin language as I could take in. It is a very long path, seemingly endless. Six years in, I feel I have only just begun. That, though, is a testament to the greatness of the endeavour. I have left the cul-de-sac of one textbook, with its narrow supply of answers, and my own routine way of teaching it, to join a very wide-open world in which I cannot possibly anticipate what will come next. Every time I learn something new, I also learn how much I still don't know. This situation is simultaneously energizing and humiliating.

As soon as I present myself to my students as someone who speaks Latin (or, more honestly, as one who is currently trying to learn to speak Latin), students want to discuss many things that are not in a textbook, like chocolate chip cookies (perhaps *crustula frustis socolatis sparsa*). And if I encourage them to try speaking, their speech will inevitably be filled with errors. Won't that cause more harm than good? Isn't this an invitation to a giant tangent? These are the kinds of worries that can prevent a teacher from venturing into new territory. Keeping my classroom in the cul-de-sac that I know so well would be so much more comfortable.

But then I reflect on these questions: Who were my best teachers? What made them the best? In every single case, the best teachers were ones who were not merely conveying information, right answers and wrong answers according to the textbook, but ones who were clearly themselves in pursuit of greater knowledge and skills, right now, and who were conducting that pursuit with humility. They were taking personal risks. One of my favourite professors, an otherwise quiet man, once hopped up onto a table and threw his car keys across the room to imitate a prehistoric oracle, consulting bones. If that sounds unnecessarily eccentric, consider this: we loved it, and we loved him for it, and I still recall the lesson thirty years later. We (my teacher, my classmates, and I) were looking at something together; we were fascinated together. The teacher may have been in the lead, but we were all on the same challenging path.

Pursuing active spoken fluency in Latin has already provided me, not just with some new teaching method, but with deeper insight into the nature of learning and teaching, because of how roundly it has thrown me back into the position of being a novice again myself. It makes great sense to me then that I see other teachers who are in pursuit of fluency developing a myriad of uses in their classrooms. I suggest that the success of these uses is not necessarily because of some new (or old) technique, but perhaps because teacher has been privately practising the spirit of humble investigation, of open-mindedness, and of risk-taking.

I am going to share with you my own teaching circumstances, along with the way that I have chosen to employ active Latin in my classroom. I ask readers, though, to realize that they are going to have to forge their own paths towards using a communicative approach in their teaching. The ways that I have so far chosen to use active Latin will not be yours. Your uses of such things will grow organically out of who you are, and out of what you already prefer to do. Change may also be undertaken gradually so that differences are almost imperceptible. The challenge for me has been to introduce that adventurous spirit of risk-taking into a conservative environment without threatening the traditional approaches of my school, for which I have great respect. Briefly stated, I surround a traditional written-translation method with spoken Latin.

I teach in a private, non-sectarian, K-12 school (ages four to eighteen) in Wisconsin named Brookfield Academy, which was founded in 1962 by a handful of families who wanted to maintain traditional approaches to education. For example, while many other schools in the United States at the time were beginning to drop formal grammar lessons, we did not. Our school continues to teach grammar (in both our English classes and in our World Language classes), and we have been cited as one of the few schools in the United States that continues to teach the diagramming of English sentences (diagramming is a method of mapping out the grammar of a sentence (Mulroy 2003: 113–14)). Along the same lines, while many schools started to abandon Latin as a requirement, all students at our school must study at least one year of Latin. We hardly ask them to become experts; in practice, we only ask them to acquire a decent familiarity with the basics of Latin (i.e., about 500 vocabulary words, the five noun declensions, verbs in all tenses of the indicative mood, adjective agreement, and translating at a level appropriate to those elements). With about seventy to eighty students per grade, and our commitment to small class sizes, it's a full-time job for me to teach just the introductory year, and we have three other full-time Latin teachers who continue the Latin curriculum after me.

Because of my situation, I have important things to consider when I choose my approach to teaching the material. As the first of four Latin teachers, I know that my choices affect them, and I would not make major changes without their agreement. None of them currently practises active Latin, so I make it a priority to teach my students in such a way that they are comfortable with either approach – communicative or non-communicative. Another consideration is that it is compulsory for all students to study Latin at our school. I therefore have a greater mix of students than many other Latin teachers might have. I would say that at least a third of each year's new class discover that they love it, and want to continue learning beyond the required amount. Yet I also teach a number of students each year who have no special love for Latin. I therefore think it is helpful (and respectful) to present a wider variety of teaching methods, so that the material can appeal to as many learning types as possible. My solution has been to avoid adhering to one single approach, but to blend together elements of both approaches – both the written translating and the communicative approach. I think it's a good idea to expose my students to both worlds, and since they are most accustomed to written work, I make that the centre of attention.

About 75 per cent of what I do in my class is the grammar-translating method, and then I add, as a non-graded portion of my class, some simultaneous exposure to spoken Latin. I rely a great deal on deciphering and parsing in my class for our daily work. I explain grammar fully, and almost always in English. I ask students to make physical flashcards for all vocabulary words. However, about one quarter of what I do is communicative, and seems to me to be enough to make a large difference. Even though I have found great joy in pursuing active Latin, and it has enhanced both my personal life and my classroom, it did not prompt me to change everything in my approach to teaching. What it did do was prompt me to take a fresh look at all of the things I was already doing. The active Latin movement has helped me see that greater excellence in my teaching can come from small tweaks that dovetail with the ways of doing things that already make sense to me in my current circumstances. When I see other fun, creative methods being used by other teachers, I always admire them, but I have to remind myself that I can only be myself. The very spirit of open-mindedness that led me to active Latin has led me to see that some of the old-fashioned methods that I know are very effective. Open-mindedness does not demand that everything must be constantly innovative. It's okay if my classroom mostly has an old-fashioned look and feel to it. It's okay if much of our time together in the classroom seems banal and quiet. It's okay to use paper and pencil. I have found a fairly productive and comfortable balance in my classroom, the likes of which Alan van den Arend eloquently describes in his article on the topic as 'something old and something new – marrying early modern Latin pedagogy with contemporary SLA [or Second Language Acquisition] theory' (van den Arend 2018: 28). He encourages all teachers of classical languages to consider 'blending commitments to a spectrum of Latin pedagogical methods' (van den Arend 2018: 28).

Much of my regular routine for each chapter of *Ecce Romani*, therefore, is very traditional. In fact, it is especially the graded work that I ask them to do which looks almost the same as what I had to do as a Latin student. But in between all of the bits of graded, written work, I am usually speaking to them in Latin. Since none of the spoken Latin that I do in class counts as part of graded material, I am able to consider communication in Latin as something happening without consequence to their grades. This, I find, relieves some of the pressure that might keep students from taking risks.

I've noticed that many students (and adults) who do not have a prior mental commitment to the pursuit of active Latin will shut down their attempts to understand me almost immediately when they think they will be required to respond. So in my classroom, if I make it clear that at first all I want them to do is listen, and if I am also very careful to use many words that I know they can understand, they can start training themselves to ignore the internal negative thoughts that hamper the listening skills. Overcoming the fear of speaking is a much larger obstacle, and I for one do not push it much on my students, especially not at the beginning. As we progress through the year, almost all students feel comfortable doing a small amount of speaking. I really want them to be comfortable in my room, as much as that's possible, so if I ever require students to speak to me in Latin, I guide them through it extensively, with formulae and repetition, which I will describe shortly. To ensure that my students are never hampered by fear, I have stopped short of taking a fully communicative approach even in the non-graded element of my teaching. As happy as the communicative world of Latin has made me, I suppose I do not subject my students to the same level of discomfort that I ask of myself, because I feel it is important for people to choose risk for themselves. I realize that I have willingly chosen all of the discomfort that I experience at a *conventiculum*, while my students perhaps would not. In this, my views are much more in accord with Krashen's comprehensible input hypothesis (Krashen 1982: 21–9) than with proponents of an active Latin approach that includes speaking and writing in interaction with others (Carter 2019: 21; Minkova and Tunberg 2012: 126) – at least for a group of students who cannot drop my class.

I begin speaking Latin to my students on the very first day of school, but since they have had almost no exposure to any Latin, I will say a phrase or sentence in Latin and then translate myself immediately in English. One sentence at a time, I go back and forth between Latin and English. It feels a little strange, but the effect has so far been very positive and successful. My new students don't have to worry too much that they are missing anything, and they are hearing lots of Latin. At first, they simply become aware that Latin can be used like any other language, which I believe is already a large victory, but soon they start picking up words and phrases. I have Latin phrases posted around the room that I can point to and use to build the connections for understanding. Every day in my room I write the day and date in English and in Latin on the board. Below that I write the *agenda* (things that are to be done) for the day, which includes words which they soon come to know, such as *audire fabulam* (to listen to the story), *exercitium* (exercise), *caput* (chapter). Beneath the agenda is the homework for tomorrow. Sometimes the agenda is in English, but more often it is in Latin, especially if I think they will be able to recognize English cognates and deduce what it means it without too much help. I write the word *pensum* (homework, task) in the same place every day to indicate the homework. The homework I always write in English, so as to be perfectly clear about what is expected of them. I teach them early what '*quomodo te habes hodie*?' (How are you today?) means, and I have made that phrase come up as the screen-saver for my computer, so that my class is rather often interrupted with the computer asking how each of us might be doing, and I sometimes take a moment to answer the computer. I have on one wall a range of faces, happy to sad, with Latin adverbs under each face, so that students can easily retrieve an answer, the most popular of which is '*bene*' (fine). At the beginning of the year they need to check the wall to be sure they are answering with confidence. Soon they don't need the wall of faces.

When I begin class, after welcoming them in Latin, I can start pointing to things, talking about the date, talking about what we will do. '*iam necesse est mihi inspicere chartulas vocabulorum quas fecisti. erat pensum vestrum. ubi sunt chartulae tuae, O Clara? optime! bene factum!'* (Now it is necessary for me to check the vocabulary flashcards which you have made. That was your homework. Where are your flashcards, Claire? Excellent! Well done!). My students have not learned enough Latin to understand everything I say, but I build their confidence with key words gradually so that they do understand enough to know what they should be doing, so long as they are paying attention. Meanwhile, they are absorbing the sentence structures of Latin thinking, even with what they do not fully understand. I try to choose vocabulary words and grammatical structures that come from our textbook lessons, and I look for ways to fold those words and phrases strategically into my own speech. In Chapter Six of *Ecce Romani*, for example, the phrase *necesse est* (it is necessary) is introduced. I begin using that phrase in my speech to them some time before they study it, so that its meaning, and usage with an infinitive, sound and feel familiar by the time we see it in the textbook. That phrase, when used with a personal pronoun (e.g. *'tibi necesse est'* for 'it is necessary for you or you must'), also helps me plant the notion of the dative, and one of its uses, long before the book shows it. By the time the students see a grammar explanation of the dative case, there is already a natural use of it planted in their brains. I try to employ clear, creative, and emphatic uses of words like *etiam, quoque, dum, igitur* (even, also, while, therefore), and others whose definitions are more abstract. I also use a variety of verb endings, tenses, and moods before we reach them in the book. This offers students the opportunity to acquire vocabulary by hearing it before seeing it in print and increases the number of times a word is met, making it more likely that it will be remembered.

I move the class along with little Latin comments and observations throughout. They often hear me grumbling in Latin about my computer not working correctly. As the year goes on, and as students grow accustomed to my routines and my commonly used phrases, I speak more without translating myself. Some classes might be entirely in Latin, but only if I can know that everyone in the room will be more or less comfortable with it. Some students spontaneously join me and will start using Latin, asking me simple questions in a very casual manner. With my Latin speaking, part of my plan is that there is no plan. There's something very joyful about casually slipping back and forth between English and Latin. It certainly makes me happy, and that really matters – to set a relaxed and joyful atmosphere in class.

I ask my students to do much more listening to Latin than I used to in the past. I always read a sentence out loud before we work on it, or I ask students to do it. I also read the sentence again after we have translated it. As I tell my students, I first want them to hear the sentence come alive, as an ancient Roman would have heard it, then we dissect it with parsing and discussion, and then I bring it alive once again. Reading, re-reading, asking students to repeat after me – I see terrific results coming from these very simple activities. In recent years, when a student brings a sentence to me that he or she cannot understand because of its complexity, I very often ask the student just to listen to me reading it once or twice with careful emphasis. It's amazing how frequently this clears up the confusion. Nothing like this was happening before I started practising active Latin on my own. I now know more about how the words should be said, because I can think the sentence in Latin better. Learning how to read the sentences of your textbook with expression may seem like a simple teaching goal, but for those not accustomed to speaking Latin, it may present a real challenge. When we read with expression, we are not merely aiming for the pronunciation of individual words. We want to communicate the sentences, with an emphasis and phrasing that facilitates understanding

(Kuhn et al. 2010: 233). Tone of voice, pauses, knowing when to slow down or speed up are all things that happen more naturally when you are thinking in a language, a skill that I found I was able to develop through my experience of using Latin as a means of everyday communication and which I found nearly impossible before attending the Latin immersion events at Lexington. This is something that I continually strive to improve on, and my active-Latin pursuit has yielded the most wonderful results in my classroom.

One conspicuous result from my use of spoken Latin in my class is that it generates excitement. Not all of my students are automatically more excited when they hear someone speaking in a foreign language, but many are, and many display a clear hunger to share in what they hear, to join in. Many students start asking me how to say this or that in Latin, and the answer always seems to delight them, and they now feel a kind of vested interest in things. One of my students asked if we could rename our textbook to the Latin version of *Keeping Up with the Corneliuses*. I gave him my best attempt (*De Corneliis Manere Certiores*) and he comes in nearly every day with something new to say about that. I keep a model of the Colosseum in my room, and this year I have been putting various characters in it who 'fight' each other (just for fun, I make clear – a contest between friends). A certain group of students comes in every day and cannot wait to see who is winning. I speak about the contests in Latin, and I even featured a paragraph for translation on one test about *Georgius Curiousus in Colosseo* (Curious George in the Colosseum). It was wonderful to see how thrilled those students were to arrive at a translation section of a test!

Perhaps the most rewarding part of my new attempts to use Latin has been to see more success with students who would not naturally find themselves at the top of the class when it comes to test grades. Once, a few years ago, a student attaining mid-level grades just uttered a little Latin sentence to me, after class, as pure communication, just to try it out. His sentence was perfect, and in it he even used a word that I had never taught him. I had asked him if he could do something, and he responded with '*laete ego facio*' ('Happily I do that'). I could tell from the way it came out of his mouth that he hadn't planned or memorized the sentence. He intuitively adapted the adjective *laetus* (happy) to adverb form, presumably based on the form of other adjective-adverb pairs that he had met, and he used it in a casual unprepared comment to his teacher. That achievement seems to me incredible. The student was very proud of himself. He realized that he was daring to do something that some of the students at the top of the class could not seem to do. In my experience, that is the sort of spark that can ignite an entire life of learning.

My use of communicative Latin in my classroom has continued to evolve, and as I dare to do more complicated things with it, I see my students risking more as well. Nonetheless, even while I was still adhering to more traditional classroom methods, as soon as I started my private pursuit of active Latin (especially as I started working on thinking in Latin), I saw an overall surge in the grades of mid-range students. I saw a rise in my year-end averages after the year 2012 (of about 4 per cent). I am certain that the surge has occurred in the middle of the group. I seem to always have some students who excel no matter what I do, and some who do poorly no matter what I do; but that mid-range group continues to achieve better results than before I was pursuing active Latin. So, what happened in 2012? Interestingly, it's not the year I began speaking to my students in Latin (remember, that was only six years ago). 2012 was the year when I had my own personal 'conversion' to active Latin. That was the year that I had discovered the joy of it all. I had attended a session at a language teachers' conference in which there were two relatively fluent speakers of Latin introducing the idea of active Latin usage in classrooms. I had heard about such people. I was intrigued during the session itself, but still mostly intimidated. It was during the luncheon when I became captivated. One of the two teachers very quietly asked the other in Latin to pass the salt. A brief conversation ensued about the salt, all in Latin. This was the moment that sold me, because they were speaking Latin for the joy of it, not as a teaching technique. I wanted that joy.

As I said, very few teachers teach under circumstances that are like mine. This is one of the reasons why I am emphasizing the mindset over the methods. I very much admire what some teachers are doing with full immersion and Comprehensible-Input reading (see, for example, Patrick (2019) and others in the *Journal of Classics Teaching* 39) because there is nothing that frustrates me more than the thought of someone who studies Latin for four or more years and cannot read texts. Both in myself and in my students, I see this inability as a failure of mindset, which has arisen because we do not expect anyone to be able communicate in Latin. Yes, many of us are teaching Latin differently, hoping to change that expectation. I do worry that an immersion method, without grammar explanations, will simply take too long. But those methods are aiming at a great good: thinking in the target language. Given more time with my classes, I might take a fuller communicative approach myself.

Whenever I work to pursue fluency on my own, which I do every day, I find myself having to navigate around my own fear of humiliation. I am never as proficient as I ought to be, as I want to be. I am not sure that I would ever have had the strength and inspiration to do this, if it weren't for the extreme joy that I witnessed in others who were already doing it. The spirit of open-mindedness and risk-taking seems to pervade the current world of active Latin – entirely dissimilar to the reputation that Latin classes have had for quite some time now. Once I discovered the world of communicative Latin, I have been gradually implementing aspects of it into my classroom. I have refrained from requiring all of my students to participate in full immersion during my classes, perhaps because I believe so strongly that for it to be a joyful and meaningful experience, like it has been for me, a person needs to come to it by conscious choice. As a teacher, I can create opportunities for my students to take risks in their learning – to challenge themselves in new ways, but I can only invite them. I believe that students will be much more willing to take risks, like daring to express one's current thoughts in a difficult new language, if they see me struggling to do the same. I have found myself following the thinking of Professor Stephen Beard, a California Latin teacher who, like me, has started down the path of active Latin usage: 'Although the teacher will not have native-level fluency, he/she will be able to do this teaching credibly and creditably if he/she makes it clear that both teacher and student are on a learning adventure' (Beard 2009). *prorsus sic sum conatus*. That's entirely what I have tried to do.

CHAPTER 3
LIVE LATIN: GLOBAL EXPERIMENTS IN SHAKESPEARE'S CLASSROOM
Judith Affleck

'Good summer break?', he asked, snipping away at the back.
'Amazing. I spent a month learning Latin in a villa near Rome.'
'I thought you *taught* Latin?'
'Yes, but I don't speak it.'
'Funny thing, we had a go at some Latin – in Shakespeare's Schoolroom.'

September 2018

Part of the tourist experience for visitors to Stratford-upon-Avon involves a fleeting taste of communicative Latin – a live Latin lesson which replicates aspects of the sixteenth-century classroom experience. The inspiration comes from the physical surroundings of the renovated Guildhall, brought to life by scholarly research and scenes like young William's encounter with his school master Sir Hugh Evans in Shakespeare's *The Merry Wives of Windsor*, Act IV Scene I. My own tourist experience proved a little disappointing, but my chatty hairdresser, in his brush with Latin, felt the adrenaline of the schoolroom, the fear of being picked on by a teacher and, briefly, the thrill that he was learning *Latin*. For tourists from countries where Romance languages are spoken, the few Latin words – even allowing for British pronunciation – perhaps feel strangely comfortable.

At the King's New School at Stratford upon Avon, chartered by Edward VI in 1553, boys were taught in Latin from the age of about seven by a well-qualified teacher. The two masters who spanned the years of Shakespeare's education there – Simon Hunt, 1571–5, and Thomas Jenkins, 1575–9 – were both educated at Oxford University. 'The principal aim of an Elizabethan education was for the student to learn not merely to read Latin with facility, but also to write and speak it' (Bate 1993: 19–20). The long hours devoted to this involved much grind, repetition and role-play.

The hours devoted to Latin in the state grammar school now called King Edward VI, Stratford-upon-Avon, where I have taught since 2007, are generous by modern standards, but insignificant compared with the long Tudor school day: our 45-minute lessons include movement around the school site to a large number of subject specialists: boys in Year 7 (aged 11–12) see their Latin teacher three times per fortnight; they then have two lessons per week in Year 8 (aged 12–13), and three in Years 9–11 (aged 13–16), shared between Latin and Classical Greek for those who opt for both GCSE examinations. Our mixed Sixth Form (aged 16–18) are allocated eleven periods per fortnight with two different teachers. On these hours, is it possible for students to learn to speak Latin while also working to excel in their public examinations? The demands of GCSE and A level Latin, particularly with their heavy emphasis on literature, are already intense. The training and experience of generations of UK teachers at all levels make this a question I have rarely heard seriously considered during my own schooling, at university or in public schools like Eton and Harrow, where I taught from 1987 to 2007. The work of the Association for Latin Teaching somehow passed me and most of my colleagues by, and W. H. D. Rouse, its founder and enthusiast for the Direct Method (Stray 1992), provided material for after-dinner talks, but not for practical application in the classroom.

Is it faint-hearted to think that the barriers of curriculum time and specification consign the learning of Latin in the UK to a largely passive linguistic experience? My own initial assumption that Latin could not be taught communicatively within our system, as a spoken language, remained unchallenged until, in 2014, a student of mine went to live and study at the *Accademia Vivarium Novum* for a year before university. At that time the *Accademia* was situated in the outskirts of Rome, but aspirational plans to take up residency in the beautiful Villa Falconieri were already in the air. I was invited to visit my student in these suburbs and it was there that I first heard Latin and Ancient Greek spoken as a natural medium for communication. My shock at experiencing this was repeated when, on his return to the UK, he visited our school and delivered a couple of stimulating lessons in fluent Latin, before asking if I could meet with him to practise Latin conversation from time to time. My stumbling attempts humbled me and the role reversal from teacher to pupil was mildly humiliating, but I also felt excited that there was – and is – somewhere out there in the Alban Hills ready to help anyone – student, teacher, retiree – to take those critical first steps in thinking and speaking this ancient and unique international language; a world where, after a few hours, people whose native languages may be mutually incomprehensible can communicate with each other: passing the cheese, finding the toilet, singing a song or exploring a story or text together.

> . . . and I went full of curiosity and the faint, unrecognized apprehension that here, at last, I should find that low door in the wall, which others, I knew, had found before me, which opened on an enclosed and enchanted garden.
>
> *Evelyn Waugh,* Brideshead Revisited

My own fabulous summer month at the *Accademia Vivarium Novum* in August 2018 was kick-started by a sense that I wanted to try to out a communicative approach to teaching with my own students. That month was inspirational on so many levels, but it pointed up for me a key difference between the examination system in the UK and elsewhere in the world: how highly unusual it is for students as young as 14–16 to study and undergo written examinations about ancient literature studied in the original language. While this is the norm in the UK, it seems to be the preserve of older students in our sister countries. Another observation was that it appeared, to me at any rate, more natural and intuitive for a native Italian or Spanish speaker to speak Latin than for those from northern Europe. There is, nevertheless, a number of northern Europeans for whom speaking Latin has become a completely natural experience; and so I wanted to find that 'low door in the wall' and 'enchanted garden' for myself, and to encourage my students to do the same.

Experiments at King Edward VI School 2018–19

Fired up by my summer experience, I settled on four ways to explore the teaching of spoken Latin in the year commencing September 2018. Two extracurricular activities were grouped under the project heading 'Live Latin': a Tuesday lunchtime club which developed into a production in Latin of Plautus' *Rudens* (*The Rope*) to be performed outside Shakespeare's Schoolroom. Two further experiments took place inside my classroom using the textbook favoured by the *Accademia Vivarium Novum*, Ørberg's *Familia Romana*; these were regular lessons with a small Year 9 Latin class (aged 13–14) and one-to-one lessons with a Year 12 student (aged 16–17), who had previously studied no language, ancient or modern, but wanted to read Classics at Oxford. My principal aim was to explore how the textbook worked in practice and to assess whether my fellow Latin teachers and I would be able to incorporate it into our regular teaching.

Live Latin

Open to anyone in the school, the Tuesday lunchtime Live Latin club was a Latin speaking group that attracted a regular group of eight to twelve students from September to February (Phase 1); in March, using the same lunchtime slot, Live Latin morphed into preparations and rehearsals for a production of Plautus' *Rudens* in July (Phase 2). Most of the students who took part in these activities were, to my surprise, A level students who were studying mathematics and sciences. They had apparently come out of nostalgia for their GCSE Latin lessons. Although not a natural group of actors, they started talking Latin with enthusiasm and formed the core of my Plautus cast.

The best stimuli for getting started were pictures and questions. *Familia Romana* begins with the geography of Rome and the Roman Empire, using maps and lots of examples of places to talk about – roads, rivers, towns and islands, large and small. It is not long before we meet the *Familia Romana* and their villa, with more opportunities for talking about place and human relationships. The technique Ørberg uses means a question is never answered with a simple 'Yes' or 'No'; instead a scaffolding is constructed that can at first seem cumbersome, but encourages accuracy and the swift construction of longer sentences, using vocabulary that fast becomes natural. This replicates some aspects of the Tudor classroom, with endless repetition that establishes useful – and, in the case of Ørberg – flexible patterns of response, by-passing translation. It also brings to the fore question words key to teacher-led sessions. This approach felt relatively safe – there was no pressure to sustain it in regular lesson time and it created a light-hearted atmosphere for our first steps in speaking Latin.

We alternated question and answer picture stimuli with chapters from *Familia Romana*. The story line, carried along by a formidable quantity of text, much of it in a question and answer format, generally proved entertaining. The textbook is supported by enthusiasts from all over the world, some of whom have produced great resources, like the charming song of the runaway slave, '*non longa via est Romam*' (Capitulum VI.82, supported by Craft 2020).

This song's catchy tune and memorable lyrics reinforce key prepositions and use of the accusative to express motion towards; viewers can also re-play the excitement of Medus' journey through a computer generated Minecraft landscape, as he hastens from Tusculum (the location of Julius' *Familia Romana*, fortuitously close to the *Accademia Vivarium Novum*) to Rome, ready to sweep his beloved Lydia off her feet. In a later chapter (Capitulum VIII) the happy couple pass a jewellery shop – big mistake if you have a small fortune (*nonaginta nummi*) burning a hole in your '*sacculus*'. The clever construction of the storyline means that some words, like *nummus, sacculus, saccus, lectica*, never need translating – illustrations alongside the text provide vivid introductions to each new word and, once in circulation, they simply become a concept or stage property – coins, wallets, rucksacks etc. (for further examples of Craft's work with Minecraft, see Craft 2019). Acting out these scenes as we read them became a natural activity in which characters had to speak, listen, think and respond in Latin.

By December my Live Latin group had started to bring in new materials of their own, specifically 'The Bobbiad', an epic my students had written together, flexing their Latin composition skills, which I observed had been greatly enhanced by the communicative approach of Live Latin. However, it was at this point that, with some relief on my part, we moved on to original Latin in the form of Plautus' *Rudens*.

Rudens is the second Latin play we have performed recently at King Edward VI. The first was Plautus' *Menaechmi* in 2016, from which I had learned how many lines a student could be expected to memorize. I chose *Rudens* in 2019 for its wide-ranging cast (lots of roles with not too many lines) and cut it down to about 1,000 lines, providing a rough parallel translation. The cast, as we have seen, was eclectic and I had to draft in some Year 10s to make the project viable, but, as with *Menaechmi*, the capacity of pupils to master the Latin lines proved formidable; something about the combination of words, movement, storyline, physical space, props, interaction and music seems to help the process along. It is hard to say what is going on in a student's mind when delivering (and not, I think, parroting) his or her lines, but there is certainly no 'translation' in the conventional sense. Some phrases became almost instinctive and could pass directly to a spoken Latin context, like '*quaeso*', '*te amabo*' ('please', 'if you don't mind'), and '*eccum!*' ('Look, that's him!'). Overall, however, the project seemed ephemeral – a high-energy, exhilarating phenomenon, forgotten almost as quickly as it was learned. I had hoped it might prove a short cut to building confidence in free-form communicative Latin, but the summer holiday intervened, Year 12 dispersed, and Year 10 became Year 11 and exclusive focus on their GCSEs made any longer-term impact hard to gauge.

Familia Romana in the classroom: A Year 12 student and Year 9 class

The key role of Trachalio, the cunning slave in our production of *Rudens*, was played by a student new to the Sixth Form who only started learning Latin in September 2018. As the textbook for our in *ab initio* sessions on Monday lunchtimes I chose *Familia Romana*. Since I had read, but never used, the book before (having attended the second month of the *Accademia* summer school, based on Ørberg's *Roma Aeterna*), it was helpful to me to be scanning ahead with a bright student who enjoyed preparing for each lesson. I was afraid it might feel dull romping through so much repetitive Latin one-to-one, but his focused commitment kept things moving and it was interesting to see how natural his language acquisition was, both of vocabulary and grammatical concepts. My teacher's instinct to draw lots of tables, to analyse and label forms and to set tests seemed somehow superfluous. So why did we eventually drop *Familia Romana* and move on to *Latin to GCSE Part 2,* Cullen and Taylor's 2016 coursebook, endorsed by the UK examining board OCR? Anxiety on my part about him being 'properly prepared', a reasonable calculation that we were not able to stay using the present tense any longer, and the urgency of tackling the original literature of the GCSE set texts in time for the summer were all reasons. My impression with this high-attaining student is that his initiation into Latin via *Familia Romana*, combined with his central role as Trachalio, helped him be more fearless and intuitive in his overall approach to Latin: he raced through '*Germanicus and Piso*' and Virgil's *Aeneid II*. Had he been taught using a fully communicative approach and without the completion of the GCSE, *might he* have learned, in the same time period, to 'write and speak' (Bate 1993: 19–20) in Latin with the fluency of our oldest alumni?

Whatever the shortcomings of our current GCSE system, it seems, from my own observations, that the rewards of studying literature at that level are considerable. However ambitious or artificial it may sometimes feel to plunge into Latin literature with students so young, it gives them a head-start at the next level and inspires many to continue with the subject; even for those who don't carry on with Latin, familiarity with their set texts may leave a richer, more lasting memory than their encounters with the language. Admittedly, my Year 12 student is older and hungrier to tackle original texts, but for him exposure to texts early in his experience should provide a long-term benefit, suited to the structure and methods of assessment in our university Classics courses.

What about Year 9? This is where my own experimenting with *Familia Romana* is likely to be most relevant to other teachers interested in pioneering a more communicative approach to Latin in the classroom. I felt happy to experiment because I was teaching an unusually small group of nine boys, the majority having opted for our combined Latin and Greek course. It included students who, as I knew from teaching them in Years 7–8, were likely to struggle and had chosen Latin as much to opt out of a modern language as to opt in to anything, least of all spoken Latin! It is probably fair to confess straightaway that, as with my Year 12 student, I eventually steered them back to Cullen and Taylor's *Latin to GCSE Part 2*, and I will explain the reasons for this before describing and evaluating what happened with this group, several of whom are now keen to continue with Latin to A level.

By March of Year 10, my colleague and I aim to have covered all the GCSE Latin language work (vocabulary and grammar) so that we can begin the prescribed literature set texts after their first set of internal exams, midway through the three-year course. We use our own Year 7–8 materials, which introduces students to first, second and third declension nouns (including neuter nouns) in all six cases and to four verb tenses: perfect, future (first and second conjugation only), present and imperfect, in that order; students are also expected to learn 222 words of Latin vocabulary, but meet many others, given as vocabulary help alongside reading passages. This sets them up well for the OCR examinations board's GCSE and in particular the restricted vocabulary list (RVL) prescribed for writing simple sentences from English into Latin. In *Familia Romana*, they see no other tense than the present until, in swift succession, they meet the imperfect, future and perfect in Capitula XIX–XXI, more than half-way through the course. Recalling the trauma of introducing the Imperfect and Perfect together in Stage 6 of the *Cambridge Latin Course*, I was not too sure about this. Moreover, when the subjunctive appears from Capitula XXVII–XXXIII, readers meet the present and perfect subjunctives (not required by OCR at GCSE level) before they meet the pluperfect. Given how little teaching time we have, this is simply not streamlined enough for the OCR Latin GCSE examination.

So, what were the advantages? Starting afresh provided a welcome opportunity to refresh what students had already covered, and the communicative approach, although limited in scope, meant that there was plenty to engage the mind. When I asked the boys (in English) what they had found most fun, they said 'acting'; when I asked what they had found most valuable about the course, they surprised me by chorusing 'use of the cases – we finally understood them'. Well, the jury is out on that, but from the start, the grammatically simple (although ethically more problematic) *'Marcus puellam pulsat'* ('Marcus hits Julia') in Capitulum III.12 gives a very vivid way of connecting with a direct object. Other moments when I felt *Familia Romana* transformed students' understanding were in the introduction of the passive *'Iulius ab Urso et Davo portatur'* (Capitulum VI.62) and Capitulum XI, where Syra, whose hearing is not as sharp it was, has to have every direct statement put into indirect speech (punctuation highlighting the original words for the reader): Aemilia *(in aurem Syrae): 'medicus 'puerum dormire' dicit'* (Aemilia (into Syra's ear): 'The doctor says that the boy is sleeping.') (Capitulum XI.63–4). Although we are still waiting to meet the Future tense, we encounter a host of other things: the subtle introduction of pronouns (should Medus buy Lydia *this* ring or *that one* (Capitulum VIII)), participles, fourth and fifth declension nouns and deponent verbs, for example, alongside a vivid array of vocabulary, memorably reinforced.

Familia Romana introduces approximately 1,800 well-selected words, far more than the OCR GCSE prescribed list, all 450 words of which turn out to be embedded in the thirty-four chapters. It proved easy to create a vocabulary-learning programme based on the whole book which differentiated between GCSE words to secure in their long-term memories, and words to recognize and use in passing. As discussed above, many of the latter did not even require translation or explanation, and my Year 9 students used the picture-help or Latin synonyms provided in the margins without seeming to notice how they were acquiring a powerful vocabulary. From the point of view of vocabulary acquisition, I believe *Familia Romana* works better than any other course I have used. Repetition of words at well-judged intervals means the core vocabulary expands comfortably, without need of much reinforcement. I formally tested students after each chapter, but they seemed very relaxed about vocabulary tests – even distinguishing correctly between frequently confused words, like *nam* (for), *tam* (so/as), *num* (surely not/whether) and *tum* (then), since they effectively already knew the words. This felt different from my previous experience of Year 9 vocabulary teaching.

I have evaded the question of how communicative my approach was in the classroom with this group. Only a little, is the honest answer. However, it takes time – more than one summer month – to gain the confidence and expertise to sustain a communicative approach as a lone Latin speaker within a school, with all the pressures of a full teaching timetable. Working at my own speaking skills is invigorating and fun and I have been given a week's leave in March to refresh my learning at the *Accademia*. The most obvious gain for the students of a communicative approach is that they can experiment; mistakes can be identified and corrected – often by peers – quickly and without red ink; they begin to internalize concepts of number, gender and case; they develop listening comprehension skills transferable to and from many other languages. The huge advantage to me as a teacher is that oral work is so much faster, more vivid and easier to react to than written work; accuracy improves because there is scope for more practice and faster feedback.

How am I taking this forward? A small group of our students will visit the *Accademia* in May and I'm incorporating picture exercises (*'quid vides?'* – 'What do you see?') and selections from *Familia Romana* into our Schemes of Work to encourage a communicative approach from student and teacher alike. We hope to see Plautus performed more regularly through a new inter-school Year 10 competition, and this should help embed greater familiarity with

Plautus' style and spoken idioms, giving a more lasting legacy than a one-off performance. I wish I had discovered 'the enchanted garden' of spoken Latin earlier in my career, but I am not sure that it existed then as it does now in the form of the *Accademia Viviarium Novum*; may this remarkable institution, which is bringing together students and teachers from around the globe, long continue to bear rich fruit!

CHAPTER 4
COMMUNICATION IN ALL MODES AS EFFICIENT PREPARATION FOR READING A TEXT
Justin Slocum Bailey

Introduction

While there are individuals and organizations promoting communication in Latin for its own sake – which can be an enjoyable pursuit – for many of us teachers the goal remains to help as many of our students as possible become skilled, confident readers of Latin texts (see, for example, Hunt 2016: 7; Lloyd 2017: 149; and others in this volume). Within this broad goal, I define three general areas of desired development:

1. general reading proficiency (that is, the ability to 'sight-read' texts with whose background one has a reasonable degree of familiarity);
2. ability to read specific target texts; and
3. ability to interact with texts written above one's reading level (for instance, to translate, comment on, or simply appreciate such texts).

This chapter deals mainly with (2), offering a flexible model for preparing to teach any given Latin text. The tasks described, however, should also improve general reading proficiency, due to the high volume of Latin with which learners interact. Students' ability to make some sense of and respond to texts above their reading should improve as their general reading proficiency improves, because the more of any given text is understood at sight, the more time and mental energy the reader will have to deal with the trickier bits. The focus in the traditional Latin class is on linguistic development (Richards and Rodgers 2009), with the assumption that coursework elsewhere has helped students develop much of the relevant non-linguistic cultural background knowledge; nevertheless, some of the strategies presented here support the gaining of this background knowledge in addition to providing linguistic preparation. I have found – and my students report – that the communicative strategies described in this chapter help students read more quickly, with greater understanding, and with less frustration than before I began using these strategies.

Preliminary analysis of a passage

When preparing communicative activities to use prior to reading a target text, I have found that it is important to identify in advance the elements of the text likely to present the greatest difficulty. Common culprits include uncommon vocabulary or morphology, complex syntax and unfamiliar background information on the original context of the text. Even if students have a solid grasp of these things, reading will be made more difficult by students' initial mental or attentional distance from the text – as students enter the classroom, they probably are thinking about things that they perceive as far removed from the content or purpose the text (for the importance of this distance in student comprehension of a text, see Nuttall 2005: 6–8). This often-overlooked fact calls for action on the teacher's part to prompt and prime students to deal with the linguistic and thematic content that they will encounter in the text.

The first paragraph of Cicero's First Catiline Oration will serve as an example of a target text for this chapter. The Latin text and translation are followed by a list of items my students would be likely to find challenging.

quo usque tandem abutere, Catilina, patientia nostra? quam diu etiam furor iste tuus nos eludet? quem ad finem sese effrenata iactabit audacia? nihilne te nocturnum praesidium Palati, nihil urbis vigiliae, nihil timor populi, nihil concursus bonorum omnium, nihil hic munitissimus habendi senatus locus, nihil horum ora voltusque moverunt? patere tua consilia non sentis, constrictam iam horum omnium scientia teneri coniurationem tuam non vides? quid proxima, quid superiore nocte egeris, ubi fueris, quos convocaveris, quid consilii ceperis, quem nostrum ignorare arbitraris? o tempora, o mores! senatus haec intellegit, consul videt; hic tamen vivit. vivit? immo vero etiam in senatum venit, fit publici consilii particeps, notat et designat oculis ad caedem unum quemque nostrum. nos autem fortes viri satis facere rei publicae videmur, si istius furorem ac tela vitemus. ad mortem te, Catilina, duci iussu consulis iam pridem oportebat, in te conferri pestem, quam tu in nos [omnes iam diu] machinaris.

When, O Catiline, do you mean to cease abusing our patience? How long is that madness of yours still to mock us? When is there to be an end of that unbridled audacity of yours, swaggering about as it does now? Do not the nightly guards placed on the Palatine Hill – do not the watches posted throughout the city – does not the alarm of the people, and the union of all good men – does not the precaution taken of assembling the senate in this most defensible place – do not the looks and countenances of this venerable body here present, have any effect upon you? Do you not feel that your plans are detected? Do you not see that your conspiracy is already arrested and rendered powerless by the knowledge which every one here possesses of it? What is there that you did last night, what the night before – where is it that you were – who was there that you summoned to meet you –what design was there which was adopted by you, with which you think that any one of us is unacquainted?

Shame on the age and on its principles! The senate is aware of these things; the consul sees them; and yet this man lives. Lives! aye, he comes even into the senate. He takes a part in the public deliberations; he is watching and marking down and checking off for slaughter every individual among us. And we, gallant men that we are, think that we are doing our duty to the republic if we keep out of the way of his frenzied attacks.

You ought, O Catiline, long ago to have been led to execution by command of the consul. That destruction which you have been long plotting against us ought to have already fallen on your own head.

Trans. C. D. Yonge 1856

Individual vocabulary
abutere/abuti (you will abuse/to abuse)
eludet/eludere (it will mock/to mock)
effrenata/effrenare (unrestrained/not to restrain)
munitissimus/munire (strongly fortified/to fortify)
machinaris/machinari (you plot/to plot)

Phrases/collocations/constructions
quo usque (how long / to what degree)
abutere ... patientia (you will abuse ... our patience)
quem ad finem? (to what end? / for what purpose?)
habendi senatus locus (a place for the Senate to meet)
quid proxima ... nocte egeris ... quem ... ignorare arbitraris? (which of us do you think ignorant of what you did last night?)
quid consilii (what [kind of] of plan)
ad mortem te, Catilina, duci iussu consulis iam pridem oportebat (you should have long since been led off to death, Catiline, by the consul's command)

Syntax
There are fairly long sentences with a delayed verb, but it helps that most of them are strings of parallel phrases.

Background topics
The Catiline conspiracy; the power and duty of consuls; Roman conceptions of shame.

The following listening, speaking, reading and writing tasks are designed to increase students' comfort with several of the above items while priming them to process both the language and the content of the text.

Listening

Rather than thinking of these strategies as 'developing listening skills' – which many Latin programmes do not count as a goal and which few major examinations assess – I think of them as supplying *focused input* or *massed input*. The need for a large amount of target-language input is undisputed (see for example, Krashen and Terrell 1983; Nunan 1989; Schmitt 2000; Richards and Rodgers 2009); the main justifications for making it auditory in this phase are:

1. healthy human brains are good at processing aural input; and
2. the teacher can script or improvise aural input that is
   a. more *focused* (i.e. contains less extraneous linguistic information);
   b. more *varied* (i.e. contains target words and forms in several contexts);

c. more *interesting* to the specific learners that are present; and
d. more *plentiful*

than the input that a typical textbook lesson, worksheet, or oral explanation provides.

Personalized questions and answers

I find that the simplest way of generating focused, interesting, auditory input – and one which requires the least preparation from me – is to devise a question whose Latin answer would contain the target grammar construction. I ask the question in English and students submit their answers in English, usually on a slip of paper. Often I write the question on the board before students enter class, having trained them to write their answers as soon as they have taken their seats. For our Cicero passage, I might ask any of these questions:

What did you do last night?
(Ciceronian phrase targeted: *quid proxima, quid superiore nocte egeris*)
Write one thing you did last night, and where.
(Ciceronian phrases targeted: *quid . . . egeris, ubi fueris . . .*)
What is something you should have done a long time ago, but haven't done yet?
(Ciceronian phrase targeted: *iam pridem oportebat*)
What is something that should have happened to you a long time ago, but hasn't yet?
(Ciceronian phrase targeted: *te . . . duci . . . oportebat*)
What is a good idea you recently had?
(Ciceronian phrase targeted: *quid consilii ceperis . . .*)

Note that these questions are ones to which every student is likely to have an answer, and for which most people will be at least somewhat curious about other students' answers. Sometimes I have students submit answers to multiple questions, both so that I have more total information and so that I can decide which question to focus on based on the usefulness of students' responses. For the purposes of this example, I will use the prompt *Write one thing you did last night, and where*.
Here are some English answers I have received for this very prompt:

I read a book in my room.
I had dinner with friends at [a particular restaurant].
I slept in the library.

Having collected and skimmed students' English answers, I select one whose Latin equivalent students will be able to understand with minimal help. I then announce, in Latin, what the student did:

proxima nocte, Anna in cubiculo librum legit.

Last night, Anna read a book in her room.

I write at least *proxima nocte*, and sometimes the entire sentence, on the board with its English equivalent. Then I can ask verification questions of the rest of the class:

> *quando Anna librum legit?*
>
> When did Anna read a book?
>
> *ubi Anna librum legit?*
>
> Where did Anna read the book?
>
> *quid Anna in cubiculo egit?*
>
> What did Anna do in her room?

However, I would like students to hear not only the temporal phrase *proxima nocte*, but also the perfect subjunctive in an indirect question. I can incorporate this construction by making the above questions indirect:

> *quis dicere potest **quando** Anna librum **legerit**?*
>
> Who can say when Anna read a book?
>
> *Silvia, potesne mihi dīcere **ubi** Anna librum **legerit**?*
>
> Silvia, can you tell me where Anna read the book?
>
> *Felix, mone nos **quid** Anna in cubiculo **egerit**.*
>
> Felix, remind us what Anna did in her room.

These are mere verification questions; I can launch a more interesting version of the entire interaction by announcing only one element of Anna's answer – the activity or the location – and asking the class to guess the other:

> *Anna proxima nocte librum legit. quis scit **ubi** librum **legerit**?*
>
> Anna read a book last night. Who knows where she read the book?

Or, beginning with the other detail,

> *Anna proxima nocte in cubiculo fuit. quis dicere potest **quid** ibi **egerit**?*
>
> Anna was in her room last night. Who can tell what she did there?

Other options in the place of *quis scit* or *quis dicere potest* include *quis divinare potest* (Who can guess?) *quis putat se scire* (Who thinks they know?), *quis **arbitratur** se scire* (Who thinks they know?), *quis scire vult* (Who wants to know?). Students raise their hands to offer guesses in Latin. Students know that, because I have asked the question in Latin, I expect an answer in Latin.

I can even incorporate the exact form found in the passage (second person singular) by asking Anna follow-up questions about her classmates' answers:

*o Anna, rectene Marcus dixit ubi librum **legeris** / ubi **fueris** / quid in cubiculo **egeris**?*

Anna, did Marcus accurately say where you read a book / where you were / what you did in your room?

Note that neither Anna nor other students need to be able to produce the target forms on demand; rather, students are exposed to the target forms by the Latin questions I pose. Students do not even have to answer in complete sentences. My purpose in taking guesses from students is simply to maximize their attention and interest and to collect ingredients for the Latin statements and questions that I, the teacher, produce. My invitation for students to supply possible answers, combined with the fact that the entire exchange centers on a student's real-life activity, demonstrates that I take interest in their lives and ideas. This, in turn, strengthens their engagement in the exchange (see, for example, Rivers 1987: 4): 'Students achieve facility in using a language when their attention is focused on conveying and receiving authentic messages (that is, messages that contain information of interest to both speaker and listener in a situation of importance to both)'.

I can generate a large quantity of focused input by repeating the process with several students' information, by asking several follow-up questions of one student, and/or by comparing several students, whether I use all of their original answers or not:

*o Anna, nonne proxima nocte librum in cubiculo legisti? fuitne aptus **locus libri legendi**?*
discipuli, qui locus est aptissimus libri legendi locus? (cf. habendi senatus locus.)
o Stephane, Anna proxima nocte librum legit. quid tu proxima nocte egisti?
*o Anna, proxima nocte librum legisti. etiam **superiore** nocte librum legisti?*
quis divinare potest, quid ego (magister) heri egerim?

Anna, didn't you read a book in your room last night? Was it a suitable place to read a book?
Students, what is a suitable place to read a book? (cf. place for the Senate to meet.)
Stephen, Anna read a book last night. What did you do last night?
Anna, last night you read a book. Did you read a book the night before last, too?
Who can guess what I (the teacher) did yesterday?

A favourite variant is to announce three activities and/or locations and identify the corresponding students as a group, without revealing which of the three students did which activity:

aliquis in popina cenavit. aliquis in cubiculo librum legit. aliquis in bibliotheca dormit. discipuli sunt Anna, Beatrix, Martinus.

Someone ate dinner in a restaurant. Someone read a book in their room. Someone slept in the library.
The students are Anna, Beatrix, and Martin.

I then have each of these three students stand in a different spot in the room and tell the rest:

si arbitraris Annam in popina cenavisse, surge et ambula ad eam. si Beatricem arbitraris in popina cenavisse, surge et ambula ad eam. si Martinum arbitraris in popina cenavisse, surge et ambula ad eum.

If you think Anna ate dinner in a restaurant, stand up and walk to her. If you think Beatrix ate dinner in a restaurant, stand up and walk to her. If you think Martin ate dinner in a restaurant, stand up and walk to him.

I have used *arbitraris* (you think/reckon) in these questions, rather than, say, *putas*, because Cicero uses this exact word and form in the target paragraph. Once students have voted with their feet, I can use their distribution for further Latin input. For instance, it may be that many students walked to Anna, but only one walked to Beatrix:

o Anna, multi arbitrantur se scire, quid proxima nocte egeris. rectene arbitrantur?
o Beatrix, unus tantum te in popina cenavisse arbitratur. rectene arbitratur?

Anna, lots of people think they know what you did last night. Are they right?
Beatrix, only one person thinks you ate dinner in a restaurant. Are they right?

I have given so many examples of questions because I wanted to emphasize how I tend to ask similar questions during almost any preparatory activity, including those described in the rest of this chapter, as well as to generate further input and personalization during the actual reading of a text.

While interactions like those described above may seem daunting to teachers who are not used to producing Latin, they are highly scriptable, and I recommend that teachers script Latin sentences in advance, both to reduce stress and to ensure the frequency of target words and forms. Collecting students' answers to the initial question(s) in a preceding class or electronically makes it easier to select which students to talk about and to script statements and likely follow-up questions in advance.

Storytelling with visual support

Another easily scripted way of providing focused aural input is simply to narrate a brief story in Latin that either is a greatly simplified version of the target text itself or provides background for the text. The teacher then tells the story dramatically while providing visual support in the form of simple drawings and diagrams on the board and/or actors drawn from among students.

olim Catilina, Romanus nobili genere natus, coniurationem contra rem publicam machinatus est. magna cum audacia multos iuvenes convocavit qui contra rem publicam pugnarent. etiam Ciceronem consulem ad caedem designavit. consilia esse callida arbitrabatur, sed consilia senatui patebant. tandem Cicero in senatu orationem praeclaram in Catilinam habuit.

Catiline, a Roman of noble birth, once plotted a conspiracy against the Republic. With great audacity he called together many youths to fight against the Republic. He even marked Cicero, the consul, for death. He thought his plans were clever, but they were obvious to the Senate. Finally, Cicero gave a famous speech against Catiline in the Senate.

Visual aids to clarify phrases in this account might consist of a simple timeline emphasizing the 60s BCE, a stick-figure drawing of Catiline wearing a toga, a thought bubble with a sword hanging over the abbreviation *SPQR*, several hastily drawn stick figures with arrows indicating their gathering around Catiline, and so on. I recommend adding each support only as the relevant phrase is said, both to maintain suspense and to allow students to associate the clarification with the exact words of the story. Along the way, I occasionally ask comprehension questions or have students turn to each other to summarize the story as told so far, either in English or in Latin. I tell the story at least twice, sometimes more, using identical or near-identical wording. Optionally, students can transcribe the story during one of the tellings, or write a Latin summary in their own words after the final telling. This technique owes much to the approach Beniko Mason calls 'story listening' (see, for example, Mason and Krashen 2018).

Speaking

I do not conduct many pure 'speaking activities' unless oral Latin proficiency is an explicit goal of the course, nor do I emphasize students' spontaneous production of Latin forms. This is because I do not find lengthy speaking activities to be *efficient* precursors to reading, which is the topic of this chapter. That is, I have observed that focused speaking activities, minute for minute, often are not good uses of class time, especially during the first several years of study. That said, students do speak Latin in small bursts as they answer questions I pose in Latin, and activities that involve students' speaking Latin can form part of the build-up to reading a passage if they prime students to think about concepts that appear in the passage. Here follows one such activity.

I project a picture, in this case, Cesare Maccari's well-known painting of Cicero denouncing Catiline in the Senate. The task then proceeds in three rounds, for which the students can be paired by any method (I like to have them walk about the room while music plays; when the music stops, they partner with the nearest classmate).

During the first round, students, working in pairs, simply make as many observations or statements about the painting as they can. I encourage students to say whatever they feel capable of saying in the moment, in order to accommodate the variation in speaking attainment among students and the fact that even any given student's competence varies as a function of fatigue, stress, and many other factors. The resulting interaction also functions as formative assessment as I eavesdrop on students, giving me a sense of how readily students can access and combine relevant Latin vocabulary. Some students may simply list words – *homines* (people), *togae* (togas), *albus* (white), *columna* (column), *antiquus* (ancient) – while others produce complete and even complex sentences.

For the second round, students form new pairs and only ask questions. (They do not answer these questions). I tell students that these questions can either be 'comprehension questions' such as *ubi sunt hi homines?* (Where are these people?) or *cuius coloris sunt togae?* (What colour are the togas?), or information-gap questions such as *quis est ille? quid ille dicit?* (Who is that man? What is he saying?). Students' questions give me a sense not only of students' oral proficiency but also of what stands out to them about the picture and what they are curious about.

Finally, students form new pairs and again make statements, this time all beginning with the word *fortasse* (maybe). This encourages students to make conjectures based on even more careful inspection of the picture and, again, gives me a sense of their proficiency and their ideas.

How is this activity an efficient precursor to reading? First, it helps me determine students' background knowledge of relevant language and history, allowing me to focus and streamline the instruction that follows. Second, if I ask students to share some of their questions with the group after the paired activity, fruitful discussion in Latin or English may ensue. Finally, the activity primes students' brains to process the thematic and linguistic features of the text: that it involves a group of men formally meeting, that it takes place in an important building (even if it actually takes place in a different building than that pictured), and that it features one person speaking harshly to another. This priming reduces students' mental distance from the text's context, an effect maximized by the fact that the task is done in Latin, the language in which the action was originally narrated.

In the process of inviting students to share some of the things they said during the activity, I can emphasize phrases from the text such as *habendi senatus locus* (a place for the Senate to meet) or *quis arbitratur se scire, quid hic (sc. Catilina) egerit?* (Who thinks they know what this man [Catiline] did?). If I have already told a simple version of the story in Latin, students and I can now connect elements of the painting to that story.

Reading

Reading course book texts that are simpler than most classical texts is a common, longstanding didactic practice in most Latin programmes. I have found a few types and treatments of texts especially efficient for developing what I call micro-literacy, that is, literacy with respect to a specific passage to be read. I subdivide such texts into teacher-created texts, student-created texts and combinations of the two.

Teacher-created text

1. The teacher can create from scratch a text that features a high concentration of words and forms found in the target text. This simpler text can be similar or identical to that used for oral storytelling (see 'Storytelling with visual support' above).

2. The teacher can create an informational text based on students' responses to survey questions: *Anna proxima nocte librum legit. ubi librum legit?* (Anna read a book last night. Where did she read her book?). An easy way to do this is to have a student transcribe the in-class Latin conversation as faithfully as possible and for the teacher then to edit the transcript to generate a relatively smooth, grammatically accurate text.

3. The teacher can create an informational Latin text containing historical or other background information for the target text. Such background knowledge makes comprehension of the target text easier (Nuttall 2005). Delivering it in simple Latin increases total Latin input and creates the opportunity for previewing some of the language of the target text. Creating background texts in Latin can be time-consuming, especially for teachers not used to writing in Latin, but some teachers have begun to share Latin background texts online (see, for example in the *Mille Noctes* online database).

4. The teacher can create a simplified version of the target text. This is a familiar practice. I find this process easiest, and most likely to prepare students for the actual text, if I create 'tiered' versions of the target text. This consists of removing bits of the original text without violating basic Latin syntax or morphology. The process can be repeated to generate ever-easier versions (see Sears and Ballestrini 2019 and Gall 2020 for information about creating and using tiered texts).

Student-created text

1. A simple, deceptively powerful strategy is to help the entire class co-create a text based on the interactions described in the *Listening* section above. On language teacher blogs this strategy is often titled, *Write & Discuss* (see, for example, Chase 2020). During this activity, I act as scribe, taking suggestions from students for what to write next. When a student's suggestion contains grammatical errors, I simply write the correct version into the text. The resulting written version of the oral input not only constitutes further input, but also allows teacher and students to inspect more closely any forms or constructions found in the text. Having the class dictate the newly created text saves the teacher time and effort and can serve as scaffolding for more complex individual writing tasks. Sometimes I have students write the text in their own notebooks as each sentence is finalized; sometimes they simply contribute ideas and focus on the copy that I write.

2. Students in a more advanced course can be tasked with writing stories that feature certain vocabulary and constructions for less advanced students to read.

Combination: Mini-scripts for micro-literacy

In order to expose students to expressions from a target text, as well as common narrative transitions, I often write a short script containing English equivalents of these items, with blanks for students to fill in details (also in English). This is a script I have used for my example Ciceronian paragraph:

Last night, _____ and _____ met in/at _____
in order to _____.
When they met, they said, 'We seem _____?'
They said this because _____.
In the end, they decided they had better _____.

After collecting the completed scripts, I use planning time to select a few that, when translated to Latin, will not contain too much obscure vocabulary or too lengthy expressions. I incorporate students' ideas from these scripts into this Latin version of the script:

proximā nocte, _____ et _____ _____ convēnērunt
ut _____ (*or* ad _____).
cum convēnissent, '_____.' inquiunt, 'vidēmur.'
hoc dīxērunt quod _____.
tandem _____ sē oportēre arbitrātī sunt.

Here is an actual version received from a student, followed by the Latin version I created:

Last night, <u>Harry</u> and <u>Sally</u> met in/~~at~~ <u>Paris</u>
in order to <u>discuss the Latin language</u>.
When they met, they said, 'We seem <u>too French</u>.'
They said this because <u>they were wearing berets</u>.
In the end, they decided they had better <u>return home</u>.

proxima nocte, <u>Harry</u> et <u>Sally</u> <u>Lutetiam</u> convenerunt
ut <u>de lingua Latina loquerentur</u>.
cum convenissent, '<u>nimis Galli</u>' inquiunt, 'videmur.'
hoc dixerunt quod <u>pilleos Gallicos gerebant</u>.
tandem <u>domum redire</u> se oportere arbitrati sunt.

Note that the first line's *proxima nocte* (last night) comes from the target text and introduces the idea of people meeting at night for some purpose, the second line answers the question *quem ad finem?* ('for what purpose?'), the third line includes the construction [nominative] *vidēmur* (we seem ____), and the fifth line includes *tandem* (finally), *oportere* (to be necessary/appropriate), and *arbitari* (to think/judge/decide) from the target text – the last in a slightly different sense, inviting some discussion of the word. Note too that I do not consider it important to convey all the details of the student's version with a literal translation.

In the following class meeting, I briefly project the English version of the script with blanks to recall it to students' memory, then project a picture emblematic of the setting, in this case, perhaps the Eiffel Tower or Notre-Dame cathedral. After briefly discussing the image with students in Latin, I reveal the Latin version of the completed script one line at a time, pausing after each line to verify comprehension in English and/or Latin and to ask students questions such as: *umquamne Lutetiae fuisti?* ('Have you ever been to Paris?') or *estne Lutetia aptus locus linguae Latinae tractandae?* ('Is Paris a good place to discuss Latin?').

Treating two to four versions of the script in this manner allows students to see and hear key constructions from the target text several times, all in the very manageable context of a five-line story.

Writing

Most of the Latin writing that my students do comes after reading a text. Writing, like speaking, may not immediately appear to be the best use of learners' time, but some low-pressure writing linked to the topic of a target passage can prepare students not only to understand the passage better, but also to gain some appreciation for the linguistic and stylistic decisions that go into writing such a passage. Some researchers have also identified a positive role for learners' production of the target language during the language-learning process (see, for example, Swain 1993). Here are some options:

Write and discuss

See 'Student-created text' above; though its primary purpose is to generate a simple text, it also constitutes a highly guided form of student writing.

Mini-scripts

After being introduced to several versions of the Latin script discussed above, students can be given a template with blanks to fill out in Latin.

Written version of picture-response activity

Give students a certain amount of time to write in Latin as many observations, questions and conjectures about a picture as they can.

Rorschach

This is named for the psychological test in which subjects respond to inkblots (see Wikipedia 2020). Rather than writing as many sentences as they can, students simply write the first three Latin words that come to mind upon seeing a projected picture. The picture can be an obvious depiction of the passage to be read, such as Maccari's picture of Cicero and Catiline, or another image that relates in some way, such as an eerie nighttime scene or a picture of people arguing. Students can share these words with the whole class while the teacher records each word on the board. The resulting list can make for interesting discussion of possible themes or the possible tone of the upcoming text. One variation is for students, rather than sharing their words with the entire class, to mingle with each other in search of students whose three words overlap with theirs.

Rorschach + sentence composition

The above task can be extended into a composition task by instructing students to write a Latin sentence that uses their three words. Often, I challenge students to write the shortest grammatical sentence they can come up with using the three words – that is, to use their three words and as few additional words as possible. This can generate another round of mingling in which students compare sentences and see if any can be linked sensibly to create longer sentences. I have seen that this task gets students to think about economy of style and some of the choices that Latin authors have available to them.

Conclusion

The strategies I have outlined can be used in a variety of combinations based on the needs and interests of the class and the teacher, regardless of the overall method or curriculum employed. The strategies are easy to vary and gradually implement as teacher's and students' comfort increases. I rarely use every strategy to build up to a single text, but I do tend to follow this trajectory:

1. listening, with some spoken interaction
2. reading preparatory text(s)
3. writing
4. reading the target text

The tasks described in this chapter occupy instructional time, which means they need to be weighed against other possible ways of spending that time. While we may instinctively wish to devote as close as possible to 100 per cent of class time to reading and discussing texts, every Latin course I know of, at every level, seems to spend time on things other than the mere act of reading Latin literature. A number of chapters in this volume suggest the value of communicative approaches involving the development of all four skills (reading, writing, speaking and listening) as beneficial in improving reading. These wider approaches may be adopted because they fulfill other goals of the Latin course or because the teacher expects them to prepare students efficiently for reading Latin literature. I submit the strategies described here as efficient preparation for reading based on my own experience in my Latin classrooms.

I have found that the feasibility and effectiveness of these strategies is maximized if students have been engaging in similar interactions from the beginning of their Latin-learning career, accumulating increasing comfort with and competence in comprehending Latin 'in real time'. If it seems unrealistic or inefficient to introduce some of these strategies abruptly into advanced literature courses, consider the potential success of students who have benefited from these kinds of tasks and interactions from the very beginning of their Latin studies. I believe it is never too late to start taking advantage of target-language communication as a strategic precursor to reading advanced texts.

CHAPTER 5
FROM READING TO WORLD-BUILDING: COLLABORATIVE CONTENT CREATION AND CLASSICAL LANGUAGE-LEARNING

Justin M. Schwamm, Jr. and Nancy A. Vander Veer

In September 2015, Nancy had recently started her teaching career at a small boarding school for girls. She was beginning to know her combined Latin II and Latin III class, who were expected to work with one of the well-known reading-comprehension method Latin textbooks. But there was a problem. She rang me: 'It's such a tiny class, but they're all over the place. A. can do this, B. can barely do that, and C. can do almost anything. But what can I do to help all of them?'

I thought back to a dreary April day several years earlier. The Latin II class in my memory was larger than Nancy's, but they too were 'all over the place', and they, too, had worked with one of the well-known reading-comprehension method Latin textbooks. 'We hate it', they told me. 'The stories are contrived and stupid, the characters are flat and dead, and the things about Roman culture are so simplistic. But we love it when . . . .'

What came after that 'when' was what led both of us on our journeys from reading to world-building. But before we describe those journeys, let us clarify the purpose and essential characteristics and desired results of such a journey. We see the study of Latin as a fundamentally communicative act, in which language-learners and teachers alike are participating in the centuries-long conversation among all Latin speakers and writers. That conversation began with the Romans, of course, but it has continued essentially uninterrupted to this day. We also see the study of Latin as fundamentally similar to the study of other languages; as Americans, we refer to the 'Can-Do Statements' and proficiency guidelines described by the American Council on the Teaching of Foreign Languages (ACTFL). For our readers in Europe and elsewhere, the ACTFL terminology is somewhat different from the terminology in the Common European Framework of Reference for Language (CEFR), but the levels themselves are similar. We aim for our students to reach an Intermediate High to Advanced Low proficiency level in ACTFL's Interpretive domain (reading and listening) and an Intermediate Low to Mid level in the Presentational domain (writing and speaking), or roughly B2 on the CEFR framework, by the time they leave us as seventeen- or eighteen-year-olds.

American students in a school such as Nancy's typically begin their study of language around age thirteen or fourteen; while timetables certainly differ from one school to another, it is not unusual for American students to spend forty-five minutes a day, five days a week, for a 36-week academic year in face-to-face contact with their language teachers and to spend fifteen to twenty minutes or more on independent homework assignments between class sessions. By contrast, my home-schooled students generally begin their study of Latin around age nine or ten. They meet with me for an hour or so per week in a live online video session and work independently for another hour or two per week until they complete their studies at age seventeen or eighteen.

In short, we aim for our students to be able to understand main ideas and important details in the texts they read and the things they hear, and we want them to be able to write connected sentences and paragraphs in which they narrate a story, express an opinion, or convey information to a reader who may or may not be familiar with the typical patterns of errors that language-learners make. Guided by the ACTFL Standards, we deliberately de-emphasize the written translation of Latin into English and the reverse-translation of English into Latin (what is often referred to as 'Latin composition'), and we emphasize *extensive* reading ('pages and pages') rather than *intensive* reading (the slow, deliberate parsing and translation of a few lines or paragraphs with which most Classicists are familiar from our university training). We emphasize the importance of grammar in context rather than grammar in isolation or grammar for grammar's sake, and we view translation (both from Latin into English and from English into Latin) as a tool rather than an end in itself.

We would note that the well-known reading-comprehension textbooks do not, in fact, advocate for an intensive or grammar-translation approach to the reading of Latin. But we have also noted, both in our own practice and in our work with other teachers, the remarkable power of teaching as one was taught. Many current Latin teachers in the US will have begun their study of Latin as university undergraduates, a setting where the grammar-translation, parse-every-word method predominates, and naturally carry over those methods to their work with younger students as 'the only possible way' or 'the best way' or 'the only way I know'.

As we and our students have moved first from intensive reading to extensive reading and then *from reading to world-building*, we have incorporated some techniques from the comprehensible input movement and from research on the importance of spaced repetition, combining them with the power of fan-fiction writing, role-play and a meaningful audience. In this chapter we describe our current processes, briefly outline their evolution, and close with recommendations for others who wish to incorporate these types of communicative activities in their Greek or Latin classes.

We return to the moment when my students shared with me: 'We love it when …'. They loved it 'when we make up our own stories and characters, because we really have to learn the vocabulary and the grammar and the culture then.' They challenged me: 'Why couldn't we just do that?' The energy in the room shifted as they began to take real ownership of the plan. 'We could have all kinds of interesting characters, not just wealthy men. They could really think and act like Romans, not like mid-twentieth-century American or British guys in togas. We could have stories from all different periods of Roman history. We could have animals as well as human characters.' I went home on that fateful Friday and spent much of the weekend developing a preliminary outline – an outline which led, eventually, to the *Tres Columnae* Project website (see http://trescolumnae.com/gamma/ and Schwamm 2019) and an ever-expanding set of additional characters and stories. Inspired in part by David Perkins's book *Playing the Whole Game*, we aimed to shift our focus from what Perkins calls 'learning about', or focusing on isolated elements of a subject, to what he calls a 'junior version of the whole game' that 'conveys the essence' of the work – in our case, the work of skilled readers and writers of Latin (Walker 2019).

By the time of that September phone conversation with Nancy, my students and I (first at that small public school in North Carolina, then in small groups of homeschooled students meeting in a virtual space online) had made significant progress toward our 'junior version of the whole game'. We had developed a storyworld or 'mythocosm' set in Herculaneum, mostly between the accession of Vespasian and the eruption of Mount Vesuvius, with 'flashbacks' and 'flash-forwards' to other periods of Roman history. We had established five primary families and some important animal-characters – with special attention on a mouse named Ridiculus who regularly gets into arguments with the *narrator* whom only he can perceive. We had also developed and begun to refine a system for creating new characters, stories, and complex storylines within that story-world and for adding them, either as supplementary stories or, if they sparked enough interest in the community, as additions to the core narrative. In brief, we would: (1) choose an interesting cultural topic or location in the Roman world; (2) divide into smaller groups to do some preliminary research; (3) see whether we needed to add a new character or characters; (4) make a short list of words or constructions that we might want to include in our stories; and (5) work together, sometimes as a whole class and sometimes as smaller groups, to write the new story or stories. For example, the *Lectio XI* story-sequence, featuring a disastrous visit to a human dinner party by our friend Ridiculus the mouse, grew out of a series of questions about the forms and logistics of Roman letter-writing. What might happen, students wondered, if someone misidentified the sender of a dinner invitation?

In 2014, I left 'physical-world' schools to work with students who, in American terms, are labelled as gifted and 'twice-exceptional' due to significant asynchronies of development or, in some cases, significant learning disabilities combined with significantly above-average intelligence test scores. As I continued to work with such students in small online groups, and as Nancy's students joined the efforts, we refined and systematized the structure described above. We also began to develop a more structured and intentional approach to what the Greek and Roman rhetoricians called *mimesis* or *imitatio* – the deliberate, conscious imitation and expansion of a prior text, undertaken by a learner who seeks to improve his or her writing. After reading an initial set of three stories, which introduce the city of Herculaneum and the family of our character Lucius Valerius Capito, students have their first *imitatio* experience. They see a picture of the family tree of another important character, Marcus Lollius Urbicus, one of Valerius' clients. Lollius, his wife, and three of his children are pictured, and there is a short list of Latin vocabulary which students have now encountered a number of times: *pater* (father), *mater* (mother), *maritus* (husband), *uxor* (wife), *filius* (son), *filia* (daughter), *frater* (brother), *soror* (sister), *infans* (baby), *est* (is). 'How many sentences,' wonders the teacher, 'can we make together about this *familia Romana*?' Having read many such sentences (and series of sentences) about the Valerius family, students find the task enjoyable and attainable. Without a word of grammatical explanation, students find themselves creating sentences that are grammatical, contextual, and meaningful. When we add the word *quis*? (who?), the activity becomes fully communicative as students are able to ask and answer questions about this Roman family and, if they choose, about their own real-world families.

As they continue to read stories about the Valerius family, the Lollius family and other Roman families set in our fictional version of Herculaneum, my students are invited to start creating their own authentic Roman family, who might be friends or clients of one of these core families or might have an independent existence, perhaps even in an entirely different part of the Roman world. They make family trees and brief Latin paragraphs (practising nominative and genitive case forms, among others) in which they introduce their *familia*, its members, and the members' relationships to each other. As they continue to read and learn about the core families and their lives in Herculaneum, my students develop more things for their new families: an authentic home, complete with a short paragraph in which someone is something in a particular part of the house, after reading a series of house-focused stories that serve as models for their *imitatio*. They decide on appropriate decorations (wall paintings or floor mosaics) for one or more rooms in their characters' homes in *imitatio* of stories where such decorations are featured. They create a scene in which a client-character and patron-character interact after reading stories about a *salutatio* or morning greeting-ceremony. Eventually they move from *imitatio* to direct creation as they write 'The Story You Must Tell', a whole sequence of stories featuring their new characters. The ultimate goal is to create a story worthy of publication as a core or 'expanded universe' story on the website, where it can be read and enjoyed by other participants.

Here is a particularly interesting example, created in Spring 2017 by an eager young Latin student in the western United States. His school had no Latin programme, but his family had a friend who had taught Latin, who contacted me and asked for permission to use the *imitatio* process and submit stories for publication. Of course, I promptly and gladly agreed. After working through several *Tres Columnae* Project story-sets, they wrote three publishable stories, of which the first can be found online at http://trescolumnae.com/gamma/de-personis-octavius-pompeius-taurus/. It begins:

> *Sub monte Vesuvio in urbe Pompeiis habitat Octavius Pompeius Taurus cum sua familia. Octavius est maritus Helviae. Et Helvia est uxor Octavii.*

> Below Mount Vesuvius in the city of Pompeii lives Octavius Pompeius Taurus with his family. Octavius is the husband of Helvia. And Helvia is the wife of Octavius.

> *Tiberius est filius Octavii et Helviae. Numerius est filius Octavii et Helviae. Pompeia est filia Octavii et Helviae. Pompeia est soror Tiberii et Numerii. Numerius est frater Pompeiae et Tiberii. Tiberius est frater Pompeiae et Numerii.*

> Tiberius is the son of Octavius and Helvia. Numerius is the son of Octavius and Helvia. Pompeia is the daughter of Octavius and Helvia. Pompeia is the sister of Tiberius and Numerius. Numerius is the brother of Pompeius and Tiberius. Tiberius is the brother of Pompeia and Numerius.

> *Turdus est psittacus Octavii. Turdus est callidus et caeruleus. Turdus exclamat: 'Da mihi cibum!'*

> Turdus is the parrot of Octavius. Turdus is clever and blue. Turdus exclaims: 'Give me food!'

> *Helvia est consobrina Vipsaniae. Familia Helviae familiam Vipsaniae visitat. Turdus exclamat: 'Trux! Trux! Veni huc!'*

> Helvia is a cousin of Vipsania. Helvia's family visits Vipsania's family. Turdus exlaims, 'Trux! Trux! Come here!'

Octavius, Helvia and their children (along with a rather insolent pet parrot) are the students' creation; Vipsania and Trux, the dog, both of whom are mentioned in the last paragraph, are core characters who appear in many published stories. Student and teacher had started working with the freely available version of the *Tres Columnae* website in mid-March 2017; they worked together for about an hour a week; and the student created this story two months later, in mid-May, 'because he enjoys Trux'. Even in this first story, he had moved from direct *imitatio* (the description of the family members in the second paragraph, and Turdus's words to Trux the dog in the last paragraph) to expressing some original thoughts: 'Turdus is clever and blue.'

In Nancy's classroom, *imitatio* continued to play a central role from day one of her students' first Latin classes, even though her schools have not used *Tres Columnae* as the primary curriculum. Latin composition based on rules of grammar and deductive reasoning is a challenging task, but even a student with a week of classroom exposure can imitate the sound patterns of a simple sentences. With an emphasis on repetition, a course like *Tres Columnae* is very helpful in providing enough models, but the early chapters of any reading method course provide enough material for fruitful imitation. Language-learners have clearly embraced various forms of *imitatio* in tribute to such textbooks; for example, a Google search for 'Cambridge Latin Course memes' in Spring 2020 returns almost two million results, and one for '*Ecce Romani* fanfiction' returns over eleven thousand. Since students are already building on these stories in entertaining and sometimes complex ways in their free time, it is entirely possible to harness this energy in the classroom in service of learning the language. One advantage of student-created characters such as those in the *Tres Columnae* storyworld is that, unlike the characters in commercially published textbooks, such memes can be created without fear of copyright infringement.

A simple exercise that Nancy used with great frequency – one that requires zero teacher preparation, but demonstrates the potential of an *imitatio*-based approach – is the following, which Nancy uses as an extra-credit question on an early test or quiz:

Write a simple story in Latin of at least four sentences. No sentence in your story should have more than four words. Simple is key! Try to imitate the Latin you have seen in [the chapters of the textbook that we have read].

Nancy has found that brand-new Latin students have no trouble following this prompt, although sometimes they require a little reassurance and reminder that the story can be simple, silly, and should not have anything to do with something complex that they might want to tell in English. With reference to the ACTFL proficiency framework discussed earlier, students are reproducing familiar words or phrases (the Novice Low proficiency level) and beginning to recombine those phrases to express their own ideas (the Novice Mid level). As they move from phrases to simple and possibly error-laden sentences, they begin to perform at the Novice High and Intermediate Low levels of the framework.

There are some roadblocks to introducing this practice later in students' experience with Latin, especially if their earlier experiences have involved extensive grammatical analysis or English-to-Latin translation. For example, in the 2014–15 school year, I worked with online groups of students at two high schools in northern New Jersey. I was familiar with the students and former teacher at one school, and they found the transition to a reading and *imitatio*-writing process relatively straightforward. The beginning students at the other school, knowing no other approach, found it as straightforward as beginning students normally do in both my experience and Nancy's. But the students in Latin II and Latin III, who had experienced a grammar-translation approach to the *Ecce Romani* textbook series, were overwhelmed. Despite their considerable declarative knowledge of Latin vocabulary, noun cases and verb tenses, they had never been asked to produce an original Latin sentence of their own without writing in English first, then translating. Faced with tasks that called for expressing their own ideas in writing at the sentence and paragraph levels – even when they had models and were shown how the *imitatio* process works – they struggled for the first few months to put away their old translation tools and use the tools I had provided for this specific purpose. Even at the end of the school year, they were less confident writers of Latin than their counterparts in the first-year class.

Many of Nancy's students, by contrast, came from middle-school backgrounds where they had learned some Latin, often finishing a first-year textbook's worth of grammar lessons. For a host of administrative reasons, many of these students were placed in Nancy's beginning Latin classes, even though they were hardly beginners. Curiously, it was rarely difficult to train these students to follow good imitation habits, as they reviewed the simplest concepts of grammar with the simplest models of language along with their peers who were encountering both concept and model for the first time. The key seemed to be to get the students used to the idea of playing with language and copying and tweaking very simple sentences while the only sentences in front of them are still simple. To continue to be a successful tool beyond the beginning stages students need to practise *imitatio* with more complex texts – after all, we do want to move our students beyond simple sentences such as those used in our first story above. But we have found that any attempt at short-circuiting the process is completely unhelpful. We believe that students need simple, frequent, creative imitative engagement with language from the very beginning, especially to avoid the pitfalls of over-intellectualizing in a misguided attempt to please their teacher.

Imitatio is, of course, possible with nearly any textbook or curriculum – all you need is a set of clear, repeatable examples for students to imitate, and such examples can be found in every textbook. But, in our experience, it feels easiest if started from the beginning or, as in the case of Nancy's students above, in a situation that feels like the beginning. As students grapple with the basics of inflection and simple sentences, their confidence improves when they can not only understand how something fits together, but also create something that is understandable and meaningful. It is hard to overstate the importance of creating sentences, paragraphs, and stories for an authentic audience, even if that audience consists only of one's classmates. When students share their creations with each other, they truly experience the power of David Perkins's 'junior version of the whole game'. The larger the audience, the more powerful the experience, as Nancy's students discovered when one class shared its products with another, and as the young creator of Octavius, Helvia and Turdus the parrot found when his story was published online.

While they are still working on the simplest items in the grammatical 'checklist' – perhaps only nominatives, accusatives, prepositional phrases and a couple of present-tense verb endings, we have shown that they are perfectly capable of expanding upon and telling simple stories. Grammatical errors in student work give information to the teacher about what students are truly acquiring and can provide signals for what kinds of further models the students need to see and, eventually, imitate. We believe that all students benefit from this approach, too, regardless of their level of Latinity or facility with applying grammar rules. With proper guidance, the teacher's and students' expectation shifts from 'Does the student understand and apply this grammar rule and this set of terminology' to 'What sounds like Latin? Why?'

For many teachers, including both authors, the challenges of *imitatio* arise not with the simplest items or the telling of simple stories, but in the not-so-simple stages that follow, as the ideas that students want to express in the language begin to outpace the language they have acquired and, in some cases, seen. The power of shared writing truly emerges at this stage. My small online groups, with four to six active participants, are an ideal environment for intermediate-level Latin readers and writers to work together on a story, or set of stories, that emerge from the shared interests of all participants. For example, in Fall 2019, my 'early Monday' group became fascinated with questions of gender identity in the Roman world. Did gender-non-binary people exist in the Roman Empire, they wondered, and if so, what sorts of experiences would they have had in a world where gender roles seem so pervasive and so fixed? Within a week or so, they had created a physically intersex character, the child of a Greek vine-dressing and sheep-herding family who work for, and live on, the estate of the wealthy Caelius family, relatives of the Valerius family mentioned above, who unfortunately live on the slope of Mount Vesuvius itself. The students quickly decided that their new character normally presents as male; named him Tiresias (in honour of the mythological character who was transformed from male to female and back again); and began creating stories in which Tiresias uses his gender fluidity to his own advantage and that of his family. In the course of creating the character, they did extensive research into the few available and relevant sources, and they also learned a great deal about subjunctive constructions that are often considered as 'far too advanced' for thirteen-year-olds. Around the same time, another of my groups was fascinated with the possibilities of a 'secretly proto-Christian' family and was working hard to create a plausible storyline around them, and another was developing a series of stories involving the character growth and change of one of the Caelius family's daughters, who realizes through a series of dreams and real-life conversations that she has been unduly cruel to her little brother. Through copious amounts of reading, accompanied by a carefully-constructed move through *imiatio* to independent writing, they had all become highly invested builders and maintainers of the story-world itself, and their eagerness to communicate their own ideas in Latin drove them to develop and refine their language skills. For example, the group that focused on the cruel sister demanded a 'really thorough explanation' of the Latin noun and verb systems. Within the first ten minutes of that explanation, they had mastered a noun-declension chart that they found incomprehensible two months earlier.

At times, my students, especially those in physical classroom settings, have wanted to move from writing about characters to performing versions of their stories and characters – in ACTFL's terms, from presentational writing to presentational (and sometimes interpersonal) speaking. One memorable class, in the spring of 2014, created videos with Latin dialogue to accompany every set of stories that we read and wrote together. Some featured live actors with masks, and a few featured paper-plate or paper-bag puppet actors; some had scripted or semi-scripted dialogue, but at least one was totally improvised – in remarkably comprehensible and grammatical Latin – in the moment of filming. For its final project, that class chose to do what we called an 'embodied role-play' in which they became members of the wealthy Caelius family, as the *paterfamilias* summons a number of neighbour-family *iuvenes* (young men) to his *villa maxima et splendida* (large and splendid villa), hoping to find good candidates to marry his rather high-spirited daughters Prima and Secunda, who by now have outgrown their earlier cruelty towards their younger brother. We wrote a story-line (now published beginning at http://trescolumnae.com/gamma/de-sororibus-cnaei-fabella-prima/); read it together; and then improvised in Latin an outcome in which Caelius' hopes – both for appropriate husbands for the girls and for a bidding war over the small and relatively useless field he wants to get rid of as part of their dowry – were hilariously and unpredictably foiled. Nancy's students, with more constraints on following a textbook, still ventured into similar forms of world-building when they construct their eagerly awaited crime scene investigations and reveal the 'real' cause of the death of the character Barbillus at the end of Cambridge Latin Course Stage 20, a task which they, too, have performed in serviceable (if not error-free) Latin.

But what is it about world-building (and, specifically, about this sort of collaborative content creation) that encourages, even compels beginning and intermediate Latin students to do so much more reading and writing than a more 'typical' US textbook-based approach in which 'coverage of the textbook' is seen as a primary goal? For my current students, as for Nancy's, the power of community and the promise of an authentic audience – two crucial features of the 'whole game' approach for which David Perkins advocates so strongly – have been key, and those promises were equally important when I was teaching in those schools in prior decades. There are as many reasons for students to consider studying Latin, or to enrol in a first-year course, as there are students who make those decisions. But once enrolled, facing a decision to continue (or not) past the requirement level, one of the most important factors our students cite is the power of the class community, and another is the power and depth of the learning process itself.

Between the first and final drafts of this chapter, schools and Latin programmes around the world found themselves in unprecedented levels of upheaval as the coronavirus pandemic swept from one country to another to another. Teachers, students, school leaders and parents found themselves facing situations that they could not have imagined even a few months earlier. In a situation where learning and teaching suddenly became remote and, in many cases, asynchronous, community and an authentic audience are even more important than they were a few short months ago, and we believe they are likely to remain important in the 'new normal' that will emerge in the coming months and years. While there are many routes to a learning community, and even more routes to a deep, powerful process of language-learning and teaching, it is our hope that more teachers will consider the route we have described above and discover for themselves the power of collaborative creation and world-building, in the context of a communication-focused and proficiency-oriented language class.

CHAPTER 6
ACTIVE LATIN TEACHING FOR THE INCLUSIVE CLASSROOM
Steven Hunt

Since Kenneth Baker's Education Reform Act of 1988 was passed, the position of Latin in UK schools has continued to be precarious. Records of how many students are learning Latin in schools are not kept, but the number of students taking Latin examinations at GCSE has remained stubbornly below 10,000 for pretty much fifteen years (Council of University Classics Departments 2020a). Some of the present challenges stem from circumstances teachers can hardly control: the competition from other subjects, especially STEM; the reduction in school funding; and the problems associated with changes in external assessment. What remedies can teachers turn to, then, to halt or maybe reverse this trend? In this chapter I suggest that UK Latin teachers could consider communicative approaches in their pedagogy as a strategy to encourage more student participation, engagement and motivation to continue Latin from Key Stage 3 to GCSE and beyond. Drawing on observations of teachers' developing practices in communicative approaches in Latin teaching, I will describe and evaluate several straightforward activities for teachers who wish to extend their repertoire of techniques.

The past has some useful lessons from which to learn. There have been three significant transformations in pedagogy since the 1960s. The first resulted from what Forrest called the 'two crises' – the removal of the Oxbridge requirement for Latin O level in 1960, and the comprehensivization of UK schools in the 1970s (Forrest 1996, 2003; Stray 2003; Lister 2007; Hunt 2016) – and led to the widespread use of the reading-comprehension method in preference to traditional grammar-translation approaches. The second transformation was brought about in the 2000s by the Blair government's forward-looking ICT policy in schools in combination with the development of Cambridge School Classics Project (CSCP) digital resources (Lister 2007; Griffiths 2008; Hunt 2016) and saw the integration of digital multimedia with printed course materials. The third transformation has been to reintroduce prose composition as an explicit, albeit optional, grammar assessment at GCSE under the 2010 Gove education reforms (Hunt 2018a). This move was part of the Department for Education's (DfE) neo-traditional education policy designed supposedly to restore rigour to national examinations in all subjects – what Ball calls a 'restoration curriculum' (Ball 2017). At the same time the DfE and ministers gave rhetorical and financial support for Latin in state-maintained schools (see, for example, the (then) Mayor of London Boris Johnson' article in the *Daily Telegraph* newspaper, in which he referred to the study of Latin and Greek as being 'the key to a phenomenal and unsurpassed treasury of literature and history and philosophy' (Johnson 2010)). This was a somewhat mixed message: the reintroduction of prose composition by the DfE *to make the subject harder* at the same time as attempting to promote wider uptake in across all sectors was – to this author at least – a somewhat contrary move.

There now seem to be no more policy changes on the horizon. Teachers have the opportunity to take advantage of the absence of further top-down policy reforms to develop bottom-up, professionally-driven means of encouraging students to study Latin. Various methods have been tried in the past – and I do not suggest that we lose sight of them. For a long time, Latin has been rebranded: its value is now perceived to lie in its contribution to cognitive development and language awareness rather than the gaining of social status (Lister 2007; Lanvers 2017; Quigley 2018). Latin is not *just* a language: learning about Roman civilization has long been shown to be attractive to students (Morris 1966; Emmett 2008; Khan-Evans 2018) and few teachers today would ignore the 'background material'. Most modern Latin coursebooks have undergone redesign and review: they aim to make Latin accessible to everyone, not just a select few (Paul 2013; Lister 2015). The examination boards for Latin (WJEC / EDUQAS and OCR) have tried to improve accessibility to a wider range of students than before: in the examination papers scaffolded response structures abound and written translation and comprehension of unseen texts is marked positively rather than negatively – that is, in the case of unseen written translation from Latin to English, students are credited for as much of the meaning of the Latin as they get, rather than for word-for-word accuracy. Most classroom teachers have welcomed these developments as necessary to widen access to students from across the ability range. Simply put, they know that schools will not offer Latin if the numbers do not make financial sense. But these changes are still not enough because they ignore the natural impulse of the students themselves actually to use languages – even dead ones.

I suggest, therefore, that a fourth transformation is now worthy of consideration: the inclusion of communicative approaches. A word of explanation before I go on: I subscribe to the view that the end purpose of learning Latin differs from that of Modern Foreign Languages. Ball and Ellsworth's (1996) article suggests that communicative Latin means the invention of what they call 'hyperfake' Latin: role-plays, Roman cookery demonstrations and general Latin mash-ups (Ball and Ellsworth 1996). Their anxiety that such activities might distract students from gaining mastery of subject and disciplinary knowledge is justified. Nor am I advocating a campaign to revive Latin as a spoken language in the classroom or beyond. I still want sixteen-year-old students to be able, with support from the teacher, to comprehend and comment in English on a passage of original Latin poetry or prose. Nor do I suggest teachers aim for fully immersive Latin experiences, because of their impracticability. Krashen's (1982) theories about the need for rich and engaging input are widely recognized and have been welcomed by many US Latin teachers and their personal experiences of employing his theory of comprehensible input are compelling (see, for example Macdonald 2011; Patrick 2011, 2019; Ramahlo 2019). However, I am anxious for practical reasons: whether a teacher can provide sufficient spoken input for every student in a standard UK Latin class of thirty-one, which meets, maybe, twice a week for an hour on a good timetable and once a fortnight on a bad one, for a maximum of five years (and more likely four or even three). In addition, time needs to be found for the preparation for the challenging examinations at GCSE, which include questions and short essays on original Latin literature, Roman civilization and prose composition. I admire what colleagues in the US are able to achieve in this vein, and am humbled by teachers' descriptions of what they are able to do in the immersive Latin classroom (see, for a very early example, Torchia (1973) and throughout this book); but I fear that full-lesson immersive approaches may be though to be unrealistic in the UK classroom, where time is short and innovation is curtailed by the outside demands of a school accountability system based on externally-set examination results. An eclectic approach seems therefore appropriate, in which communicative, reading and grammar-focused tasks are brought into play by the teacher depending on the aim of the lesson and the needs of the students (Nunan 1990). If that seems in the spirit of Rouse rather than Krashen, so be it.

Access to ideas and experiences of communicative Latin teaching have grown enormously since Torchia's 1973 article. Publications are now easy to find online. US teachers, less hidebound in many ways than their UK counterparts, have been more open-minded about different approaches to teaching Latin and the majority of the literature has come from across the Atlantic. Early criticism of communicative approaches such as that seen in Ball and Ellsworth's (1996) diatribe has been thoughtfully answered by Wills' (1998), Coffee's (2012) and Owens' (2016) more measured responses. Pre-eminent among those basing their arguments around second language acquisition (SLA) theories are those by Carlon (2013), Rasmussen (2015) and Van Den Arend (2018). They are all well worth reading. Teachers' experiences of communicative approaches to Latin teaching are becoming more widely shared (see, for example, Patrick (2015), Miller (2018), Sinclair (2018) Hunt et al. (2018) and special editions in the *Journal of Classics Teaching* 22 and 39). Increasingly the lived experiences of the students themselves are shared through a rich collection of blogs and social media (see, for example, the Facebook group Teaching Latin for Acquisition 2020). As yet, however, there is too little qualitative research or comment on students' attitudes to the use of communicative approaches to learning Latin. Lloyd's 2017 thesis provides some good examples of adult students' practices in using Latin communicatively, and this volume also contains samples from individuals and small groups. However, analysis of transcripts of students' 'Latin talk' in more school settings, with large groups, would be a valuable contribution to the field and might provide the evidence to convince more teachers to try.

As the Subject Lecturer for the Postgraduate Certificate in Education (PGCE) course in Latin, I maintain a keen professional interest in classroom practices from all over the world. My position requires me to train teachers not just in the way that suit the classroom now, but also to explore alternative approaches which might better suit their students' differing needs and interests (see, for example, Deagon 2006 for an excellent overview, with examples of activities). I am also a trainer for the charity Classics for All, working with teachers who are not trained Classicists (Hunt 2020b). Training directly with established teachers in their places of work (and I have done so with some sixty-two such schools since 2018) often offers a very different perspective on the way in languages can and need be taught, because many of the schools where these teachers work are non-selective, mostly urban and socially-disadvantaged in many ways. They often operate under very different conditions to the selective grammar and independent schools where Latin remains strong (Lanvers 2017) and the students I see in them represent more fully the social and cultural diversity of the UK population. In the 1950s, when Latin was only available in the academically-selective schools, it was almost acceptable that teachers could forge on with the 'impersonal rigours of grammar': only the 'convergent' students would be expected to continue (Stray 2018: 327). Such an attitude would rightly be questioned today. According to the DfE teachers must 'Set high expectations which inspire, motivate and challenge pupils' and 'Adapt teaching to respond to the strengths and needs of all pupils' (Department for Education 2020: 10–11). Teachers in all schools are highly aware of the different types of students in their classes and their responsibilities to each one of them (Sawyer 2016). But traditional coursebooks and lectures can act as monolithic barriers to the personalized learning styles of students and often demotivate them. Deci and Ryan's (1985) work on motivation in general and Dörnyei's (2011) work on student motivation in the SLA classroom both point to the idea that increased student participation in personalized activities in lessons is a powerful incentive to successful learning. Teachers could therefore consider relaxing the stranglehold of the coursebook awhile and investigate whether communicative approaches provide greater inclusivity.

Wills (1998), for example, listed four reasons why he saw that communicative approaches engaged students: they appealed to different learning styles; they increased the number and variety of activities in the classroom; they offered enjoyment; and they encouraged student participation. Rasmussen (2015) draws on her experiences in the classroom as follows:

> The final motivation that I have found among those who use any aspect of oral Latin is simply that it is enjoyable and fosters the joy of learning … When they realize it is a possibility, many students request the use of oral – especially conversational – Latin in their classes; they recognize the joy and value of communicating in the language they are learning. They see students of modern languages learning to speak and communicate, and desire to do so themselves.
>
> *Rasmussen 2015*

Both authors' experiences of using communicative approaches draw attention to the students' enjoyment. Communicative approaches are attuned to students' natural disposition to use language and are a successful way to engage and motivate learners.

When my teacher trainees and I have tried to communicate in Latin in the comfort of the university, it has been generally agreed that the experience has been enjoyable and it has led to lively discussions about practicability in the classroom. However, from the scores of classroom observations which I make each year, I perceive communicative approaches are rare and very limited. For example, it is common practice for teachers to read aloud and to ask students to read aloud, sometimes chorally, sometimes individually, or in pairs or small groups (especially with dialogues and playlets). From what I have seen, however, the practice seems to be used more to provide variety in the lesson rather than with any particular learning objective in mind. Sometimes the teacher starts the class with a traditional, '*salvete, omnes!*' ('Hello, everyone!') and gets the choral response, '*salve, magistra!*' ('Hello, Miss!'). All of these activities impress on students that Latin was once a spoken language. But that is the limit. Indeed, my observations show me that most contemporary Latin teaching gets out of the Latin and goes into English as soon as is practicable. Lesson activities principally involve students completing oral or written translation or comprehension of a Latin text from a coursebook or anthology of practice examination texts. Then the Latin is, as it were, put to one side. There follows a sometimes lengthy discussion in English of the meaning of the passage or an element of grammar within or something of socio-cultural interest. Sometimes these discussions happen before the students work on the Latin text, so as to set the text in its socio-historical context and aid comprehension. English is the medium of these discussions. A further observation: scanning the Facebook threads, one is amazed at how many activities in the Latin classroom are quizzes, the drawing of cartoons or storyboards, essay-writing practice and so forth. Very rarely are any of these in Latin: they are occasionally 'about' Latin (such as grammar notes or exercises), or they quote from the Latin text which has been recently studied; but it is almost as if the aim is to get out of Latin as soon as possible. Learning Latin seems not so much to be a learning a language as much as learning a language system – a list of rules to remember, mnemonics to help you remember the rules, vocabulary lists to work through, charts and tables to learn. And when the activities *can* be described more broadly as being directed towards learning how to read Latin, instead they consist of translations of Latin to write down into English, English gap-fill exercises (translation in all but name), drawings and cartoons with Latin tags and labels to make. None of these are wrong in themselves – indeed, they are very useful and engaging activities – but the more of them that are done, the further away from learning how to read and comprehend written Latin the student gets.

I am going to describe two simple communicative activities which I have seen in action in the school classroom recently. After each I shall provide a commentary and suggestions for further thinking. Both activities and their sub-activities seem to me to entirely suitable for the Latin classroom today.

Teaching talking

Communicative approaches offer the opportunity for teachers to interact with students and make them feel that they are creative participants in the development of their own knowledge rather than passive recipients of pre-packaged information. It is a potentially highly inclusive activity because it entails personalized learning through question-and-answer routines and therefore encourages proficiency at multiple levels. The best example of this is through 'circling' activities. I have seen examples of 'circling', where the teacher strikes up a simple Latin 'conversation' with individual students about a topic of interest or their likes and dislikes. Patrick (2015) and Bailey (2016) give good descriptions of the practice. Simple questions of the yes/no types can lead gradually up to alternate question phrases and finally very simple extempore responses produced by the student. The teacher controls the questioning and keeps the vocabulary range small enough so that the number of repetitions is sufficient for retention. Circling also allows the teacher to modify their questions to the students' declared personal interests and to recast the student's responses if appropriate, while still focusing on the desired vocabulary.

Some teachers (including myself) have worried that the use of non-classical vocabulary to incorporate students' personal experiences is problematic in that it may lead students astray into learning Neo-Latin vocabulary unsuitable for reading original classical texts prescribed for examination (Morris 1966; Owens 2016; Hunt 2018b). Recent (April 2020) Facebook threads have asked for the Latin for 'to spend time' and '2020', for example (Teaching Latin for Acquisition 2020). I have come round to this. Such vocabulary 'favourites' are exactly the sorts of things that can connect with students' everyday worlds and can motivate them to want to find out more. While personally meaningful to the students at the time, they can be considered in the long term to be 'throwaway vocabulary'. This is much in the same way, I feel, that a reading-comprehension text often provides an extra vocabulary gloss (in English) to support the understanding of the narrative of the text and to meaningfully stitch together the higher-frequency Latin vocabulary that teachers do want students to recall.

Another anxiety is that maintaining that sort of dialogue for more than a few minutes is tiring for the teacher and the students involved: engaging a class of thirty-one students is challenging, even for a very experienced teacher. I have noticed a tendency for the teacher to try the following practices: (1) to maintain a dialogue with one student alone, with the intention that the rest should look on, listen and learn; (2) to attempt to ask all students at least once a question or two with the intention of allowing everyone to participate at least once. Neither approach is particularly successful with a large number of students: how can teachers include as many students as possible? An obvious alternative might be that, once the model has been demonstrated, students ask one another questions in similar style. The teacher's role then becomes one of facilitator and monitor rather than demonstrator. The audience changes – students can be less reticent when their performance takes place not in the full glare of the whole class, but in the pseudo-privacy of a paired conversation.

However, although students usually yearn to talk about themselves, they are often limited by the vocabulary they can recall for themselves and so lasting or meaningful *extempore* dialogue can be impeded. Further models might be to ask students to recall characters from a text which they have previously studied and to ask them to come up with the sorts of questions and answers which they can ask amongst themselves. Assuming the *persona* of someone within a text is a familiar pedagogical device for encouraging reluctant or insecure speakers (Cresswell 2012). Talking about someone else, using vocabulary which they can draw on from the printed text, is an effective way to stimulate Latin conversation. The teacher would need to model the process first and maybe provide some help-notes such as a list of interrogatives. In this way the students practise the vocabulary that is needed in the guise of characters whose dispositions and motivations are already known and where vocabulary is easily accessible.

Teaching culture

One of the reasons that the reading-comprehension courses have been so successful is that they blend language-learning within a culturally authentic setting. The problem, as any teacher will tell you, is that the cultural materials are often considered by the students to be much more worthy of discussion than the Latin itself and it is easy for the class to get distracted from the Latin and instead focus on English. In order for students to spend more time in Latin rather than divert to English, background cultural material can also be delivered in Latin. However, for most teachers the fear of being unable to sustain talking in Latin without errors prevents them from trying. The following observations are based on lectures of various sorts given in Latin which I have witnessed.

The first thing to remember is that communication is more than just words: tone of voice, gesture, speech patterns and eye contact are all important cues to understanding and can be very useful to support students who are beginning to listen to Latin speech. The second is that there should be something to talk about. Hearing is so important; but it seems to me that it is the combination of hearing and seeing actions or especially images that works. Four examples. The first: an experienced Latin speaker in a class of twenty Year 11s discussed the content of a Latin text *which the students had already translated*, using synonyms for poetic vocabulary. The second: a novice Latin speaker in a class of thirty Year 7s asks students to pick out details in Latin about the Roman family using the text and pictures *Ørberg's Lingua Latin per se Illustrata*. The third: a medium-proficiency Latin speaker asks students to annotate an illustration from a scene from the Latin text and gets them to describe the scene in short but complete sentences using the same vocabulary. The fourth: an experienced Latin speaker gives a thirty-minute talk on a subject with which everyone in the class is familiar. In each of these cases the subject matter makes an enormous difference – if we know what the topic is, it is far easier to engage with listening and to understand the most of what is being said. The repetition of key words and syntactical features – discourse markers, if you like – also aid understanding considerably. I don't think that keeping strictly to Latin word order matters especially: the students are listening for meaning and – certainly in the beginning stages – they will find English word order helpful. This plays into the hands of the teacher who may be a novice themselves. Pauses help both teacher and students: few teachers today would talk continuously to their students in English for more than five minutes, much of which would in itself consist of pauses. I've noticed that certain phrases are common 'fillers': *ut opinor* (as I think); *ut dicitur* (so to say); *nescio quis* (someone or other). Simple syntactical constructions are easier to handle than complex ones – although supposedly complex ones often fall into usage quite naturally (I am thinking of some ablative absolutes and ablatives of the gerund which seem to slot neatly into conversational usage as pre-formed vocabulary items). Indeed, this is normal communicative practice: lexical strings of words are heard as single lexical items – and they are easy to say too (see, for example, Nation (2001 317–43) for an overview). There is also the chance to recast phrases which the students themselves use and thereby increase the number of repetitions of key vocabulary. It is also clear that gesture and physical movement add saliency to meaning and act as interpretative guides to the meaning of individual words and phrases.

So, one of the starting points must be that there is something of interest to the students to talk about (Rivers 1987). If the subject matter is not familiar, however, then I have seen teachers make use of a large-scale image on the whiteboard. It is easy to maintain the conversation if there is an image to talk about and go and point to. With my teacher trainees I have taken images of wall paintings from Pompeii from standard Latin coursebooks, for example, and described the scenes in Latin, eliciting responses ranging from the shaking or nodding of the head, to repetitions of phrases, to the production of simple sentences using the vocabulary learnt in the activity, and to short stories built up using simple sentences and the vocabulary which describe the scene. We have also used standard coursebook material to explore how to introduce spoken Latin into the everyday classroom. One of the biggest fears I have found among beginning Latin teachers is about having something to talk about. Starting with the familiar is a comfortable way in. Here is an example with Cambridge Latin Course Stage 1 material, for example:

Images of Caecilius and Metella from the Cambridge Latin Course are projected on the board.

Teacher	[points to Metella] quis est? Caecilius an Metella?
	(Who is this? Caecilius or Metella?)
Students	Metella.
	(Metella.)
Teacher	[smiling] Metella est. [points to Caecilius]et quis est? Metella an Caecilius?
	(It's Metella. And who is this? Metella or Caecilius?)
Students	Caecilius.
	(Caecilius.)
Teacher	[smiling] Caecilius est. [pointing] haec est Metella et hic est Caecilius. [to the class] dicite omnes: haec est Metella.
	(It's Caecilius. This is Metella and this is Caecilius. Everyone say: this is Metella.)

Students	[repeating] haec est Metella. *(This is Metella.)*
Teacher	[pointing] et hic est Caecilius. *(And this is Caecilius.)*
Students	[repeating] et hic est Caecilius. *(And this is Caecilius.)*
Teacher	[pointing] Caecilius scribit an dormit? [acting out the verbs] scribit ... an ... dormit? *(Is Caecilius writing or sleeping? Writing ... or ... sleeping?).*
Students	scribit. *(Writing.)*
Teacher	[smiling] Caecilius scribit. non dormit. dicite omnes: Caecilius scribit [acting out the verb]. *(Caecilius is writing. He isn't sleeping. Everyone say: Caecilius is writing.)*
Students	[repeating] Caecilius scribit [acting out the verb]. *(Caecilius is writing.)*
Teacher	non dormit [acting out the verb]. dicite omnes: Caecilius non dormit [acting out the verb]. *(He isn't sleeping. Everyone say: Caecilius isn't sleeping.)*
Students	Caecilius non dormit [acting out the verb]. *(Caecilius isn't sleeping.)*
Teacher	[pointing] haec est Metella. [To the class] est pater an mater? *(This is Metella. Is she a father or a mother?)*
Students	mater. *(Mother.)*
Teacher	[pausing, as if something is not quite right] dicite mihi: Metella est mater. *(Everyone say: Metella is the mother.)*
Students	Metella est mater. *(Metella is the mother.)*
Teacher	[relaxing] Metella est mater. Caecilius est pater. [points] mater. [points] pater. Caecilius scribit? *(Metella is the mother. Caecilius is the father. Mother. Father. Is Caecilius writing?)*
Some students	Caecilius scribit. *(Caecilius is writing.)*
Some students	scribit. *(He's writing.)*
Teacher	[points] mater scribit? an sedet? *(Is the mother writing? Or is she sitting?)*
Some students	mater sedet. *(The mother is sitting.)*
Some students	sedet. *(She's sitting.)*

Teacher	[smiling] mater sedet. dicite omnes: mater sedet.
	(The mother is sitting. Everyone say: the mother is sitting.)
Students	mater sedet.
	(The mother is sitting.)
Teacher	[points] et Caecilius quoque sedet et scribit. [To the class] pater dormit? in pictura? pater dormit?
	(And Caecilius also is sitting and writing. Is the father sleeping? In the picture? Is the father sleeping?)
Some students	pater scribit.
	(The father is writing.)
Some students	pater sedet.
	(The father is sitting.)
Some students	pater sedet et scribit.
	(The father is sitting and writing.)
Teacher	[Pleased] ita! pater non dormit. sed sedet et scribit. dicite omnes: pater non dormit, sed sedet et scribit.
	(Yes! The father is not sleeping. But he is sitting and writing. Everyone say: the father is not sleeping, but sitting and writing.)
Students	pater non dormit, sed sedet et scribit.
	(The father is not sleeping, but he is sitting and writing.)

Note the way in which the vocabulary is used to create meaningful discourse; the small set of words used by the teacher and by the students; the number of times those words are repeated; the ways in which questions, positive and negative statements, and synonyms build word knowledge by repetition; the use of gestures by teacher and students; the positive affect of the classroom, evidenced by the teacher's demonstrations of enthusiasm and students' participation.

Even better is if the teacher adds a small number of key words in Latin on a side board or to the word-wall. These are not like the glosses in coursebooks or the 'throwaway' vocabulary used in circling, however: they are the key words which students need to be grasping as part of their other language work. They might act as a silent scaffold to support student understanding or for them to recall and use in later activities. It is important that students make their own responses to the description. I've seen students answer chorally; or the teacher has prompted individuals to respond. There remains an anxiety among UK teachers that senior leadership personnel want to see written evidence of measurable outcomes and that listening and speaking is difficult to capture and quantify. The use of mini-whiteboards for students to jot down phrases or to briefly answer questions given by the teacher is a proxy for actual speech, but might be seen as a partial solution. It is very easy today to ask students to record their voices reading, asking questions, engaging in classroom dialogue with a fellow member of the group. If teachers are careful, it should be possible to store such communicative practices digitally.

Further experiments might take the form of students describing their own choice of images, their classrooms or even their own homes in Latin. The ubiquity of the internet and the simplicity of video recording and editing makes this increasingly possible. Might Justin Slocum

Bailey's (2020) 'Journey to the Bathroom' video and its like inspire a whole craze for student-made descriptions of home, pets and pop stars?

Conclusion

The communicative transformation I propose differs from other shifts described in the introduction to this chapter in that it is not in response to a sudden external turbulence over which Latin teachers have no control. Government is presently too busy to bother itself with Latin teaching in schools and teachers may be able to grasp a rare opportunity to chart their own course while attention is elsewhere. Communicative approaches, at least at the simplest level, require a certain amount of determination, some self-training, but no special or expensive resources. They are, if anything, the most bottom-up creation of all – produced by teachers collaboratively with the students themselves as active participants and contributors. To my mind, the moment is right: there is now no extra funding for Latin from government, no matter how kindly the (present) prime minister, Boris Johnson, might look upon the subject. But there is a real need to attract more learners to Latin if the subject is not going to follow ancient Greek down the road to become the prerogative of the tiny number of elite schools which can afford it. Latin cannot be seen as an option only for those of a certain disposition, for the gifted and talented corps, for those destined to scholarship in the languages at university. Teachers need to build a broader base through more inclusive practices. Communicative practices give teachers a chance to make that base more secure in all our schools and colleges.

PART 2
INTRODUCING COMMUNICATIVE APPROACHES IN UNIVERSITY SETTINGS

CHAPTER 7
EXPLORING COMMUNICATIVE APPROACHES FOR BEGINNERS
Mair E. Lloyd

Introduction

In October 2017, I taught a non-examined beginners' Latin course for postgraduates in the Modern Languages Centre (MLC) at King's College London (KCL). The course comprised weekly two-hour lessons held over two terms and had an intended duration of twenty weeks. In this chapter, I present an exploration of the teacher and student experience of the communicative aspects of this course, drawing evidence from lesson recordings, student comments, and from my own recollections and reflections.

It was a requirement of the MLC course that I should attempt to teach Latin in a way that was similar to that in which other Modern Foreign Languages (MFL) were being taught in the Centre. That is, I was asked to take a communicative approach to Latin teaching. My previous doctoral research exploring communicative approaches through the perspective of modern language-learning theories (Lloyd 2017) was a key factor in my being offered this extraordinary opportunity. Based on data gathered at the full Latin immersion event held annually in Lexington, my PhD thesis had claimed benefits for attendees in terms of development of reading skills, intrinsic motivation (taking pleasure in learning for its own sake) and enhancement of affective factors including increased confidence and reduced fear of making mistakes (Lloyd 2017). It also called for teachers to take on researching the effects of communicative approaches in their own classrooms and to share and debate their findings with the Latin teaching community, so that, based on the evidence of benefits they demonstrated, a wider variety of teaching practices might become available for future generations of teachers and students. The opportunity at KCL provided me with a way to take forward some of the research and debate I had wanted my thesis to inspire.

The postgraduate beginner MFL courses in the MLC are taught by native or near-native speakers, and students are expected to reach the equivalent of A1 Basic User Breakthrough level of the Common European Framework of Reference (CEFR 2020). Criteria for that level include being able to '... interact in a simple way provided the other person talks slowly and clearly and is prepared to help' (CEFR 2020). Another specified learning outcome for MLC courses is that students 'communicate in everyday situations using mainly two language skills of speaking and reading at a basic level' (MLC 2016: 2). Classes are largely taught through the medium of the target language (MLC 2016: 3). Ideally then, drawing both on the MLC teaching model and on my own evidence for the benefits of full language immersion, I should have been a near-native Latin speaker and I would have delivered my classes predominantly through the medium of Latin.

I found myself with conflicting feelings about this prospect. I was concerned about how well teaching through the medium of Latin would work for my absolute beginner students, and about the practicalities of carrying out lessons entirely in Latin as a relative newcomer to Latin speaking myself. I had observed beginner students being taught successfully through the medium of Latin in the *scholla aestiva* at Poznań (see Part 2 of Chapter 16 of this volume). However, the Lexington *Conventiculum* that I attended as part of my doctoral research mandated 'at least a passive understanding of the structure of Latin' and the ability to 'read unadapted Latin texts of the simpler kind' before taking part (see Part 1 of Chapter 12 in this volume). Convener Terence Tunberg does not recommend full immersion for complete beginners but suggests that the 'teacher ... should have ready recourse to the native language to explain things' (Lloyd 2016: 47). In the field of English as a Foreign Language (EFL) recent research also highlights 'increased acceptance of own-language use' and its potential as a 'cognitive tool [...] through which learning is scaffolded' (Hall and Cook 2012: 298 and 291). I resolved that rather than striving for an unattainable (for me), and possibly undesirable (for my students) goal of Latin monolingualism, I would use a 'bilingual approach' (Hall and Cook 2012: 271). I decided that this was feasible given my own capability as a Latin speaker, and that flexibility in language use would allow me to remain responsive to the needs and progress of my students. It seemed very important to me that the introduction of communicative approaches in the Latin classroom could be shown to be possible for teachers who have not practised Latin as a spoken language to the highest level. I therefore set out to discover the extent to which the benefits I had seen delivered by expert speakers in immersive Latin gatherings could be provided by a relatively inexperienced Latin speaker in a mixed language environment.

In the event, my two-hour classes were held with slightly less than half the time spent 'in English' and slightly more 'in Latin'. These estimates are based on the recordings I made of two of my lessons. Transcripts show a good deal of alternation between short segments of each language, with the longest time spent consistently in either language at approximately twelve minutes. This statistic pleases me enormously as I had not imagined at the outset that I could keep things going in Latin for so long nor use so little continuous English. A good proportion of the uninterrupted 'in Latin' time (about 30 per cent of the total lesson) was made up of reading (and re-reading) aloud stories from Ørberg's *Lingua Latina per se Illustrata: Famila Romana* (*LLPSI* 2011), along with dialogues from the companion volume *Colloquia Personarum* (Ørberg 2006). My students and I also occasionally read stories from other books including *Cambridge Latin Course, Book 1* (CSCP 1998) and *Epitome Historiae Sacrae* (Lhomond 2009). The other 'in Latin' segments, taking up just over 20 per cent of the total lesson time, were made up of a mix of the following:

- extemporized introduction of vocabulary supported by slides with images and Latin labels;
- scripted or extemporized Latin questions about the stories we had read;
- conversation on everyday topics, supported by slides with useful phrases.

While I did also make use of English in my classes, I want to concentrate in this chapter on these 'communicative' Latin portions of my lessons, that is the times during which my students and I used Latin as a means of interacting with each other, and on the techniques I used to make sustained Latin exchanges possible for us. I will therefore present transcripts of excerpts from these parts of my lessons alongside commentary informed by MFL and ancient language scholarship, a research method used in my doctoral thesis (Lloyd 2017) and based on discourse analysis techniques recommended for teachers (see, for example, Demo 2001). Recordings are from week 12, when we revised Chapter IX and read Chapter X of *LLPSI*, and week 17, when we revised Chapter V and covered Chapter XIV.

Communicative activities

Introducing vocabulary 'in Latin'

In the first few lessons of the course, I relied on reading Ørberg's stories and his vocabulary hints in the margin to make the texts comprehensible for my beginner Latin learners. This 'reading approach' (Wilkins 1969; Celce-Murcia 1991) can be considered from the perspective of Krashen's Comprehensible Input hypothesis in which he claims that '[we] acquire [language] only when we understand language that contains structure that is "a little beyond" where we are now' (Krashen 1982: 21). The *LLPSI* stories progress in such a way that new linguistic material builds gradually on what has gone before and comprehension is maintained through a combination of the hints in the margin and measured introduction of new elements. Though this approach seemed to be effective for some of my students, others told me that they found it very difficult to deduce meanings of new words in context. Difficulty with 'guessing' meaning was particularly evident among beginner students whose first languages were unrelated to Latin (these made up about half of enrolments), possibly because they were not familiar with some Latin/English cognates nor with the geographical features that are designed to make the initial chapters of *LLPSI* readily accessible to those with English or Romance language backgrounds. For example, a sentence such as '*Nilus et Rhenus fluvii sunt*' ('The Nile and the Rhine are rivers') is readily understood by students familiar with the Nile, the Rhine and the English word 'fluvial', but difficult to decipher for others. To help students who were struggling, I began to spend a few minutes before each reading introducing new vocabulary and (incidentally) grammar that it would introduce. I prepared images labelled in Latin presenting words or phrases from the story we were going to read so that I could make their meaning more obvious in advance. I then extemporized Latin descriptions and questions around the images, a technique I had seen used to great effect with beginner Latinists in Poznań (see, for example, Loch's (2018b) video from 5:20 to 12:24).

The transcript and commentary below are based on a recording of me preparing students to read *LLPSI* Chapter X, *bestia et homines* (beasts and men). I had previously briefly explained (in English) the meaning of the verb *possum* (I can) and its use with the infinitive. I use *Maria*, the Latin equivalent of my Welsh name, for myself and the names Fabia, Lucia, Victor and Augustus for the students. Although the students did each choose a Latin name for themselves to use in Latin classes, I have changed them, and sometimes student genders too, to preserve anonymity. Although the class was aimed at complete beginners in Latin, Fabia had studied Latin for one or two years at some time in the past. The other three students mentioned here had little or no previous experience of Latin study.

Transcript of lesson segment introducing vocabulary   Projected in front of the class is an image from *LLPSI* (Ørberg 2011: 69) that includes three birds in a blue sky with a few clouds. Next to one of the birds I have added a pink (to emphasise gender) label *avis, avis,* f. (bird) in Latin only. Underneath the birds is the sentence *aves in aere volant* (the birds fly in the air). New vocabulary that I am introducing is marked in bold in the transcript.

[pointing to picture of single bird] Maria: **avis** . . . *ecce* **avis** *et* . . . [pointing to three birds together] **aves** . . . *tres* **aves** *in caelo sunt* . . . *in caelo sunt* . . . (Bird . . . look at the bird . . . and the birds . . . three birds are in the sky . . . they are in the sky.)	It is easy for me to extemporize here because I have the label on the picture as well as a sentence for me to read and embellish using vocabulary met previously (e.g. *in caelo* used in the previous week and reviewed in the first part of this lesson).
[flapping arms like wings] *et* **aves** *in aere* **volant** *in aere* – *aut in caelo* – *sunt* (and the birds are flying in the air in the air – or in the sky – they are)	Here I mean the visual gestures to help with comprehending the new word '**volant**'. I offer *aut in caelo* as an alternative to *in aere* to give a further clue to its meaning in addition to the image since students have already met *in caelo*.

The projected picture also shows a group of three **homines** (humans) and three **pisces** (fish). I introduce these words as well as **natant** (they swim) in a similar way using the sentences *homines in terra ambulant* (humans walk on the earth) and *pisces in aqua natant* (fish swim in water). These words are reinforced as the segment progresses.

Maria: *aves* **possunt** *in aere volare* . . . *aves* **possunt** *volare* . . . *et homines* **possunt** *ambulare et pisces* **possunt** *natare* . . . *natare* (Birds can fly in the air . . . birds can fly and humans can walk and fish can swim . . . swim.)	Pointing in turn at the same images, I now go on to extemporize sentences using **possunt** (they can) with the infinitive (introduced earlier in the lesson in English) reinforcing this usage and the newly introduced vocabulary.
Maria: **possuntne** *homines natare*? (Can humans swim?) [Students nod signalling assent.] Maria: *ita* . . . *sic*. (Yes.) Maria: *homines* **possunt** *natare et* . . . **possuntne** *homines volare*? (Humans can swim and . . . can humans fly?) [Students shake heads, laughing.] Maria: *minime*. *non* **possunt** (Not at all. They can't.) Maria: *et pisces* **possunt** *volare*? **possuntne** *volare*? (And fish can fly? can they fly?) [Students nod and laugh.] Maria: *fortasse*. . . (Perhaps. . .)	Now I am ready to extemporize questions using the new vocabulary and the cognitive effort required is reduced because I can see the slides illustrating vocabulary, meaning and usage. This also makes responding easier for students, boosting their confidence. I do not pick out individual students to answer here but let them shout out or nod or shake their heads. This reduces pressure on them, lowering the affective filter (Krashen 1982: 29–31) as their laughter indicates. When students answer non-verbally, I model verbal answers that they can use in future.

I continued introducing vocabulary in this way, alternating between pointing and explaining and asking questions. Among other vocabulary introduced was ***ala, alae*** f. (wing) with accusative plural ***alas*** that I will refer back to later in this chapter.

Listening back to recordings of myself introducing vocabulary in extemporized Latin, and the apparent ease with which I produce correct Latin utterances, I would definitely recommend this as a confidence-building way for new or less-experienced Latin speakers to introduce communicative Latin into their classrooms and to improve their own language production. This type of activity could be used with any Latin textbook as long as the teacher projects suitable images annotated with noun labels and sentences. For example, the 'model sentences' and illustrations from the Cambridge Latin Course would be eminently suitable for this treatment (see, for example, CSCP 1988: 84–5).

In the lesson segment partially transcribed in above, the class and I worked on new vocabulary 'in Latin' for almost eight minutes. We then moved on to reading, still only in Latin, and we then used questioning about the story (described below) to sustain our Latin bubble for over twelve minutes. Although students had contributed little Latin input in the vocabulary introduction phase, the amount they had learned became obvious when they answered and extemporized questions themselves.

Questioning based on LLPSI *stories*

After the first couple of weeks, during which I read the Ørberg's stories out loud myself, the class and I would take it in turns to be narrator or to read the parts of different characters. This meant that students alternated listening (while following along in the book) and reading aloud. I encouraged them to put a lot of expression into the readings, in part to rehearse for expressing themselves in Latin, in part to make the reading comprehensible for their listening peers, and in part to let me gauge by the way they delivered the reading whether there were parts that needed explanation, either in English or through Latin questioning or rephrasing. We interrupted the readings at various points, usually at the end of a paragraph, and I would spend a few minutes asking the class questions in Latin or English about what we had just read. Sometimes, and particularly in the earlier lessons, I would use the Latin questions from the *pensum* C exercises of *LLPSI* that comprise Latin questions about each story (see, for example, Ørberg 2011: 76). Sometimes I would make up questions on the spot. I also invited students to make up questions (or read them from *pensum* C) and we would take turns posing and answering questions. I present here extracts illustrating each or these activities.

Teacher-extemporized questions   I extemporized the questions transcribed in the following segment after Augustus had read lines 19 to 25 of Chapter X of *LLPSI*, a paragraph that used some of the vocabulary covered in the transcript above. New vocabulary is again shown in bold and I address the class as a group rather than singling them out for questions.

This type of questioning is not difficult for me as a teacher because it relates to a relatively short piece of text, and vocabulary and phrases are fresh in my mind from the reading. As long I stay close to content of the extract and use familiar ways of forming questions, answering is also manageable for students.

Maria: ***potestne*** pastor ***volare***? (Can the shepherd fly?) Students: (quietly) *minime*. (Not at all) Maria: *et **potestne** canis **volare**?* (And can a dog fly?) Students: [quietly] *non potest.* (It cannot.)	Having rehearsed this vocabulary thoroughly before the reading, it is reasonably straightforward for me to make up simple questions relating to the section that we have just read. Students answer quietly at first, but clearly demonstrate understanding of the questions and the story content.
Maria: *cur canis non **potest volare**?* *cur non **potest volare** canis?* (Why can the dog not fly? Why can the dog not fly?)	Here I repeat the question (with a variation in word order) to give students time to think and to look at the text if they need to.
Lucia: [confidently] *canis non **alas** habet.* (The dog does not have wings.) Maria: *optime!* (Excellent!)	Suddenly, Lucia answers with a complete sentence. This is not simply read from the text, which actually says *canis alas non habet,* but extemporized, showing active command of the vocabulary, including the new word *alas.*
Maria: *Lucia, visne legere?* (Do you want to read?)	I keep us in the Latin bubble inviting Lucia to read.

Lucia demonstrates that having met the word *alas* for the first time in the earlier vocabulary introduction session, she has – through a combination of interaction using this word, and hearing it read – acquired confident production of the new vocabulary without being asked to consciously learn it. This active production takes place approximately fifteen minutes after the word was first introduced. It is not possible to say whether this could have been achieved without a communicative approach, but it is promising to see production of new vocabulary after so little time, and confident use of Latin to express an idea in only the twelfth two-hour session. I suggest that, though I started introducing vocabulary communicatively for the benefit of students whose first language was not Latin-related, it became a valuable addition for the whole class, making new vocabulary readily comprehensible, facilitating active production and, *a fortiori*, contributing to reading skills by promoting vocabulary recognition. This segment also demonstrates students' developing the ability to 'interact in a simple way' as required by CEFR (2020) and the MLC syllabus and so making progress with the original aims of ancient and modern language pedagogy.

pensum C In the following transcript, I use questions taken from *pensum* C of Chapter IX of *LLPSI* to promote interaction around the story. While Loewen has argued persuasively for 'judicious error correction' in second language classrooms (2007), some meta-analyses have judged this practice 'ineffective and possibly harmful' (Truscott 2016: 1). Having observed the demotivating effect of correction on myself and on others, I side with Truscott's judgement. I do not correct student mistakes but praise successful expression of meaning.

Maria: *Auguste, ...num pastor solus in campo est?* (Augustus, ...surely the shepherd is not alone in the fields?) Augustus: *pastor non solus in campo est sed cum canis et ovis.* (The shepherd in not alone but with the dog and a sheep.) Maria: *optime! optime!* (Very good! Very good!)	Using scripted questions makes it very easy for me to provide accurate input, and addressing individuals provokes much more Latin use than addressing the class in general. It is harder for students to get all the Latin endings right when they reply using phrases that are not in the question (for example *canis et ovis* should be *cane et ovibus*), but grasp of the vocabulary is very evident and meaning clear so I respond with praise.
Maria: *quot oves habet pastor?* (How many sheep does the shepherd have?) Fabia: *centum oves habet.* (He has 100 sheep.) Maria: *et suntne albae?* (And are they white?) Fabia: *undecentum oves albae et una ovis nigra.* (Ninety-nine white sheep and one black sheep.) Maria: *bene, optime!* (Well done! Very good!)	Fabia is a more experienced Latinist than the other beginners and she answers well and confidently here, giving peers an opportunity to learn from her example as well as mine.

[a number of other questions are negotiated successfully]

Maria: *Lucia, cur pastor umbram petit?* (Lucia, why does the shepherd seek the shade?) Lucia: Er ... *quia* ... *pastor* ... er ... word what's the word .. *iac* ... *iac* ... *iacet* ... no ... (Er ... because ... the shepherd ... er [...] li ... li ... he lies [...].) Maria: *sed cur umbram petit? ubi est sol?* (But why does he seek the shade? Where is the sun?)	At this question, understanding temporarily breaks down. Although Lucia seems to have understood that *cur* (why?) requires an answer beginning with *quia* (because) and that the question is about the shepherd doing something, she is not clear what that 'something' is and is trying to say what the shepherd does (i.e. lies under the tree). My attempt to introduce the idea that the answer is connected to the sun does not help.
pastor umbram petit ... cur? (The shepherd seeks the shade ... why?)	Nor does repeating the question in a different order.

Lucia: I can't find the word I want. [Lucia looks for the segment in the text to find the word she wants to say and uses it to make this sentence] *iacet . . . pastor iacet sub arbore.* (The shepherd lies under the tree.)	Lucia feels free to break into English to seek help and is given more time to check the word she is looking for in the book. She verifies that it is *iacet* and puts together a new sentence (not in the original story) that admirably conveys what she means. I wish I had praised this more.
Maria: *iacet quia sol in caelo lucet. sol in caelo lucet. itaque pastor sub arbore iacet in umbra.* (He lies down because the sun is shining in the sky. So the shepherd lies under the tree in the shade.) *ita? bene?* (OK? Good?)	Instead, I try to bring us back to the original question. I check for comprehension with *ita?* and *bene?* but it still is not clear to me that Lucia has really understood this exchange.
Fabia: *in caelo . . . in caelo nubes non sunt.* (In the sky . . . in the sky there are no clouds.) Maria: *ita vero nubes non sunt in caelo. sol lucet. sol splendet in caelo.* (Indeed there are no clouds in the sky. The sun is shining. The sun is bright in the sky.)	Fabia tries to help with explaining why the shepherd is seeking the shade, but eventually we move on, unsure whether comprehension has been restored.

It is not clear whether Lucia, having missed the previous lesson where we first read this chapter, has less grasp of its content than Augustus (a beginner) or Fabia (more experienced) nor whether she has understood that the question asks 'Why?'. With hindsight, I could have been more helpful by breaking into English myself to give the meaning of *cur* or even of the full question. This extract illustrates some disadvantages of a beginner-speaker teacher staying too rigidly 'in Latin' with beginner Latinists when a 'bilingual approach' (Hall and Cook 2014) could release them from a breakdown of communication.

Another feature to notice here (and in the next transcript) is that students have begun to actively support each other in their learning, deliberately intervening to try to help with comprehension. This demonstrates 'scaffolding' among peers to achieve more than each individual would manage alone (Foster and Ohta 2005). Communicative tasks provide ample opportunities for the provision of such support. Viewed through Lave and Wenger's (1991) model of learning as a social process, Fabia's behaviour also displays characteristics of 'apprentice' progression in a 'community of practice', in which members become more capable as they progress towards gaining mastery and become mentors to others. There is further evidence of peer support and mentoring in the following exchanges.

Turn-taking questions In this communicative activity, the students and I sat in a circle and took it in turns to ask each other questions. Though we sometimes used *pensum* C to do this together, in the transcript shown below we are all extemporizing our own questions. This exercise took place in Week 17 of the course, after the class and I had re-read the whole of Chapter V to ease ourselves in after a three-week strike-induced gap between lessons.

Maria: *Victor, estne Aemilia femina pulchra?* (Is Aemilia a beautiful woman?)	Victor and I begin the activity with a successful exchange.
Victor: *est.* (She is.) *Aemilia est femina pulchra.* (Aemilia is a beautiful woman.) Maria: *bene!* (Good!)	
Victor: *Lucia, in villa Iulia . . . Iulii . . . er estne impluvia?* (Lucia, is there a rainwater pool in Iulius' villa?) Victor: [whispering under his breath]: Is there an *impluvium*?	Here Victor makes two self-corrections: first he converts *Iulia* to the correct genitive *Iulii* and later he replaces *impluvia* with the correct form *impluvium*. He also mixes languages to help Lucia.
[Victor points to page with impluvium] Maria: *in illa picture, fortasse.* (In this picture perhaps.) Victor: *estne impluvium?*	Victor and I try to repair communication with a visual clue from page 33 of *LLPSI*. Victor repeats his question using the correct form *impluvium*.
Lucia: Yeah? [laughing] *certe!* (Sure!)	At first uncertain, Lucia then realizes she does know what the question means and what the answer is.

[Now it is Lucia's turn to ask a question.]

Lucia: [laughing after a long empty pause] The weak link in the chain here. Victor: It is usually me, don't worry. Lucia: I can't think of the question word.	Lucia breaks into English to ask for help and Victor is ready with reassurance, which it is easier for him to give quickly in English.
Maria: You can cheat and pinch some from the story if you like. There are some on page 34. Lucia: I can't think what 'what' is. Maria: *quid.* (What.)	I also break into English to help more effectively. Lucia then feels she can ask in English too and is able to go on and ask her question in Latin once I supply the word she wants.
Lucia: er, *quid est in hort . . . ?* (What is in the garden?)	Lucia seems aware of her uncertainty of the right Latin ending for *horto*.
Fabia: *ah, multi arbores sunt in horto.* (There are many trees in the garden) Lucia: [whispering and pointing to the picture of a villa in the garden] I was looking at this, but yeah! Fabia: *villa Iulia in horto est.* (The Julia villa is in the garden.)	Fabia understands the question and gives a valid answer, but Lucia uses English to help Fabia find instead the answer that she was originally looking for. Although Fabia should ideally say *villa Iulii* rather than *Iulia*, she now gives the answer Lucia was after and successful communication is restored.

During this exercise, I found that I felt more relaxed sitting and working with students in a circle rather than standing in front of them as a class, and I believe I could more easily laugh with them over any difficulties. Again, the community of practice model fits this experience well, with me mentoring other apprentices while acknowledging my own ongoing development. Victor shows how fellow novices can generously support each other in progressing or, through a Vygotskian Zone of Proximal Development perspective (Vygotsky 1978: 86; Lantolf, Thorne and Poehner 2015: 208–13), scaffold each other's performance as he supports Lucia's understanding by whispering his question to her in English.

It is evident that this exercise is more prone to mistakes in Latin than the two illustrated previously. This is as true for me as it is for the students, though my errors occurred outside the transcribed segment. Without close scaffolding from a relatively small segment of text or from vocabulary slides, this was a challenging exercise all round. Use of some English rescued us from being altogether stuck and I would recommend this as an acceptable escape route for beginner students and new-to-speaking teachers.

This extract also shows students' awareness of the need for appropriate word endings and effort to move towards accurate use of Latin despite me refraining from correcting them. Although it is not evident here, later transcripts also show me correcting myself in an effort to provide a better example. We are clearly monitoring our production (Krashen 1982: 18–21) to make our Latin more accurate.

Finally, there is evidence for my students' reading comprehension skills through the confidence and expressiveness with which they read on recordings, and through largely successful exchanges about content in these transcripts. This may not be solely attributable to communication in Latin, but the eclectic approach I took clearly facilitated progress with reading as well as with simple interactions in Latin.

Conversation on topics relating to everyday lives   My closest approximation to the MLC's requirement that students 'communicate in everyday situations' was to promote conversations about personally relevant topics such as greetings, families and origins etc. The inclusion of personally relevant topics is supported by Rivers' assertion that students 'achieve facility in using a language when their attention is focussed on conveying and receiving authentic messages (that is, messages that contain information of interest to both speaker and listener in a situation of importance to both)' (Rivers 1987: 4). In addition to being relevant to students' lives, each topic had the potential to highlight similarities and contrasts between Roman daily life, as represented in *LLPSI*, and the daily lives of students, fulfilling another requirement of modern language syllabuses at the MLC that students 'develop knowledge and understanding of the societies of the countries where the language is spoken' (MLC 2016). This aim is equally valid for students of classical languages, where one of the reasons for studying the language prioritized by university teachers is to 'understand ancient culture and thought' (second only to 'reading, accessing or appreciating ancient texts') (Lloyd 2017: 149). Research has also indicated that awareness of the culture of origin aids reading (Wilkins 1969: 175) and that bringing together an understanding of the culture in which texts are situated with a reader's own world experience is key to facilitating reading competence (Nuttall 2005: 6–8). The practice of using Latin to bring ancient and modern schemata (i.e. world-views) together promises a very powerful way of focussing effort towards the twin university teacher aims of engaging with ancient texts and understanding ancient culture.

To scaffold student language production in talking about Roman and contemporary life, I projected a 'cheat sheet' of phrases (in Latin only) that students could use. I built up the number of phrases each week repeating earlier ones to reinforce memorization as well as adding new phrases that reflected material met more recently in the *LLPSI* chapters. For example, in the lesson where we read Chapter IV of *LLPSI* that introduces Roman numbers and *quot* (how many), I added the following new items on our *colloquium parvum* (little conversation) slide.

quot liberi sunt in familia tua? (How many children are in your family?)
in familia mea sunt xxx liberi / in familia mea est una filia / unus filius.

(In my family there are xxx children / in my family there is one daughter / one son.)
The 'little conversations' had two different formats. Sometimes, I asked the class questions individually. At other times I asked them to talk to each other in pairs or threes and then feed back to me what they had found about each other. I have taken part as a student in this kind of activity in both the Lexington *conventiculum* and Poznań *schola aestiva* (see Chapters 12 and 16 of this volume).

Sadly, I do not have transcripts of this type of session, because the lessons in which I made my recordings (in weeks 12 and 17) did not include this activity. Nonetheless, there is one part of the recording of the week 17 lesson where I attempt to engage students in a conversation about where they live. We had practised questions relating to home locations in the previous week when the following had been added to the *colloquium parvum* slide:

ubi habitas? habito in oppido xxx quod in Britannia est.

(Where do you live? I live in the town of xxx, which is in Britain.)
We had not previously practised talking about the types of houses in which we lived though. Nonetheless, at the beginning of lesson 17 we re-read chapter V which mentions the Roman villa, and, on an impulse, I decided to ask some questions about students' homes. The following dialogue was then extemporized without the 'cheat sheet' and without practice by me or the students.

Maria: . . . *habitasne Victor in villa?* (Do you live in a villa, Victor?) Victor: *non . . . er, . . .* Maria: *in domo fortasse? . . . sed non in villa.* (In a house perhaps? . . . But not in a villa?) Victor: [in English laughing] No.	Initially Victor does not seem entirely sure about the meaning of the question, so I go on to try to make this clearer by suggesting he lives in a house (*domo*). However, I have forgotten that students have not met *domo* (or *domus*) before so this does not help. Victor does understand my *sed non in villa* and laughs and confirms this in English in a tone that suggest humour.
Maria: *et in domo tuo suntne multi cubiculi?* (And are there many bedrooms in your house?) Victor: Oh, erm . . . [long pause]	I plough on, still using the unknown word *domo*. Other vocabulary has been revisited in reading Chapter V.

Maria: *quot cubiculi sunt in domo tuo? . . . sunt fortasse er . . . unum cubiculum?* (How many bedrooms are in your house? There are perhaps, er . . . . one bedroom?)	I persist in Latin repeating the question. Now my own Latin is suffering, and I match a plural verb with a singular subject.
[showing picture of bedrooms] *hae sunt cubiculi* (These are bedrooms.) *quot in domo tuo sunt?* (How many are in your house?) [long pause]	I try using a picture as a prop to explain *cubiculi* (mismatching gender of *hae* and *cubiculi*).
in domo meo sunt duo cubiculi, unum cubiculum meum et unum cubiculum. . . er. . . er. . . filii mei. (In my house there are two bedrooms, my one bedroom and one bedroom . . . of my son.)	I give a further clue by responding to my own question using words that *are* known to Victor.
Victor: *ah! unum cubiculum . . .* (Ah! One bedroom.)	Now he understands the question and can respond.

This shows that I have some difficulty staying accurate when extemporizing unaided, and that Victor finds it harder to join in with this discussion in the absence of further scaffolding from known vocabulary and slides. I do eventually find a way of helping him with known vocabulary, though. This exchange continued successfully with more experienced Latinist Fabia, who (having perhaps learned or been reminded of the meaning of *domo* through listening to Victor and me struggle) was able to reply to *quot cubiculi sunt in domo tuo?* with *sunt tres cubiculi, unum cubiculum magnum et duo cubiuli parvi* (there are three bedrooms, one big bedroom and two small bedrooms). At the end of the course, Fabia commented that she would have liked to have more of this type of interaction. The other students involved in these transcripts also made very positive comments about the approach taken in this course, but one beginner student, who withdrew after eleven weeks, explained that he did not like being asked to respond in Latin in front of the class and would have preferred a more traditional approach. Communicative approaches, like any others approaches to teaching, may not suit every student. Also, pushing beyond the communicative level at which the teacher is comfortable and competent may lead to loss of confidence all round. Communication of this sort can best be successfully undertaken at a level appropriate to student stage and teacher capacity for spoken language. This does not mean teachers should avoid facilitating everyday topics of conversation, but they should be appropriately scaffolded to make them productive for both teacher and students.

Conclusions

Transcripts of recordings of teaching sessions have been used to reflect on challenges and successes in my own introduction of communicative approaches into my Latin classroom and to explore what student responses and language pedagogy scholarship tell us about how and what they are learning. From this exploration, I draw the following conclusions:

Teachers with relatively little Latin-speaking experience can successfully introduce communication in Latin as part of a wider approach that includes reading Latin stories and interaction in English. Holding part of the class in Latin can be enjoyable and effective in terms of learning for both teacher and students. If communicative approaches are to become more widely used, we need to accustom the next generation of teachers (who are sitting in our classrooms now) to be ready to carry these approaches forward. If we wait till our own speaking ability is perfected, we delay the opportunity to deliver benefits through bringing ancient language communication into mainstream activities.

Ideally, though, teachers should be happy and reasonably relaxed in their teaching so that they can establish a supportive classroom community in which individuals feel free to make mistakes and to break into English (or another language) if they need to. It is not necessary to stay 'in Latin' all the time and, for beginner Latinist students and teachers relatively new to spoken Latin, there are good reasons for not doing so. Pushing too hard towards ideals of ubiquitous Latin usage can take both teacher and students unproductively outside their comfort zones and the extent of their current abilities.

I do, however, urge those who take on teaching Latin communicatively, regardless of current skill level, to increase their own speaking ability throughout their teaching careers, ideally by attending immersion events and conversing with other Latin speakers. There are many excellent organizations mentioned in the chapters and reference list for this book that make this possible. If this ideal is out of reach, progress can still be made through continually trying to use spoken Latin in class with appropriate scaffolding. Introducing vocabulary interactively, as described in this chapter, is a very good way for beginner-speakers to start.

Finally, I have found that for my own benefit as a teacher, it has been valuable to record lessons and to build up my own knowledge of modern and ancient language pedagogy. Playing back and critically reflecting on my own and students' performance in the light of language-learning scholarship have improved my own understanding of the benefits and challenges of different activities and let me refine my teaching strategies in line with my competence and my students' learning level. I hope that my reflections and the evidence presented here will encourage others to take the leap into introducing communicative approaches into their teaching and ongoing learning practices, to the ultimate benefit of our ancient-language-learning community.

CHAPTER 8
COMMUNICATIVE LATIN FOR ALL IN A UK UNIVERSITY
Clive Letchford

Why change?

Five years ago, I would not have expected to be contributing a chapter to a book like this. Indeed, I would probably have passed the book by without a second glance. In this chapter, I adopt a practical approach. I will describe what has changed my mind so significantly; how I have put myself in a position to be using spoken Latin in my classes; the benefits for my students; and what I have done in the classroom on a practical basis.

The route to becoming a teacher of Latin, let alone one taking a more communicative approach, has been a long one for me, with an unconventional starting point as a Chartered Accountant in the City of London. I followed this direction for fourteen years before deciding to come back to Classics. I studied full time for a PGCE to gain Qualified Teacher Status. I was gratified that my Latin and Greek returned quickly and that the more I used them, the stronger they became. After teaching in UK secondary schools, I switched sectors and began teaching Latin and Greek at beginner and intermediate levels at the University of Warwick as a Teaching Fellow.

During my time at Warwick, there have been three events that have been significant in making me rethink my teaching methodology:

1. I enrolled in an accelerated German language course for beginners, putting myself in the position of a student again. The experience of being in a learning environment was very helpful, reminding me what it is like to start a new language from scratch. I wondered whether I could adapt any of the techniques used for modern languages for my teaching. At that time, we were using a Latin course that had been developed in-house, which took a traditional approach akin to that of Wilding's *Latin Course for Schools* (1995). I could not see how I could use modern techniques using this particular course, but it left me wanting to rethink my own approach.

2. In a Latin language class, I asked my students to work in pairs to translate a handful of straightforward sentences (subject-verb-object structure) into Latin, a thing they had done regularly between classes but not during a class. The time taken to achieve this, and their apparent lack of confidence, were revelatory. It made me think how much more could be achieved in the limited time available if only we worked orally. The following year, therefore, I encouraged them to translate some simple sentences in chorus fashion (that is, the whole class together). This seemed artificial and I did not repeat it subsequently.

3. The third, and by far the greatest, event was my visit in 2016 to the *Accademia Vivarium Novum* in Italy with my wife (also a Latin teacher), to visit a former student. Once

there, we were invited to observe lessons and reflect on them. The teachers and students not only tolerated our stumbling attempts at conversations in Latin but positively encouraged them. It seemed appropriate that we had our first discussions about the benefits of communicative pedagogy through the medium of spoken Latin. We both found this visit opened our eyes and provoked some fundamental questions about Latin teaching and learning. What do we mean by 'knowing' Latin? Are our expectations too narrow, too low in the UK? Our education system is driven by external exams, but do these exams promote confident and fluent readers of Latin? Is it really impossible to read a Latin text with fluency?

With such thoughts, I considered how I might change my teaching approach. I needed to consider the type of students I had, my own skills, and the extent to which change would fit with the progress we wanted them to make over the year.

The students at Warwick

The Department of Classics and Ancient History at Warwick offers three main undergraduate degrees: Classics (Latin and Greek languages must be studied in each year); Classical Civilisation; and Ancient History and Archaeology. All our courses are multi-disciplinary and most modules are common to all three degrees. While the department maintains a focus on material culture, it strongly believes that classical languages lie at the heart of the discipline. For this reason, all first-year undergraduates must take one of the classical languages at an appropriate level. This language is a core module which a student must pass. Our beginners arrive with a wide range of experience in language-learning. The increasing diversity of students was another important factor in my wish to change my approach to teaching beginners.

Previous approaches

In previous years, I had used our in-house Latin course, developed because my predecessors had found no published course which was a good fit for our students' ability and the available time. *Reading Latin* (Sidwell and Jones 1998), in use before my time at Warwick, had not been popular or successful among the students. I tried *Wheelock's Latin* (2011) for a couple of years but it seemed to suit only a minority who liked a grammatical approach to Latin. Wheelock's lack of continuous passages did not provide text which engaged students, and the allure of 'real' Latin from the earliest stages appealed much more to me than to them.

Our in-house course had twenty chapters, one per week to be taught in three one-hour classes. It covered all the basic accidence and main syntax. When written, it had been benchmarked on the language content of GCSE Latin, but GCSE requirements had subsequently been reduced in terms of accidence, syntax and amount of vocabulary. A typical chapter comprised two sides of A4 explanations and examples, drills to practise new accidence, some Latin sentences to provide further practice, a passage of continuous Latin (a retelling of Roman history or myths without an over-arching narrative across the chapters), and around ten English sentences based on the Latin passage to be translated into Latin. The vocabulary expected to be known amounted to a little over 500 words.

Those who ended up in the top half or so of the cohort each year flourished with this course. It seemed to be well-structured, clear, and introduced few exceptions to the 'rules' (since we felt these could be introduced in the subsequent year). However, up to 25 per cent in some years did not engage as well as I wanted. The course was dry and did not have enough engaging content to motivate them. Despite a lot of guidance on the type of skills and approaches needed for success, a number fell behind each year. Feedback on the module each year, formal and anecdotal, suggested that some of them resented being asked to memorize tables of endings and did the minimum required to get through the module. It was clear that if I wanted to engage them more, I needed to investigate a different approach.

Teaching myself

Trying to take a more communicative approach to teaching Latin presupposes some ability and confidence in speaking it. With a grant from Warwick's Institute of Advanced Teaching and Learning, I attended the first four weeks of the summer course in 2017 at the *Accademia Vivarium Novum* (Letchford 2017). There were two purposes: to provide me with some ability to speak basic Latin, and to let me put myself in the position of a student working systematically through Ørberg's *Familia Romana* (2011). I was already considering using this in my own teaching because my research had suggested that this was a course that could work well with communicative approaches and I had seen impressive results from my previous visit. A revelation that I had not anticipated was the impact on my own learning of the games and songs we enjoyed each evening. I could see how these could be very powerful additions to my classroom pedagogy.

Planning a new approach

On my return to Warwick, I had several decisions to make. I was confident that I could make *Familia Romana* work as my module textbook and that I would get as far as *Capitulum 25* at the end of the first year. This would cover basic nouns, adjectives and the indicative mood of verbs. It would not reach the subjunctive and its associated uses nor align with GCSE requirements as my previous course had done; however, the students would have read very many times more Latin and would have a vocabulary of around 1,200 words at the end of the first year (compared with around 500 in the previous course). I considered that this was an acceptable trade-off, since in my experience a good working vocabulary is at the heart of linguistic confidence.

I decided to deliver the course through spoken Latin as much as I could, at least initially, but to give back-up support with supporting written materials in English as necessary. I would not ask students to speak Latin extempore but focus their attention on the way the book introduced vocabulary and grammar in a way that they could deduce from the context. They would understand how it used repetition to help them gain familiarity with the forms and structures of Latin.

I would keep our existing assessment structure (one end of year exam plus four short exams throughout the year worth 10 per cent each). Over the years, students had given feedback that they appreciated the regular shorter exams to show that they were on track. The exams would give the majority of marks for translating from Latin into English and there would be some grammar questions, such as filling in endings. Whilst I was open to changing assessment methods in the future, I wanted to see whether a more communicative approach could achieve results that were at least comparable to a more traditional method.

Using *Familia Romana*

When I first saw *Familia Romana* in a bookshop, I put it down almost straight away since it was not at all clear to me how it could be used. This will probably be the case for anyone who has not experienced this type of approach, so in the following section I set out how I used it in the first year. In the following section, I describe the outcomes.

My approach over the year had three main elements:

1. reading and understanding the passages (in class and in independent study);
2. consolidating new material by doing exercises (written and oral);
3. singing songs in Latin.

Chapter 1 of Ørberg is important for understanding how the method works. It is basically a geography lesson about the Roman empire, amounting to a little over 600 words of Latin. I spoke almost entirely in Latin – the text is very intuitive for anyone if their attention is directed to the map of Europe. At this stage, I modelled the pronunciation orally, getting the students to repeat after me. Using intonation, I got them to understand words like *quoque* (also) and the interrogative particle *-ne* (expresses a question). I also focused on the additional information given, showing that the pictures that Ørberg uses in the margin to introduce vocabulary were there not to leaven the text or to be a starting point for discussion of Roman life but to help them to understand the text. Because these are such an integral part of the course, I used English to explain how they needed to be used.

I have long been keen on students reading the language aloud. With a language which has such regular relationship between letters and sound as Latin, this is not challenging. From my classroom experience, it has become clear to me that students find it difficult to learn vocabulary if they cannot confidently match the written word to its sound. But with Ørberg it also means that learners can understand as they read, at least in the early stages, helping to remove the 'crossword puzzle' mentality encouraged by other approaches. To help develop this skill and to emphasize its importance, I sometimes dictated a sentence to check on their progress. It was always a key sentence from the chapter we had just read, thus stressing that language is about communication rather than a series of phonemes.

I made recordings of myself reading all the text of each chapter for them to use. My recordings in the first term also included recitations of nouns and verb endings. In my experience, I have found that some students find an aural element helpful and that having a distinctive rhythm helps students to memorize case and verb endings. Some communicative methods eschew this, but Ørberg tabulates them and the exercises explicitly test them. At the pace I needed to adopt, I considered that this would be helpful and I also wanted to provide a safety net for those students who would benefit from security and reassurance. I encouraged them to download the recordings onto their smartphones so they had access to them wherever they were. One benefit of new approach over the old was the confidence, fluency and accuracy with which the students read the text. Even if they were reading aloud at sight, the large majority read with a high degree of accuracy, and showed an appreciation of the structure of the sentence as they read – even though the sentences show sophistication in matters of subordination and varied word order from the earliest chapters. This is such an important skill if our ultimate goal is fluent reading.

Many of the chapters include a significant amount of dialogue. I asked students to read these out, each one taking a character. In the earlier chapters, where the ideas are simpler and the passages shorter, I always brought my students to the front of the room to read directly from the book 'in character' and to react to what they were reading. This was challenging since it involved them reading out loud, understanding what they were reading and reacting appropriately all at the same time. In the first term, however, this was well within their capability. From my observation over the year and from the end-of-module feedback, it was clear that a significant minority were reluctant. First-year students have always been self-conscious, but our department has seen an increase in the number with specific anxiety issues. To encourage them to be more playful, I had a range of simple costumes and props to use – coins, money bags, roses, a sheep fleece and a dog mask. Some engaged very enthusiastically once prevailed upon.

After acting out a passage for the first time, we read the passage again. We typically focused on the new vocabulary, looking at the information and context, and I often repeated the sentences and helped point up the meaning by gesture and vocal inflexion. The book introduces vocabulary and repeats it in ways that helps students to retain it. First, each chapter has a particular situational focus (such as travel, the countryside, or the human body) which means that a lot of the vocabulary is introduced in a lexically coherent way. The second way is that the course frequently defines vocabulary in terms of Latin words which have already been met, through synonyms and antonyms. This has the advantage of revising vocabulary as well as making links within the language. Current models of long-term memory suggest that building up of a mental lexicon is important and that this is a matter of making multiple connections within the second language (L2) as well as between the first (L1) and second language (L2). (For an introduction to the role of memory in learning classical languages, see Carlon 2016.)

For all written exercises, I use a flipped classroom model. I put up answers online so that students could check their work in advance. In the follow-up class, I would draw attention to key concepts exemplified in the *Pensa* (*Exercises*) I would also spot-check, asking them to reperform the exercise from the book without their written answers in front of them. My intention was two-fold: to get an impression of how well the work had been done; and also because the I considered that the act of trying to recall the answer from memory was very valuable in getting it into their long-term memory.

I found that I needed to adapt my approach in the second term. As the vocabulary became more abstract and the load became heavier, it was difficult to keep the focus on communicative methods because I needed more contact time. The students also made it clear that they felt they needed more traditional support. I started to speak in English more often to check their understanding, and I gave out a list of new vocabulary for each chapter together with English meanings. (The book itself is entirely in Latin: it lists vocabulary, and gives a reference to the line where a word first occurs, but does not give the meaning in English.) The reason for this was that I sensed that many of the students needed this if we were to reach my target chapter by the end of the module.

In the second term, I also started to give a short explicit overview in English of the main grammatical items in each chapter. If I did this before reading the text, I would give a very brief explanation along the lines of 'if you see this, think this' and I would leave brief notes on the whiteboard for reference. In addition, I produced a series of booklets leading up to each short exam with the main grammatical concepts and endings set out chapter by chapter. As the concepts became longer and more demanding, the students wanted me to use more English as I had done with vocabulary.

We also sang songs. I was introduced to most of these on the summer course at the *Accademia*, and for much of the first year they are related to the stories in the chapters of textbook. In the first term they were written specifically for the book; in the second term we added some medieval Latin lyrics, mainly from *Carmina Burana*. I explained at the outset that songs helped by repetition, melody and rhythm to fix some key structures in their minds. We went through the text of each song to establish the sense, keeping within Latin for this, using synonyms and antonyms as appropriate. I told them that I did not expect tunefulness or a good voice from everyone, but I expected them to contribute to the best of their ability. Some of them very much enjoyed this unexpected activity. I was lucky in being able to lead this confidently, as I am an experienced semi-professional singer. I am aware that some teachers would not want to use this technique.

Outcomes: subjective

From my perspective, I could see the following advantages of the new approach:

1. The continuous story line is very engaging for the students. Although simple on the surface, there is subtle characterization and the reactions of characters can be brought to the fore.
2. The approach involves making connections within L2 and using contextual information, rather than reverting to a dictionary or the 'meaning' of a word learnt from a list. My experience suggests that this a more efficient way of learning vocabulary. Although I was requiring students to learn twice as much vocabulary as on the previous course, none of them commented in the module feedback that there was too much to learn (as had been the case in previous years where the number of words to be mastered was much smaller). This suggests learning vocabulary required less conscious effort under the new approach.
3. The course demands active engagement with the content – the passages have real meaning with students frequently speculating on how the characters will act. The fact that we do not formally translate any passage means that they know that there is no expectation of one 'correct' translation from Latin into English. They have to negotiate their own understanding.
4. Classes are livelier and more varied. Using a wide range of aural and oral activities offers more ways of accessing the language. It is helpful to those who like to learn less

analytically. It is particularly helpful for those who need more repetition. In particular, I saw less evidence of the typical sorts of difficulties that dyslexic students following a more traditional course display.

5. Latin has a reputation for being hard. With anxiety and stress among students becoming increasingly prevalent over the last five years, this approach provides an easier, less threatening introduction and challenges their preconceived ideas of what learning Latin entails.

I gathered feedback from students at the end of the first year of teaching the module in May 2018.

'What do you think are the most important things you have learned from this module?'

1. 'Basics of the Latin language' was a common comment, but some widened this out to 'grammar', which included English grammar as well.
2. Time-management.
3. More experienced linguists commented on the way the coursebook introduced vocabulary, the inductive but structured way accidence and syntax were set out in the narrative, and the explanations which had many examples taken from the narrative.

'Please tell me what you liked about the course.'

1. Half of the responses specifically mentioned the story as being something they enjoyed and/or found helpful.
2. Many mentioned the narrative format helped in the retention of vocabulary.
3. Almost half mentioned the acting/props/songs and the interaction in the classroom.
4. One-third referred to the extensive use of Latin in the book (entirely in Latin) and in my delivery as being helpful in learning and consolidating the grammar of the language. One said how they felt at times they were 'thinking in Latin'. Another (who has studied several European languages as well as classical Greek) commented that it was the best textbook they had met in any language.

'Please tell me what you didn't like about the course.'
The feelings about the module were almost entirely very positive. A handful commented on:

1. Fast pace of the course.
2. Difficulty of having grammar explained in Latin.
3. Difficulty of differentiating which grammar points were really important from those which were more matters of idiom.

Outcomes: examination results

In the first year of trialling this approach, there were three groups of beginners. Two groups used Ørberg's *Familia Romana*, but a third had a more traditional introduction using the Warwick Latin course. Students were assigned to groups randomly, with the exception that my groups included those who had been diagnosed as having dyslexia. (Past experience shows that they find language-learning at university-level difficult.) The end-of-year exam for everyone comprised two unseen passages for translation and a third question specifically testing grammar. The first unseen passage was common to both courses.

I was apprehensive before seeing the marks, since the focus of my students had been on understanding the Latin to their own satisfaction rather than traditional practice in oral and written translation. I was pleased to see that on the common translation question, the mean mark for those taught using *Familia Romana* was 72 per cent, while those who had followed the traditional in-house course had a mean of 68 per cent. My students all showed that they expected the passage to make sense as a narrative. Some of the less high-attaining students following the traditional course offered a translation that was at times incoherent, but which managed to hit the mark scheme sufficiently often to get a pass. It was also noticeable that the students with dyslexia, who had followed *Familia Romana*, did better than I would have expected them to do if they had followed the Warwick Latin course. This suggests that more extensive exposure to the language which had been made possible by the use of a more communicative approach had benefitted them.

Beyond beginners

Although my project was aimed at rethinking my beginners' module, I have taken this further. This is partly so I can think how best to extend this approach to the next level of Latin teaching and partly to develop my own skills to do so. For this reason, I have worked with small groups of Latinists post-A level, showing them that it is possible to understand Latin without translating into English. We have read a variety of texts, from medieval historians, stories of saints, Erasmus' letters and selections from Boccaccio's *On Famous Women*. I have led these, keeping entirely in Latin, using the Renaissance technique of *enarratio* – rephrasing in simpler Latin. For students reared on word lists and running vocabularies, this has been an eye-opener. Particularly striking was their comment that their vocabulary became much better – even though we had spent time learning vocabulary in the traditional sense.

Future directions

As I explained at the start of this chapter, I came to use a more communicative approach to Latin teaching from a practical perspective. Having become more immersed in the literature of classics pedagogy and second language development theories, I have seen why the approach I have taken has improved the experience and attainment of many of my students. I am also aware that there are no hard and fast answers that work for every student and teacher. Theories can give us some insight into the factors that lead to success in learning a second language, but they are no guarantee of universal success.

My Ørberg-based course is now in its third year. It has been less communicative perhaps than I had anticipated because of the time needed to use a fully communicative approach and feedback from students. Even so, I have seen huge benefits in terms of the confidence, fluency in reading and, especially, engagement of students. It has made the classroom a more creative and enjoyable place for me and has made me see Latin as a real living language.

I remain committed to this approach for my beginners and continue to think about how I can extend these techniques at Warwick at a more advanced level given the constraints within which I work. Finally, I continue to work on my own spoken Latin with other Latin speakers, sharing the delight and friendship that characterizes language-learning at its best.

CHAPTER 9
ACTIVE LATIN IN THE TROPICS: AN EXPERIENCE WITH NEO-LATIN IN BRAZIL
Leni Ribeiro Leite

The last few decades have seen slow but steady changes in how Classics in general, and Latin language more specifically, are taught. The limits of Classics as a discipline have been challenged (Martindale and Thomas 2006: 2), and the understanding of which texts can or cannot be used in the classroom under that label has been disputed (Verbaal et al. 2007: viii). At the same time, another well-documented change in the teaching of classical languages has been taking place: the varied practices performed under the label 'Active Latin' are also the subject of recent scholarly interest (such as Coffee 2011; Minkova and Tunberg 2012; Lloyd 2017; Bailey 2017; Kuhner 2018 and other authors in this volume). As the terminology regarding the use of Latin is not unanimously accepted and still awaits the development of a body of scholarly work that will help in the evaluation and, perhaps, agreement on terms – active Latin, oral Latin, communicative Latin are just a few of the most common ones – we need to spare a few words on what I mean by the expression 'Active Latin' in this chapter's title. Following Minkova and Tunberg (2012: 121–4), I use the term to mean the interest in the use of all aspects of the Latin experience – reading, speaking, listening and writing. It is worth noticing that in this definition, I do not understand translating as an equivalent of reading, but as a fifth skill that may or may not be used in the classroom. I also follow those authors in understanding Active Latin not as a teaching method, but an approach to Latin in general, to be contrasted with the nineteenth and twentieth centuries' traditional view that foregrounds the skill of reading. Active Latin, according to my definition, can therefore be employed with a variety of teaching methods, as long as one is adding classroom activities that involve the use of the language in all four forms, but particularly in using communicative approaches.

Teachers at university level in Brazil face challenges of various sorts. One of these has emerged recently and relates to how the profile of the university student in Brazil has undergone significant changes over the last twenty years. Between 2005 and 2015, the student enrolment in Higher Education dramatically increased, from around five million to eight million undergraduates (INEP 2015). Professors have also been learning to deal with students from the sort of backgrounds who have not traditionally attended university (Ristoff 2014). For example, two in every three students enrolled in federal universities come from underprivileged socio-economic backgrounds (ANDIFES 2018). These changes mean that professors in Brazil have been learning to deal with students who comes from families whose members have been traditionally excluded from higher level education, as Ristoff (2014) discusses. When these students arrive at the Latin class, many of them had not only no previous knowledge of Latin but had never even heard of the language before.

This is a crucial moment in the history of Brazil, in which the creation and negotiation of identities of social groups and the maintenance of memories are fluid and contested. As Schwarcz and Gomes (2018: 3) observe, the history of Brazil is being rewritten, with new discourses emerging regarding slavery, the black population, the silencing of groups such as Amerindians and their descendants, and women. In such an environment, the study of Latin and the Classics in general might seem irrelevant or even detrimental to the construction and understanding of Brazilian identities. It is therefore essential that Classics teachers and scholars preserve and promote awareness of the ways in which Classics, alongside other elements, is actually an integral part of what has formed the Brazilian society and culture.

An important part of this challenge is confronting the perception that Latin is something disconnected from our students' lives, something that belonged only to men from another time and place (Fortes and Prata 2015; Pinto 2015). This view was evident in several of the meetings conducted between 2010 and 2014 by the Brazilian Latin Teachers Association (https://www.magistri.org/documentos), as well as in research carried out by Miotti (2006) and Maranhão (2009) with undergraduate Latin students. It is my goal to show Latin as a language that everybody can take possession of and use, just as many other people have appropriated and used it, throughout the centuries and lands that separate us from the Romans. I contend that, by restricting themselves to the ancient authors and stressing only the skill of reading, Latin teachers will miss opportunities, not only of presenting to students a wealth of works that have helped shape vernacular literatures, but also of creating cultural and temporal bridges that are in many cases meaningful to the students. In my own teaching, my desire was twofold: both to explore texts that were relevant to the undergraduates' own cultural heritage but also to encourage use of Latin as a means of communication.

The change was slow but steady. First, I decided to focus on the use of Neo-Latin texts produced in, or about, Brazil between the sixteenth and eighteenth centuries, while also including ancient and medieval sources. I was thus building a language teaching curriculum in which all periods of Latin literature were represented in a more balanced way than in my previous textbook dependent approach. I was using texts that, according to Dinter and Khoo (2018) 'transcend time by harnessing shared historical intertexts to express contemporary anxieties and identities'. This approach, which could be termed hybrid since it does not fully follow any particular teaching method, was instigated in 2013 with groups of students in their first or second year of Latin instruction in college, and who had arrived at university with no previous knowledge of the language. The approach grew out of making non-canonical texts a central element during one or more classes that were part of various courses, and emphasizing the use of the language as a means of communication, both from the authors to the students and between the students.

I started by creating reading, speaking and writing activities that were used sparingly as review work, and progressed to developing full units that could either replace or complement the more traditional regular course. The units I have now established do not all earn equal amounts of credit; nor do they follow one format – much is decided depending on the theme and texts. However, each unit is always composed of:

1. at least two excerpts from Latin texts, either unadapted or 'normalized', that is, with complex phrases or sections replaced by simpler yet grammatically sound formulations;
2. at least two components of writing in Latin undertaken by the students at home or in the classroom;
3. at least two classroom activities involving spoken questions and answers in Latin;

4. at least five exercises on form and vocabulary; and

5. at least one element of 'connections'.

To me the importance of enabling students to make a 'connection' with some aspect of Portuguese or Brazilian literature and culture meant that I wanted there to be a strong element of communication in Latin, both as the language of the works being studied and also because of the heritage of Portuguese and Brazilian culture.

All units start with a 'teaser': an image, text, song or some other element that grabs the students' attention. The function of this is to create a non-linguistic reason for learning, so that the students' feeling of personal involvement and belonging are emphasized. For instance, some teasers that have been used include: a poem by a twentieth-century Brazilian writer that references Horace; a comic-book version of the Trojan War; Catullus' tortured love poem (85) in translation; a newspaper article with tips on how to buy a house; and two movements of Orff's *Carmina Burana* performed by the Berlin Philharmonic Orchestra. After each of these has been introduced, the students are usually required to do some related research, sometimes done at home, in order to make subject content relevant to their lives. Based on the research, they exchange information or opinions on the theme in the classroom, and only after this do we move on to the first reading. The research activity also helps students to build a bridge between their own culture and the language and literature they are studying.

The reading activity is always done orally in Latin. Sometimes I, as the teacher, read and the students follow in their texts; sometimes the students are asked to listen with their books closed, so they can experience the story only by listening. The first time, the text is always read continuously at a moderate pace, without pauses. The reading is then repeated, sentence by sentence, with breaks to check comprehension, either by the teacher again or with the students re-reading it aloud, sometimes individually, sometimes as a group. Whether the text is read by teacher, students in groups or students individually is determined by the teacher, and depends on level of difficulty of the written piece, familiarity with the vocabulary and students' wish to participate. This is followed by questions and answers about the text. At this stage, students can resolve any doubts about the text, either in Portuguese or in Latin, and the teacher also poses a few questions, always in Latin, that the students can answer either in Latin or in Portuguese. This is the modus operandi of most sessions: students are always invited to participate by speaking in whichever language they find comfortable at the time. This choice is offered for two reasons: first, we want to avoid anyone feeling he or she is prevented from participating for fear of not knowing how to say something, or by worrying about saying it wrongly. Engagement with the activity and encouragement to participate in expressing one's own thoughts and opinions is more important than correctness at this stage. Second, since not all Latin teachers in our university use active practices, it is common in second or higher levels to have students who are used to the question-and-answer sessions in Latin alongside others who have not had that experience, and allowing a choice of languages avoids embarrassment for the less experienced speakers. Practice has shown that this method ensures all students feel welcome, since their affective filter (according to Krashen 1982) is lowered, and all engage in the class. By the middle of the term – that is, after about thirty hours of class time – most of them will be able to attempt answers in Latin whenever they are addressed in it. Since the use of spoken Latin has been added to classes, we have observed that many students (mainly those majoring in Modern Languages) enjoy the opportunity to speak the language, and frequently address the teacher in Latin even outside the classroom. The oral repetition of words and structures is also a facilitator of memory, for many students spontaneously report being able to remember meanings and sentences from hearing them and using them orally in the classroom. The benefits of even just repeating the structures in the spoken word is observed even by those who do not enjoy the idea of conversational Latin.

After the question-and-answer session, other activities follow in which the students engage with the theme while also learning new language structures. The texts have been selected to display particular linguistic structures that are then reinforced in exercises that often require the students to read further texts with related topics and to write in Latin using the newly seen structure. This can also pave the way for them using these structures to express their own thoughts in question-and-answer sessions. Whenever possible, the activities include audio and visual material, such as YouTube videos, drawings and pictures with Latin-only labels made by the teacher and by the students, and sometimes even involve some movement around the classroom. The *active* aspects, that is, reading in Latin (without necessarily resorting to translation); listening to Latin; speaking in Latin; and writing in Latin, are always balanced throughout each unit. A second reading related to the same theme always follows the first. Sometimes there is a third reading and each of them has their own question-and-answer session and subsequent activities on listening, speaking, linguistic structure and writing.

It is a goal of my Latin courses to set firmly in the students' minds the fact that Latin is not the exclusive property of the Ancient Romans, but a language with an extremely rich history that has had an impact on all periods of Western civilizations and through which they too can express themselves. Therefore, I have dedicated time specifically to creating units that display the connections between Latin and other disciplines of their curriculum, such as Portuguese and Brazilian literature, or that can be immediately related to some aspect of the students' lives. This 'connection' aspect is always highlighted in some activity at the end of the unit, to wrap it up. Some of the most successful units include those on the Sermon on the Mount (based on St Matthew's Gospel); on the palm tree (based on Gellius 3.6); on the atom (based on St Isidore's *Etymologiae*, 13.2); on college education in sixteenth-century Portugal (based on two poems written by George Buchanan while a professor in Coimbra); and a unit on the armadillo, using parts of a letter written by Joseph de Anchieta, a Spanish Jesuit, not well known abroad but very familiar to our students. A fuller description of this final unit is given here as an example of how my approach to Latin teaching works, combining a selection of texts that can spark interest and familiarity in the students, with the active use of Latin, which makes Latin more of a means of communicating interesting ideas of personal relevance to the students and less of a code for deciphering. This unit, together with others, have been collected in a publication entitled *Latine Loqui* (Ribeiro Leite 2016).

Josephus de Anchieta was born in the Canary Islands in 1534. After studying in Coimbra, he was sent to Brazil, where he stayed until his death in 1597. During his life in the colony, Anchieta played a part of its most important events. He is also considered to be the first Brazilian man of letters. He was the first to learn, transcribe and standardize Old Tupi, the lingua franca of the Amerindian coastal tribes of Brazil. He wrote plays and poems in that language, as well as in Spanish and Portuguese. A great number of his works were in Latin, however, including poetry and all his correspondence with other Jesuits in Brazil and in Europe. Anchieta spent his final years in the state where my school is situated, in the city now called Anchieta in his honour. All of this makes him a very important figure in Brazilian history and literature. Most people will have at least heard of him or seen him in a book or on a statue, coin or stamp. Students from our state may even have visited his place of death and his monument.

Perhaps unsurprisingly, though, most of our students are unaware that Anchieta ever wrote in Latin. The fact that his name is very well known locally, however, does encourage an immediate connection for many of them. The names of authors such as Horace or Catullus can never match this, since they mean nothing to most of the class. Some students were born in the city now named Anchieta; they all know that the seat of government of the state is called Palácio Anchieta. Suddenly, the Latin class has a connection with their daily lives.

The teaser in this unit, though, did not begin by presenting the author, but an armadillo. This New World animal is one of the many strange and surprising creatures that Europeans found in their voyages to the unknown. Native to all Americas, the armadillo is very common in South America, and very well known to Brazilians; the animal was even chosen as the mascot for the football World Cup took place in Brazil in 2014. The students taking this unit in their fourth semester of Latin, were invited, in the last fifteen minutes of a previous class, to look at the picture, identify the animal and imagine the connection between the animal in the picture and Latin. The lessons are thus predicated on the assumption that Latin is relevant to and belongs in Brazilian culture and that there will actually be a link between the ancient language from a distant land and this familiar and nationally iconic animal. Many interesting ideas were discussed, and pupils were then asked about what the Europeans might have thought when first seeing this animal, and how they would have described it. They were then told that someone had actually done that, and in Latin. The discovery that Joseph de Anchieta was the author in question was a surprise, because even though they were familiar with him as a historic figure, they did not know he was a Latin author. That gave the students, as they later reported themselves, a sense of discovering a hidden secret about a well-known personality, and also stirred up anticipation of the next class. The Latin language was suddenly less strange and distant because it had been used for communication about their own country by one of its own famous inhabitants.

In the next session, I brought in a small text in Latin about the author, with just a few general remarks on his life and works. After reading the information about the author, the class was asked to describe, in Latin, the picture of the armadillo used in the previous class. Here I was setting up the expectation that students were going to be able to express ideas about elements of their own culture by using Latin, just as Anchieta had. This was done orally with students suggesting words they already knew in Latin or asking me how to say the word they had in mind. I wrote the students' suggestions on the board, but also threw in a few of my own, so that some words that would later appear in the Latin chapter they were about to read were made familiar at that point. These included *cauda* (tail), *concha* (scale), *antrum* (cave) and *lacertus* (lizard). The text used in the sessions is a collection of excerpts of Joseph de Anchieta's *Epistola quamplurimarum rerum naturalium quae Sancti Vicentii (nunc Sancti Pauli) provinciam incolunt sistens descriptionem* (Epistle including a description of the many natural things that inhabit the province of St Vincent (now called St Paul)), one of the many letters that the author wrote to inform friends and colleagues in Europe about his life and work in Brazil.

The paragraph named *De Dasypode seu Tatu* (On the Armadillo or *Tatu*) was selected as the first reading because, in spite of its brevity, it contains one gerund and a few uses of the subjunctive of purpose, which were the structures I wanted to review in that unit. Also, it is worth noting that in Portuguese, the armadillo still goes by the native American word *tatu*, as in the title of the *caput*, which points to the fact that the Portuguese invaders kept the native name of the animal, and this made the topic immediately transparent and familiar. So, during the oral activity, I also asked questions and made suggestions about where the students would use the gerund, and about sentences in which the subjunctive with idea of purpose would be used. The students were then given a few minutes to write their own descriptions of an armadillo, in simple Latin sentences, and a few of them were invited to share their descriptions with the class by reading them aloud. Preparing in advance helped students feel less pressured about communicating their ideas to their classmates, while still encouraging them to express their own thoughts and ideas in Latin. Only after doing this were they introduced to the text as written by Anchieta in 1560, as follows:

> *Josephi de Anchieta epistola, quamplurimarum rerum naturalium*
>
> *quae Sancti Vicentii (nunc Sancti Pauli) provinciam incolunt sistens descriptionem*
>
> *XXVII – De Dasypode seu Tatu*
>
> *Est et aliud animal satis frequens apud nos (Tatu vocant) in cavernis subterraneis per campos habitans, cauda et capite lacertis fere similis durissima concha sagittis impervia, armaturae equi persimili, totum desuper corpus contectum: velocissime terram effodit, ut se protegat; cum vero se intra sua tecta receperit, nisi crus arripias, frustra in ipso extrahendo fatigaberis, tam pertinaciter enim conchis ac pedibus adhaeret terrae, ut etsi caudam apprehendas, eam potius a corpore quam ipsum ab antro posse divellere: gustui est satis delectabile.*

Epistle of Joseph de Anchieta including a description of the many natural things that inhabit the province of St Vincent (now called St Paul)

XXVII – On the Armadillo or *Tatu*

There is also another animal quite common among us (they call it Tatu), which lives in subterranean caves in the fields. It is quite similar to a lizard in its head and tail; its whole body is fully covered by very strong scales, impenetrable to arrows, very similar to the armour of a horse. It digs the earth very fast in order to protect itself. Truly, once it has entered in its burrow, unless you catch a leg, you will tire yourself in vain trying to extract it; for so tenaciously does it attach itself to the ground with its scales and feet, that even if you catch its tail, you will be able to separate the tail from the body before you can retrieve it from the cave. It has a very pleasant taste.

Author's translation

At this point in the course, students had become accustomed to the question and answer section being conducted entirely in Latin, so the reading was followed by questions such as *quomodo dasypus apellatur?* (What is the armadillo called?), *ubi dasypus habitat?* (Where does the armadillo live?), *facilene ex antro extrahitur dasypus?* (Is it easy to remove the armadillo from its cave?), *quomodo homo dasypodem ex tecto extrahere potest?* (How can someone remove the armadillo from its burrow?), *cur Josephus de Anchieta de dasypode narrat?* (Why does Joseph talk about the armadillo?). The questions are intended to be easy enough to be understood just by listening (i.e. they do not require translation) and the answers are supposed to be simple enough to be given in Latin without much difficulty. This activity was planned deliberately to ensure the speaking aspect was not a source of anxiety. My goal here is not to form masters of extempore Latin prose, but to provide more contact with the target language and to foster appreciation and experience of its use as a vehicle for communication of ideas with others: it should not always be closely analyzed or transposed into the students' first language to facilitate comprehension. However, even at this stage, if the student so chooses, the answers can always be given in Portuguese. Even when they do not speak, students are witnessing Latin as a communicative tool when their classmates and teachers do.

After the question-and-answer sessions, students compared their own armadillo descriptions with the one written by Anchieta, and were encouraged to change their own texts by adding some of the target structures to make their writing more complex, thus refining and extending their own powers of expression. As preparation for the second reading in the same unit, I then presented a list of titles of other sections from the same letter. The students were asked to choose one of a number of titles of other Anchietan descriptions that they thought would be most interesting for them personally. The titles of the other sections of the same work offered to the students as second reading were: V. *De Bove Marino* (*manatee*); IX. *De Crocodilo* (crocodile); X. *De Glyre Capiuara* (capybara); XVIII. *De Araneis* (spiders); XIX. *De Scorpione* (scorpion); XXI. *De Myrmecophaga seu Tamandua* (anteater); XXII. *De Tapiiara* (tapir); XXIII. *De Bradypode seu Pigritia (sloth)*; XXVI. *De Simiis* (monkeys); XXIX. *De Parvo Camelo Glama* (llama). The list presented to the students did not contain the translations in parentheses but, as the list was read, students tried to guess what the animals were, which was not overly difficult, as many keep their Amerindian names in Portuguese. This ease of recognition increased their confidence and reinforced the idea that Latin 'belonged' in Brazil.

During this stage, the students discussed their familiarity with these animals and shared their experiences about them. That led to lively discussion, during which I suggested they describe the animals orally in Latin and Portuguese and I directed the students to vocabulary that would be useful for the following activity. While talking about their preferences and experiences, the students were also learning vocabulary in Latin about those animals and preparing their own phrases to reinforce what they had learned.

After each student had picked the animal they preferred, they were asked to bring, for the next class, a draft of a Latin description of that animal so that they could read Anchieta's description in groups and, based on that, improve their own. The structures being focused on in the unit – the gerund and purpose clauses – are quite useful when describing the physical appearance and habits of an animal, and so the students were encouraged to use those structures when writing their descriptions. In the third session, small groups of two or three students read each others' descriptions of the animals they had picked, and sometimes, without being asked to, spontaneously corrected each other's Latin writing. The writing activity was done at home, so that the students had time to think about and develop more complex sentences, but the comparing and rewriting activity took place in the classroom and served as a review of the target structures. After they were happy with their work, they shared their texts by reading them aloud. Sometimes, if one student did not understand the other's text, it was repeated and discussed, so that the class listened to the Latin again and interacted with it. They were then given the paragraphs of Anchieta's text that corresponded to the animals that each student had previously selected and, still working in groups, read and compared his writing with their own.

Finally, a third activity with the same letter was carried out as follows: once more working in groups, the students were given other paragraphs from the letter in which native Brazilian animals and plants are described but not mentioned by name. The goal was to determine to which animal the author could possibly be referring. Not all animals and plants are easily identified, but negotiating conflicting suggestions about the creatures' identities was a key part of the activity, as the overall goal was to have the students make conjectures about the animals' and plants' identities while reading in Latin. In this way they were encouraged to relate reading in Latin to expressing their opinions about their own experiences with familiar plants and animals. Here is an example of some text from the third reading:

Gignuntur in arundinibus Vermes quidam teretes, et oblongi, albi toti, unius digiti crassitudine, quos Rahu appellant Indi: hos igni assos et tostos solent comedere, tanta vero est eorum multitudo, acervatim congesta, ut ex eis fiat liquamen, quod liquato ex sue non est dissimile, cujus et ad emollienda coria, et ad vescendum usus est.

Found in the swamps are certain plump worms, long, all white, of the width of a finger, called *Rahu* by the Indians. They are used to eating them baked and roasted. Such is their number, found in huge heaps, that a sauce is made out of them, which is not dissimilar to pork sauce, and which is used to soften leather and to eat.

Author's translation

During the unit, which lasted four and a half hours divided across three sessions, the students were able to:

1. review and strengthen their knowledge of recently learned Latin structures and improve their mastery of these by seeing them used and also by using them to express themselves in their own writing;

2. perceive Latin as a means of communication: they were able to convey their own ideas in the language by first of all thinking of vocabulary appropriate to the task. They then used that vocabulary in the construction of their own description of an armadillo and further enhanced their work by reading the texts composed by a man that they admired and who lived almost 500 years ago in the place where they now live. In so doing, they were led to understand that Latin is first and foremost a language via which a long deceased person talked to them of his own experiences and through which they could, by putting themselves in the young Anchieta's place, communicate to each other or with friends and family far away the wonders of what he and they saw;

3. observe the connection between Latin and their mother tongue, Portuguese, and its role in the history of Brazil and of their own state. Through the elements presented in the unit on Josephus de Anchieta and Brazilian fauna and flora, they could see that Latin played an important role in the literary, cultural and political formation of the colony.

Could these goals have been achieved satisfactorily through studying the works of a classical author alone? Possibly. Would they have resonated as well? Would they have created such an immediate connection? From what I have observed in my classrooms, the long-lasting effect of experiences with non-canonical authors such as Anchieta is that they make abundantly clear to modern students the idea that the Classics are deeply embedded in our culture and everywhere around us, even in names and characters they thought they already knew about beforehand. Today's teenagers in Brazil will (understandably) find it harder to connect with distant events relating to classical Rome, such as say, the construction of a bridge over a river in Europe, as described in Caesar's *De Bello Gallico*. However, once they see the connection between the Latin texts and their own lives, once the spark is struck, they start to see for themselves the permanence and impact of the Classics everywhere – and want to see more of it. And, at that point, this intensity of impact can happen with the most intricate and allusive of Horace's Odes, whereas, in my own experiences, this happens very rarely when Latin is presented exclusively as the language of a distant culture. And, while I do also want to give my students access to and a feeling of belonging with the long and fruitful series of classical authors, I have seen that texts written not only in Brazil, but about Brazil, can be used very effectively as an immediate bridges towards those more distant authors.

At the same time, when Latin is seen more as a code to be deciphered than a language through which we can all express thoughts, opinions and emotions, the feeling of strangeness is stronger than the possibility of identification. That is why the understanding of Latin as a language for communication has been the main guideline in determining the development of units. It has influenced the following:

1. the selection of texts with appealing themes and language that can be understood and used as models for the students' own writing and speaking;
2. the contact with the text, always carefully prepared, curated and mediated to guarantee and emphasize the understanding and communication between text and student, teacher and student, and student and student;
3. the extent to which students are encouraged to use Latin themselves, actively, writing and speaking the language. The active aspect, mainly the speaking part, is not enforced but always encouraged and emphasized as an enjoyable and important part of making Latin one's own. The exercise of trying to express one's ideas in Latin – in writing if not in speaking – ensures that students think in the target language, which makes them more familiar with vocabulary and grammatical structures. However, the more important benefit is that it turns Latin from a distant, almost mystical, language from the past, to a common, quotidian tongue that was (and is still) used by humans from all walks of life – including less affluent students from Brazil – who can then access the vast array of cultural background that, together with so many other influences, has shaped their world today.

It is certainly challenging to construct teaching units that promote high levels of identification between learners and the Latin language and its texts, because cultural context is unique to each situation and group; it is even more challenging to combine it with a more communicative approach that many students might not be used to, but which includes developing a closer personal connection with the language: listening to it and speaking it to communicate as well reading and writing it. But since these changes have been introduced in my classes, they brought with them a level of meaningfulness to the Classics in the eyes of my students that I had not seen there before, and a level of identity between Latin and the twenty-first-century learners that I hope to continue to foster and keep alive.

CHAPTER 10
THE USE OF *LUDI DOMESTICI* IN COMMUNICATIVE LATIN
Daniel B. Gallagher

One of the biggest challenges of using spoken Latin in the classroom is deciding what to assign students *outside* that space. What kind of 'homework' not only complements, enhances and improves the spoken Latin used in class, but the students' overall mastery of the Latin language? By 'mastery' I mean a complete command that includes not only the ability to speak fluently and to understand spoken Latin, but also to read readily, speedily and accurately a never-before-encountered text by any author from any time period, prose or poetry, classical or Christian. What type of outside-the-classroom exercises help students achieve this mastery in courses that focus on a communicative approach?

In my experience, whatever those exercises consist of, they are best designed directly by me specifically for the students sitting in my classroom at any given time. They build on conversations that have actually taken place in the classroom, they draw on readings suggested by the students, and they assess skills that the students have already acquired but need to work on further. In short, the more time and effort I have spent on customizing these out-of-the-classroom assignments, the more readily the students have achieved the course outcomes.

But first, a word about my role at Cornell University and the two courses I teach that focus on oral comprehension and expression, and therefore use a communicative approach. As the Ralph and Jeanne Kanders Associate Professor of Practice in Latin, I specialize in helping students achieve Latin fluency through communicative Latin both inside and outside the classroom. In addition to a variety of courses on Latin prose and poetry, I teach two courses entitled 'Conversational Latin' that utilize a communicative approach to, as Lloyd says, 'promote authentic functional and interactional use of language between participants' (Lloyd 2017: 88).

Students may elect Conversational Latin I and Conversational Latin II after having completed at least two years of Latin grammar. Some students in Conversational Latin have had as many as five or six years of formal Latin training. In short, these are not introductory courses, but courses for those with a working knowledge of Latin but who have never had the opportunity to speak before. Presently at Cornell, there is no option for beginning Latin *ab initio* using a communicative approach.

According to the course description, the aim of Conversational Latin I is to acquire the skills of oral comprehension and oral expression that will enhance a student's ability to understand every Latin genre from every time period. The outcomes of Conversational Latin I are fourfold. By the end of the course, students are able to:

1. comprehend spoken Latin;
2. express themselves in spoken Latin;
3. compose their thoughts in written Latin based on models from various authors and time periods;

4. re-assimilate the structure and functions of the Latin language through these newly acquired aural and oral skills.

The aim of Conversational Latin II – which, unlike Conversational Latin I, is conducted entirely in Latin – is simply *fecundia Latina* (Latin fluency). The outcomes of this course are also fourfold:

1. *legendi et capiendi opera Latina sine adiumento versionum vulgarum* (reading and understanding Latin works without the help of vernacular translations);
2. *recapitulandi Latine personas, narrationes necnon argumenta magnorum Latinorum operum* (recapitulating in Latin the characters, stories and topics of the greatest Latin works);
3. *exprimendi verbis Latinis animum tuum sententiasque tuas* (expressing your own mind and opinions in Latin); and
4. *nominandi et imitandi proprietates orationis Latinae purae ac integrae* (identifying and imitating the characteristics of pure, integral Latin).

The lessons for Conversational Latin I consist of a combination of material from Traupman's (2006) *Conversational Latin for Oral Proficiency* and primary texts from Latin literature. Each unit consists of a chapter from Traupman's book and at least one passage from primary literature that deals with the same topic. Chapter 1 of *Conversational Latin* on 'Greetings', for example, is paired with passages from Erasmus's *Colloquia Familiaria*. Chapter II on 'Family' is paired with Cicero's letter to Paetus in *Ad Familiares,* XXI. Chapter 3 on 'School' utilizes Letter 88 of Seneca's *Epistulae Morales*. Each unit is covered over two class periods. The first class period generally begins by reenacting a dialogue or two from Traupman's book and then offering prompts to stimulate a conversation with and among the students. These conversations take place in pairs, threes, and as a whole class. In the second class session, we read aloud the assigned passage(s) from the primary literature. A series of questions is then used to assess the students' understanding of the passage. We then practise the vocabulary learned from the corresponding chapter in *Conversational Latin* by talking about the primary text using that vocabulary. Many of the words given in Traupman's book appear in the primary passage. When necessary, we review grammatical and stylistic points that students have been introduced to in previous Latin courses. By the end of the second class period, conversation tends to focus on the students own experiences and thoughts on the primary text and on the topic in general. They are encouraged to imitate the style of the primary text as much as possible in these conversations.

The approach to Conversational Latin II is similar to Conversational Latin I, but by that point the students are able to engage in conversation more readily and confidently. Accordingly, the course relies more heavily on conversation-stimulating activities already introduced in Conversational Latin I, including visual works of art, news stories about current events, and video/audio recordings of lectures given in Latin.

Although I have been producing my own out-of-the-classroom activities for years, only by teaching Conversational Latin I and II at Cornell since autumn 2017 have I been able to hone my *ludi domestici* (home games) by building on the students' experience of spoken Latin in the classroom and challenging them to remain in the target language outside the classroom. Prior to that – mostly at various Roman institutions and at the University of Notre Dame – I was designing *ludi domestici* for classes that utilized spoken Latin, but were not conducted exclusively in Latin as in the case of Conversational Latin I and II. I would like to share the results of my experience in using *ludi domestici,* emphasizing that my arguments for using them and for customizing them is not based so much on theory and research as on trial and error.

The structure and focus of a *ludus* can vary depending on when it is assigned within a given unit. Nevertheless, there is a basic structure to all *ludi* regardless of whether they are entirely in Latin or use a combination of Latin and English. A *ludus* generally:

1. gives an original passage from literature;
2. insists that the student read the passage aloud three or four times;
3. leads the student through a careful analysis of the text;
4. in some cases, asks the student to translate the text; and
5. asks the student to say something in Latin using the words – and often imitating the style – of the author.

Currently, I create and assign *ludi* through the online teaching platform Canvas. I use the Quiz function to create and post the *ludi,* and students may access and open them whenever they are ready. There is generally one *ludus* assigned per class session. In most cases, students are allowed to take as much time as they need to complete the *ludus,* provided they turn it in by the established due date. Some *ludi* are timed, however, meaning that students must complete them in one sitting and within a specific time frame from the moment they open it, usually sixty minutes. I use a variety of question formats on each *ludus*, including multiple choice, multiple answer, true/false, fill in the blank, short answer, matching, and essay. Once students turn in the completed *ludi*, I review them manually and provide significant feedback.

I have found that producing my own *ludi domestici* rather than relying on textbooks or other outside resources is the best way to facilitate my students' achievement of Latin mastery. Only in this way can I target the specific skills, needs and interests of my individual students, not to mention my own strengths and weaknesses as a teacher. I was first introduced to the *ludus* as a student of Reginald Foster, who has been teaching for years using only three elements: a dictionary, primary texts ('reading sheets'), and *ludi domestici* (home games). Foster's approach is fleshed out at length in the first volume of his series on teaching and learning Latin, entitled *Ossa Latinitatis Sola* (Foster and McCarthy 2016). Among the succeeding volumes to *Ossa* will be a new publication (expected in 2020) in which Foster explains more fully the pedagogy underlying *ludi domestici* and provides copious examples of *ludi* developed through his years of teaching.

A *ludus domesticus* is precisely that: a game played at home. It is a series of exercises based on an original Latin text that require students both to comprehend the meaning of the text and to use the text actively to express their own thoughts in Latin. By 'actively,' I mean students are asked (1) to answer, in Latin, a series of questions given in Latin, and (2) to formulate Latin sentences using the vocabulary from the passage based on English prompts. The former can take the form of true/false, multiple choice, fill in the blank, short answer, or another format. The latter generally take the form of short answers or fill in multiple blanks.

Here is an example of the former (the primary text for this *ludus* was Virgil's *Eclogue IV*):

quarta in Ecloga, quod signum est quo gentem vel aetatem auream advenisse sciemus?

A) *sol nubibus operietur.*

B) *vela a sutore dabuntur.*

C) *coluber numquam morietur.*

D) *color arietis ab ipso mutabitur.* (CORRECT)

Here is an example of the latter:

danda est tamen omnibus aliqua remissio, non solum quia nulla res est quae perferre possit continuum laborem, atque ea quoque quae sensu et anima carent ut servare vim suam possint velut quiete alterna retenduntur, sed quod studium discendi voluntate, quae cogi non potest, constat.

Quintillian, Institutiones Oratoriae, I

Quickly use <u>Quintilian's highlighted vocabulary</u> to say the following in Latin:

'Teachers give rest to all so that continuous labor may not be endured (use the word in the text) by them.'

ANSWER: *magistri dant omnibus remissionem ut continuus labor ab iis non perferatur.*

These are but two examples of a plethora of question formats I use on my *ludi*. The ever-expanding options offered by Canvas make it possible to use interactive images, audio and video recordings, and live-time encounters with the instructor and other students outside of class. I particularly chose the second example above to illustrate a distinctive feature of the *ludi* which may be controversial among proponents of a communicative approach: i.e., the use of English. The reason for this is actually twofold, as I explain in what follows.

First of all, the infrequency with which Conversational Latin meets imposes significant time restrictions. Both Conversational Latin I and II meet only three times a week for fifty minutes. Each semester runs for approximately fifteen weeks. By comparison, modern foreign languages at Cornell meet at least four to five times a week for an hour at least. The amount of time allotted for class sessions significantly affects my planning for the Conversational Latin courses as well as the role of the *ludi domestici* in contributing to the courses' aims and outcomes. I am convinced that the *ludi* are effective tools no matter how much class time is available for Conversational Latin, but, given the limited class time, the ways in which I design and construct *ludi* revolve around my ongoing task of prolonging the communicative experience of the classroom and extending it into the home. Somewhat counterintuitively, however, the communicative approach I use in the classroom is drastically enhanced if the *ludi* allow students to drill themselves not only in the target language but, to a limited extent, in English as well.

If Conversational Latin I were to meet five days a week for an hour, students could more easily be 'immersed' in the language. We strive to speak Latin exclusively during Conversational Latin I sessions, but occasionally I must revert to English for very brief periods (no more than five minutes) to make sure students have grasped an important grammatical or stylistic point. In any case, when we reach the end of each lesson, it seems as if we have barely begun, and it will be at least another forty-eight hours until we meet again. Moreover, there may be as many as twelve to fifteen students in the classroom, making it difficult for each student to have sufficient time to practise speaking Latin with the entire group. Time in class is devoted, of course, to conversation and exercises in smaller groups. Nevertheless, it is difficult to consider a course that meets so infrequently a 'language course' on a model similar to modern languages. Even in the course catalogue, Conversational Latin I and II are described as 'lecture' courses, simply because, from the registrar's point of view, that is the default classification of classes that meet three times a week for fifty minutes.

If, however, the *ludi domestici* are designed with care and include some English, I find that it is much easier to stay exclusively in the target language in class. As I have shown above and will show more fully below, most of the exercises in the *ludi* are performed in Latin only, but occasionally students are asked to demonstrate their comprehension of Latin with English prompts or even by translating short passages into English.

For example, Chapter IX in *Conversational Latin* is dedicated to 'Days, Weeks, Months, Years'. I routinely pair this chapter with passages from Suetonius's *De Vita Iulii Caesaris* on the measures Caesar took to reform the Roman calendar. Short passages on time and dates from Cicero, Livy, and Plautus are also included in this unit. I find this unit extremely valuable to students since they invariably lack the ability to quickly render Roman dates into English. This is not a hard skill to learn but is of immense value when working with primary texts. Our department does not require students to learn how the Roman calendar works, and this is why I require them to learn it in Conversational Latin I. Students simply must learn how to do this sooner or later, and sooner is better since it is not hard to do. Moreover, if you are going to talk about time in any language, you simply have to know how to say days, months, and years.

The first class session of the unit on 'Days, Weeks, Months, Years' is conducted entirely in Latin using a printed calendar, the basic vocabulary given in *Conversational Latin,* and several fun exercises, including interviews with other students about birthdays, favourite US holidays and noteworthy dates on campus such as Cornell's annual tradition of 'Dragon Day'.[1] Students can easily learn the otherwise arcane system of Kalends, Nones, and Ides *Latine tantum*. To reinforce this learning, however, I ask students to complete at least three *ludi* that utilize both the target language and English, prompting them to put English dates into Latin and Latin dates back into English.

The first *ludus* for this unit is entirely in Latin and is based on exercises we have previously completed in class. Students are asked to write dates in Latin in response to questions in Latin. So, for example:

1. *quo die celebramus diem festum Sancti Valentini? scribe modo Romano sine litteris compendiariis!* (On what day do we celebrate Valentine's Day? Write your answer using the Roman method and with no abbreviations!)

2. *in Civitatibus Foederatis Americae Septentrionalis, quo die celebratur dies anniverarius Libertatis Nationis? scribe modo Romano sine litteris compendiariis!* (On what day is Independence Day celebrated in the United States of America? Write your answer using the Roman method and with no abbreviations!)

3. *anno praeterito, quo die honoratus est Martinus Luterhius King? scribe modo Romano sine litteris compendiariis!* (On what day was Martin Luther King Day celebrated last year? Write your answer using the Roman method and with no abbreviations!)

4. *anno insequenti, quo die celebrabitur Festum Gratiarum Agendarum? scribe modo Romano sine litteris compendiariis!* (On what day will Thanksgiving be celebrated next year? Write your answer using the Roman method and with no abbreviations!)

5. *qui est dies quo cives Civitatum Americanarum Americae Septentrionalis ad comitia eunt? id est, quo die habetur dies comitialis? explica scribendo sententiam completam.* (On what day do citizens go to the polls in the United States of America? That is, when is Election Day? Explain how it is calculated using a complete sentence.)

The first two questions ask for a fixed date. The second two ask the dates of moveable feasts. The last question is the most complicated in that it requires students to explain how to calculate a date rather than give a set date or calculate a moveable feast within a certain year. In Latin, they must explain that, in the United States, Election Day is set as the Tuesday following the first Monday in the month of November. They might add that this means the earliest possible date is 2 November and the latest possible date 8 November. In responding to each of these questions in Latin, students will most likely calculate the date in English and then convert it into Latin. There is no problem with that procedure initially, but I want to lead them into the habit of thinking about the calendar in Latin without having to convert it from English. They must tackle these computations from various angles, and the use of fixed, moveable and calculable feasts is precisely what allows them to acquire this habit. Notice also that they are not allowed to abbreviate dates but are required to write them out in full, including numbers. So, for task 4 above, they must write: *ante diem VII Kalendas Decembres*, or better yet, *ante diem septimum Kalendas Decembres.* Only in this way will they develop the habit of thinking in the accusative case in a way entirely foreign to English. Requiring them to write the numbers out in full also reinforces the habit of speaking Latin numbers in their head rather than muttering X, L, V, I.

In the next *ludus* for this calendar unit, students must express dates of greater personal interest to them. So, for example:

1. *quo die inceptum est semestre autumnali apud Universitatem Cornellianam hoc anno? scribe modo Romano sine litteris compendiariis!* (On what day did the autumn semester begin at Cornell University this year? Write your answer using the Roman method and with no abbreviations!)

2. *quo die natus es, vel nata es, tu? scribe Romano modo!* (What is your birthday? Write your answer using the Roman method!)

This *ludus*, in fact, most closely resembles exercises done in the first class of the unit. There are two advantages to this type of question, both in spoken and written form.

First, it is special and unique to each student, giving him or her a sense of self-importance – and therefore confidence – and it encourages fellow students to take personal interest in that person and stimulate conversation with her. In class, we often hear something like, '*ego quoque nata sum mense Novembri!*' Second, students memorize these special, personal dates in Latin more quickly, moving them away from the habit of converting English dates into Latin. Interestingly, students tend to memorize their birthdays and the birthdays of friends and family directly in Latin rather than converting them into Latin.

Given these two advantages, I make a deliberate effort to bridge the personal interest factor modelled in these in-class exercises with the intrinsic motivation that enhances reading comprehension. As Mair Lloyd, referring to the research of Linda B. Gambrell (2011: 172) and others, writes: 'L1 reading researchers claim that engaged readers are intrinsically motivated – that is they enjoy reading for its own sake, and that enjoyment of reading is linked with development of reading skills and essential for achievement of a student's full literacy potential' (2017:71).

The third *ludus* is the surprising one, and it best illustrates my main point that the use of English in *ludi domestici* greatly enhances Latin oral fluency, regardless of the time restrictions I discussed above. Students – albeit only in written form – are required to move out of the target language back into English. They are simply asked to translate dates as found in the headings of some of Cicero's letters:

1. *scr. Brundisii pr. K. Mai. a. 696, CICERO ATTICO SAL.*
2. *scr. Thessalonicae Id. Iun. a. 695, CICERO ATTICO SAL.*
3. *scr. Thessalonicae a. d. iv K. Quint. a. 696., CICERO ATTICO SAL.*

Through experience, I have learned that the students' ability to give dates spontaneously in Latin is greatly enhanced if, in the end, they have done this final written exercise of translating dates back into English. After they have done the final of the three *ludi* for this unit, they should have reached a point where they will not have to translate dates from English to Latin in their heads before they speak; rather, they should make the computation directly in Latin without ever having thought of how to say the date in English. In my experience, that point is reached *precisely because*, in the third *ludus*, students must now transfer the date back into English.

I wish I knew the psychology and science behind this phenomenon. I can only speculate and leave that for a future article based on a more thorough investigation of student capabilities before and after undertaking the various *ludi*. I will say, however, that, given the limited class time each week, this final of the three *ludi* on days and dates seems to contribute invariably to the students' oral fluency. I have used this unit several times *without* a third *ludus* to test my hypothesis informally, and the results are invariably the same: contrary to what I expect, students are less confident and less able to say dates in Latin without having gone back to the beginning, so to speak, and come full circle, translating dates – real dates occurring in real Latin literature – into English: not in the classroom, but in the *ludi domestici* administered through Canvas.

Let me offer another example taken from a unit on 'The Weather' (*Conversational Latin*, Chapter XV). Students are assigned a *ludus* in which they play with a passage from Virgil's *Georgicon*:

frigidus agricolam si quando continet imber,
multa, forent quae mox caelo properanda sereno,
maturare datur...

As in the unit on dates, the initial *ludi* for this unit stay focused on the target language. So, for example:

1. *cuius generis imber continet agricolam?* (What kind of rain keeps the farmer inside?)

    Students supply a fill-in-the-blank response, and they must respond in one of two correct grammatical cases: *frigidus* or *frigidi* are both acceptable. Similarly:

2. *Cum agricola imbre contineatur, quanta ei datur maturanda?* (When the farmer is closed indoors, how much is given him to prepare?)

The correct response is *multa*.

Some questions on this *ludus* require a student to choose an appropriate image. For example, they may be asked, *Quae imago optime repraesentat hos Vergilii versus?* (Which picture best represents these verses by Virgil?). They will then be given a series of four photos depicting various farming activities including ploughing, sowing, harvesting and pruning vines. Only one of the photos, which shows a farmer repairing woven baskets inside a barn, displays an activity that can take place while it is raining outside.

Other questions related to this Virgilian passage prompt more personal answers. For example, students are shown an image of a young lady looking forlorn, gazing out the window at the falling rain. Accompanying the image is the question: *Si continet te frigidus imber, quid tibi placet facere? explica in duabus vel tribus sententiis Latinis!* (If cold rain keeps you indoors, what do you like to do? Explain in two or three Latin sentences!)

In the final *ludus* of this unit, however, students must do more a careful textual analysis, and do so in English. Once again, I have repeatedly noted a more fluid and elegant way of speaking in class after students have completed this final *ludus*; indeed, a greater fluidity and elegance that I do not notice if they have not come full circle and forced themselves to think carefully about the same or a related passage and analyzed it thoroughly. So, for example, staying with the same section of the *Georgicon* in the unit on weather:

vere nouo, gelidus canis cum montibus umor
liquitur et Zephyro putris se glaeba resoluit,
depresso incipiat iam tum mihi taurus aratro
ingemere et sulco attritus splendescere uomer.

In the early Spring, when icy waters flow from snowy hills, / and the crumbling soil loosens in a westerly breeze, / then I'd first have my oxen groaning over the driven plough, / and the blade gleaming, polished by the furrow.

Virgil, Georgicon, *Book I*

1. What kind of grammatical construction do you see in *vere novo*?
2. Explain what *cum* is doing in the sentence?
3. What mood do you see in the verb *incipiat* and what reason can you give for that mood?
4. Using Virgil's vocabulary, how would you say in Latin: When (use *cum*) the bulls moan, the ploughs will glisten (*splendesco, splendescere*) while (use *dum* + indicative) the furrows are being sunk into.

I have yet to understand a full linguistic explanation of why exercises like this seem to enhance both oral fluency and listening comprehension when they are assigned toward the end of a unit. But I initially adopted this approach for a very practical reason: I needed students to recognize the details of Latin grammar and style, and I needed a means of assessing their grasp of grammar and style in a course conducted entirely in Latin.

In observing students who take either or both Conversational Latin I and/or Conversational Latin II and then go on to take an advanced Latin course with me, I have also noticed that their ability to speak Latin continues to improve by doing these 'full circle' or 'back to the beginning' type of exercises. Another comparison with modern language instruction may help to clarify why this is so. When students finish Conversational Latin, they can find ways to continue practising spoken Latin – including participation at various *Conventicula, Bidua,* and *Rusticationes* – but they will never be able to travel to a foreign country where Latin is spoken. This makes learning Latin drastically different from learning German, Spanish, French or any other modern language. When it comes to Latin, they will primarily be experiencing the language by reading texts. Indeed, that is presumably why anyone studies Latin in the first place. The skills students gain from speaking Latin are ultimately geared toward more efficient and rapid reading. Capping a unit with carefully crafted exercises that aim to assess a student's grasp of how the language functions seems to feed back into the student's active use of Latin and to foster an integration of oral fluency and reading proficiency.

It is not a matter of not being able to do grammatical exercises in Latin. In Conversational Latin, prompts are easily given during class that allow students to do grammatical drills entirely in Latin: *'verte hanc sententiam in numerum pluralem!'* (convert this sentence into the plural) or *'dic mihi hanc sententiam voce passiva'* (tell me how to say this in the passive voice)! Granted, this is not the kind of 'natural' exercise that can be done in modern languages, but it does give students a command of the language that they need to have to become better, more efficient speakers and readers. Because we tend to focus so strongly on the importance not only of grasping but of *explaining* Latin grammar, students feel all the more empowered in their mastery of the language if they are able to talk about Latin grammar in Latin. And when it comes to talking about Latin grammar in Latin, students are much better equipped to speak with authority if they have run a fine-toothed comb through their understanding of Latin grammar at home in the *ludi domestici* rather than breaking into English in class to make sure they have grasped difficult grammatical concepts and recognized them and used them when reading and speaking Latin. If nothing else, it saves time in class for *Latine tantum* fun if the final *ludi* of any given unit utilize some English to polish the details of understanding and writing in Latin.

As for *ludi* assigned in the middle of a unit, I have also found that a combination of Latin and English greatly enhances the spontaneous speaking ability of students in class. This is particularly the case when it comes to learning vocabulary that students have never encountered before and are unlikely to encounter again in their reading. In my experience, visual prompts work extremely well in *ludi domestici* that furnish students with a primary text and ask them to engage with that text actively by identifying objects that connect with the words in the text. In a unit on Animals (Chapter 16 in *Conversational Latin*), for example, the following passage from Virgil's *Georgics* is assigned on the *ludus:*

1. Read the following text in which Virgil talks about the best livestock:

seu quis Olympiacae miratus praemia palmae
pascit equos, seu quis fortis ad aratra iuuencos,
corpora praecipue matrum legat. optima toruae
forma bouis cui turpe caput, cui plurima ceruix,

et crurum tenus a mento palearia pendent;
tum longo nullus lateri modus: omnia magna,
pes etiam, et camuris hirtae sub cornibus aures.

Georgicon III, 49–55

Whether you choose to nurture horses, in admiration / the prize of Olympia's palms, or sturdy oxen, for the plough, / select the mother's stock carefully. The best-shaped cow / is fierce, her head ugly, with plenty of neck, / and dewlaps hanging down from chin to leg: / then there's no end to her long flanks: all's large, / even the feet: and there are shaggy ears under crooked horns.

The student is then given a series of photographs showing farmers pointing at various parts of a cow. Students are asked to fill in the blank with a word from the above text that matches the photograph. They must write the word in the case that correctly answers the Latin question, and either keep or change the word from singular to plural or plural to singular, depending on which grammatical number correctly answers the question. So:

(Image 1 showing a famer touching the cow's chin)
quam partem tangit homo palma?

> [mentum]

(Image 2 showing a farmer touching a cow's neck)
quam partem tangit homo digito?

> [cervicem]

(Image 3 showing a farmer touching a cow's legs)
quae sunt haec?

> [crura]

(Image 4 showing a farmer touching a cow's feet)
et qui sunt hi?

> [pedes]

Homework exercises such as these are heavily complimented by class activities. Photographs and paintings of various animals are presented to students for identification. These activities are carried out *Latine tantum,* but, due to time constraints, not all students are able to respond in detail to questions about the animals, their body parts, their habitats, diet and so on. The *ludus* gives both students and teacher an opportunity to put their active Latin skills to work in understanding a text and activating real Latin vocabulary. In the exercise above, there are no direct questions about Latin grammar, but the student obviously must have a command of grammar to arrive at the correct answers. Putting words found in the text into the correct case when answering a question may seem trivial, but it is not. I have observed that even the most advanced students will not master vocabulary until they have declined or conjugated a word at least once. When they have, their ability to recall the word is enhanced immensely. Writing rather than speaking certainly seems to have much to do with that. Whatever the case, it is only by breaking out of the target language in at least a few exercises on the *ludi* that my students are able to cope with staying exclusively in Latin in the classroom.

Another important practice I have adopted is never recycling a *ludus*. *Ludi domestici* are dynamic, meaning that a consideration of the students' performance on one *ludus* is the basis for deciding how to design the next one. If students are strong and confident in their grammar but weak in metre, then I design a *ludus* that exercises and assesses meter. Texts, of course, are also constantly changing from one course to another depending on the students' interest (in line with Gambrell 2011). If they adore love poetry, I give them Ovid in a *ludus* rather than Caesar. When it comes to speaking Latin, students can only be inspired to say something about things they like to do, read and talk about. I accordingly design my *ludi* so that they reflect these topics.

Furthermore, I have found it most effective to design *ludi* for *a particular group* of students at *a particular time*. Not every group of students needs to be exercised in the same way. Some are stronger and more experienced with certain points of grammar, others with others. In an ideal world, each student would be given a separate, customized *ludus*, but it is admittedly hard enough to come up with forty new *ludi* every semester for each class. I find it humbling that in over forty years of teaching, my teacher Reginald Foster has never recycled a *ludus* and continues to produce them on a manual typewriter rather than a computer (I again draw attention to Foster's forthcoming publication with the Catholic University of America Press).

I should emphasize that, even in courses in which I am not teaching through the medium of Latin, translation is the least important activity of any *ludus*. In Conversational Latin – with the exceptions given above – there is generally no translation section at all. The reason for this is twofold. First, I have discovered that even if students render decent translations, those translations do not necessarily reveal whether they have understood how the Latin functions. It is one thing to offer a 'perfect' translation of '*permagni nostra interest te, si comitiis non potueris, at declarato illo esse Romae*' (Cicero, *ad Atticum*, II, 23) as 'it is of great interest to us that you be in Rome after the elections, if you cannot be there before', it is quite another thing to understand and articulate the reason for the case and gender in *permagni*, *nostra*, and *te*, the time in *potueris*, and the time indicated by *declarato illo*. Second, when working on Latin composition, it is important for students to avoid being 'infected' by English so that they may write pure, elegant Latin idioms.

I should also note that *ludi domestici* take the place of written examinations in Conversational Latin I and II (i.e. they are a form of assessment as well as a learning opportunity). Among other activities, students are required to give a final oral presentation to the class and sit through an oral examination with me, but they are free of any other form of Latin examination at the exact time that they are cramming for other exams. Students generally appreciate this, although the *ludi domestici* do require them to work harder and more consistently from day to day – and that is precisely what allows them to learn in a way that endures rather than fades away within months after the course is over.

To make progress and improve in using communicative Latin to enhance reading and speaking fluency at all levels, I have had to think carefully about what I require students to do at home. I certainly want them to speak and write text messages and emails to one another in Latin outside the classroom. I similarly want them to find enriching video and audio content on the web to continue hearing and speaking Latin. I constantly encourage students to read aloud at home, be it poetry or prose, even when there is no one but the cat to listen. But I have also found that I must give attention to written exercises and assignments that enhance and maximize the effectiveness of classroom time, especially when classroom time is limited. I have discovered that to do this, a combination of Latin and English is needed in *ludi domestici* to ensure that my students correctly analyze Latin structures and that I accurately assess my students' strengths and weaknesses so that I can support them appropriately by providing targeted activities in and out of class.

I believe that more scientific research should be devoted to understanding why this is the case. I have my own hypotheses, but I will need to extend my own linguistic and psychological training to test those hypotheses. For now, I can only speak from my experience of carefully designing both in-class and out-of-class activities in a way that I believe maximizes oral comprehension and fluency for my students. I am convinced that any language must ultimately be taught and learned through a communicative approach, but my hunch is that Latin – even though alive and well – should not be taught in exactly the same way as Spanish, French, German or any other modern language. I know I disagree with several colleagues on this point, and I continue to learn much from my discussions with them. In my opinion, communicative Latin has never had a brighter future. I only hope that as we continue to increase the load of spoken Latin inside and outside of the classroom, we pay attention to those *loci* where a combination of Latin and English – such as in *ludi domestici* – will ultimately help our students achieve the loftiest outcomes that best serve them in Latin and beyond.

Note

1. Dragon Day, observed on the Friday before spring break, features a procession through campus of a mechanical dragon built by first-year architecture students. In class that day, we read and discuss Phaedrus' Aesopian fable *Vulpes et Draco* (The Fox and the Serpent).

CHAPTER 11
TEACHING LATIN COMMUNICATIVELY TO POSTGRADUATE STUDENTS
Cressida Ryan

Introduction

This chapter explores a number of the issues I have encountered when making use of communicative methods in teaching Latin to postgraduate students. Two years ago, I changed my approach to use *Lingua Latina per se Illustrata* (hereafter *LLPSI*) (Ørberg 2011); but this is more than an extended book review of my experience in doing so. I reflect on issues about theories of input and output, introducing compelling reading, the use of textbooks and resources, dictation, pronunciation, and student psychology, within a framework of considering what students are learning for, and how the overall set-up of a group affects the type of teaching which best suits it. This is not a comprehensive account of my experiences of embedding communicative elements in my teaching, but it does highlight some of the challenges and points of interest in working with communicative approaches.

My main case study involves teaching Latin to postgraduate students in the Faculty of English Language and Literature at the University of Oxford. A significant number of sources, including letters, wills, other legal documents and introductions to editions that postgraduate students on the 1550–1700 Master's course might want to read are in Latin, and so students find they need to learn the language to make progress with research. They are not a group whose needs have been much considered by teachers of Latin, but they are a group for whom Latin is important, and important in a different way to the average Classicist. The University of Leicester, which has no degree programme in Classics, runs a module which covers Latin from classical to early modern, but does not focus on postgraduate education for research purposes, or solely on the peculiarities and idiosyncrasies of this kind of Latin (see Foxhall, Story and Knight 2012). To this end, I think it is especially important that we consider what forms of teaching activity and resources might help them, broadening access to Latin to new audiences.

There are many challenges to such a programme. I cannot teach my students much Latin in the time allocated (sixteen weekly classes of ninety minutes). Much of the published discussion about communicative methods presupposes a significant amount of contact time with students, and students under the age of eighteen (see, for example Piazza 2019, who suggests a daily / weekly schedule, Carter 2019 writing about William Stevens' plan for two-and-a-half hours daily, and Chambers 1992 on the general problem of time constraints). Carter suggests the extensive reading method recommended by Stevens might work with *ab initio* university students, but that Stevens over-estimates the contact time most of these have, and even Tunberg – a major proponent of communicative Latin at the university level – is unsure about its place in beginners' courses (Lloyd 2016).

Because of my own time constraints, I need to maximize the impact of my teaching, so as to equip my students with a level of procedural knowledge about reading Latin which they can then develop themselves in order to access their texts. My students have a clear goal: being able to read the particular texts pertinent to their research. This is unlike other Latin-learning contexts, where the goal may be to pass a public exam, or gain greater understanding of the Roman world more generally. Students have varying levels of prior language experience, ranging from no prior foreign language study, to Latin A level many years ago. They come from a range of international backgrounds, which further diversifies the kinds of language teaching they have previously encountered. The timespan (1550–1700) covers a range of forms of Latin, which makes it hard to focus on any one style of Latin (classical, medieval or other). The textbooks available demonstrate this point: *Reading Medieval Latin* (Sidwell 1995), *Latin for Local History* (Gooder 2013) and *A Primer of Ecclesiastical Latin* (Collins 1988) all describe their specific purposes in their titles, but cannot possibly cover all Latin designated 'Neo-Latin', a term used broadly to refer to Latin after about 400 CE, or sometimes more specifically after about 1500 (post-medieval). The Society for Neo-Latin Studies has published an anthology of resources to support the teaching of Neo-Latin, but these all presuppose a strong knowledge of primarily classical Latin being adapted to a new reading purpose, rather than being appropriate for an *ab initio* group. (See the Centre for the Study of the Renaissance at https://warwick.ac.uk/fac/arts/ren/snls/snls_teaching_anthology/.)

My initial approach to the course was to use grammar summaries I had written myself to outline a map of what Latin looked like as a system. I interspersed this with some class time on how to use both Early Modern and contemporary lexica and grammar books in order to make sense of texts. In each class we focus on a short passage of a particular student's chosen text, which would be directly relevant to that one student, and model ways of approaching Latin for the others. Trying to cover all the foundations of Latin grammar in sixteen weeks, putting grammar into a sequence to teach from while still teaching real texts whose language was anything but 'stepped', proved challenging. The students found themselves overwhelmed, surrounded by a sea of language tables they would try to navigate while having a text in front of them, and never feeling able to acquire proficiency in using the language.

Two years ago, the class remit changed. It now included those studying English 650–1550, and the Latin texts written in that period, thereby increasing student numbers and further diversifying the types of Latin I needed to teach. I decided that a change of approach was needed. Having visited the Polis Institute to learn more about communicative methods, and having reviewed their Greek textbook (Ryan 2017), I considered teaching Latin communicatively myself. In addition to teaching my group, I have also been attending the beginners' classes in the Oxford Latinitas Project (OLP). The OLP facilitators are experienced in communicative Latin and have had much to teach me (see Chapter 17 in this book). They are less experienced in classroom teaching, however, and I have learned much from this experience about the practical implications of taking a communicative approach in the classroom. The rest of this chapter discusses the challenges and benefits of such an approach with my postgraduate students.

What do I mean by communicative approaches?

When I surveyed the literature on second language teaching, I quickly realized that a variety of approaches were available. Modern foreign languages books talk mainly about Communicative

Language Teaching (CLT) with a view to developing students' communicative competence. They make an assumption that all four skills (reading, writing, speaking and listening) are used (Richards and Rodgers 2001). This immersive experience is sometimes used in the teaching of Latin. In a series of articles, Carlon articulates the roles of memory and translation in the Latin classroom, and in particular, in achieving meaningful assessment. She argues that using more immersive and communicative approaches improve student engagement and performance, and offer a way to maintain Latin's strength and credibility in an educational climate which does not always seem to value it (Carlon 2013; 2015; 2018). Part of this package, as she mentions, has included a move towards Comprehensible Input (CI) approaches on the basis that students do well when not pressurized to produce Latin, only to consume it, in the first instance. Rogers introduces a special issue of the *Journal of Classics Teaching* dedicated to this topic (Rogers 2019), but elements have been included in that journal far earlier. A good summary of the different elements and their history can be found in Hunt (2018). CI may only explicitly include Latin input, but I include discussion of its elements here for three reasons. Students instinctively move to produce Latin, whether or not I actively encourage it. *LLPSI* may not demand Latin output, but when I talk to students about it, ask questions, or generally address them in Latin, they instinctively try to answer in Latin. Second, in acting out the roles of *LLPSI* they are taking on the Latin and making it more active, sowing seeds of production. Third, reading Latin in such a fashion is very far removed from standard grammar-translation models, providing at least part of a CLT package. My interest has been in how this exposure to using Latin differently changes student progress, and CI is a part of this. I am reminded by Richards and Rodgers (2011) that communicative teaching is an approach rather than a closed method to be adhered to in an all or nothing fashion. I have therefore chosen to blend elements of CI with CLT in a kind of hybrid communicative teaching approach. I therefore use the term loosely throughout this chapter, clarifying in each case which element I am referring to.

What are we learning for?

I initially want to think about why my students are learning Latin, and how that shapes the way I teach them. In her blog post summarizing a recent talk, Whyte charts the tension between English for Specific Purposes (ESP) and Teaching English for No Other Reason (TENOR) (Whyte 2019a). She argues that the ESP approach to language teaching raises issues over course design, methodology and evaluation. My students need to learn to read their own texts as quickly as possible, with far less concern for Latin as a language more broadly. While they may not be learning to pass a test, they are learning for a specific goal. Students therefore risk failing to understand their texts in the broader linguistic context. Their goal-orientated motivation may be less productive than an internal motivation. They may achieve the goal, but without the levels of communicative competence needed to be able to read any other Latin. Their specific textual needs change every year, placing a significant workload burden on a teacher. I would like students to learn Latin for its own sake, and then apply what they have learned to their own texts. This tension between my pedagogical values and their academic needs is hard to reconcile in the time available. Using a communicative approach has provided me with some means to achieve this to a greater extent than in previous years.

An early proponent of the Direct Method of teaching Latin in England, W. H. D. Rouse, was criticized for not teaching students to pass standard school tests. Stray charts the problems he faced in convincing people that conventional assessment was not appropriate (Stray 1992; see also Hunt 2018). One benefit I have is that students do not have a standardized test to take. To this extent, they are an excellent group to experiment with, learning Latin for its own sake. In teaching students to read just the texts their own research demands, however, I risk creating an excessively focused corpus-driven course which fails to do justice to Latin more broadly. I also risk alienating most students in any given class, as the level of academic altruism needed to focus on other people's research at the expense of one's own interests may be beyond them in this challenging and time-pressured environment.

One particular challenge I face is the nature of the Latin my students need to read. Take a student studying Thomas More, for example. They might want to read the introduction to *Utopia*. This masterly passage contains an opening sentence of ninety-nine words. For a beginner, it is a nightmare. I have mocked it up with vocab, brackets and arrows in a multitude of colours in order to help students try to comprehend the meaning of it. As Lloyd discusses in her PhD, however, this is not reading so much as deciphering, or unpicking a text (Lloyd 2017). Such a text could become a chore, no more than a puzzle to solve, a slow exercise, and probably not an enjoyable one. Moreover, this is only page one of a much longer text. Unlike the Classicist who is at liberty to contemplate only a few hundred lines of verse, and for whom that contemplation may be the point of their studies, my students need Latin as a tool at their fingertips, so that they can read a whole text in order for it to form part of their greater study. The study of the language itself is a mere footnote to their overall project aims. As Gratius Avitus (2018) and Lloyd (2016) argue, there is a need to engage in scholarship that has been written in Latin, and this need is very real for my particular students.

With the aim of fluent and extensive reading in mind, communicative approaches are very attractive to me, and lead to a new set of pedagogical questions. My students do not need to learn to speak Latin. Doing so might, however, aid their language development in general and their appreciation of Latin texts in particular if they could learn to express themselves in Latin, as a creative part of their learning. It may also help students to learn Latin using techniques similar to those of authors they are studying, in order to access their texts with a similar linguistic perspective. Erasmus' letter on how squalid and unhealthy British houses are, for example, is a good read, however awkward, and demonstrates how Latin was used communicatively by the kinds of people most of my students are interested in. I have excellent material at my fingertips, but how to use it most effectively remains the ongoing question.

Compelling reading

This concept of a good read brings me to the next aspect of teaching my students communicatively. My students are learning Latin because they want to, and because they do have very specific goals in mind, namely their research texts. If I can harness their inherent interest in their subject by using texts relevant to them, then I have already invoked their intrinsic motivation, which Ash (2019) notes as important (although Ryan and Deci 2000 remind us that the differences are neither clear-cut nor necessarily as important as is sometimes made out). Following the work of Krashen (1981), in the literature on CI, the need for texts to be compelling is always made clear (Ash 2019; Bracey 2019; Patrick 2019; Rogers 2019). The texts my students bring me, however, are far beyond the linguistic level they will achieve over the course. The extent of the challenge risks being extremely demotivating. I have so far dealt with this issue in two ways. First, I have been using *LLPSI* to give the students exposure to comprehensible Latin building from the beginners' level every lesson, to build their fluency. With their Latin antennae tuned in for the day, I have relied on high motivation levels and a willingness to be led carefully in their reading in order to then approach original texts. Secondly, I have bridged *LLPSI* to their chosen texts by using some texts of my own finding. These include Alcuin's riddles for teaching Charlemagne. They are largely simple, elegant, and charming, and make an excellent starting text:

quid est littera?	*custos historiae.*
What is literature ?	The guardian of (hi)story.
quid est homo?	*mancipium mortis, transiens viator, loci hospes.*
What is man ?	A slave of death, a passing wayfarer, a guest in the place.
quid est somnus?	*mortis imago.*
What is sleep ?	The image of death.
quid est luna ?	*oculus noctis, roris larga, praesaga tempestatum.*
What is the moon ?	The eye of the night, full of dew, who warns of storms.
quae sunt stellae ?	*nautarum gubernatores, noctis decor.*
What are the stars ?	Sailors' helmsmen, the ornament of night.
quid est nebula ?	*nox in die.*
What is cloud ?	Night in day.

Waddell 1932; all translations are mine

The vocabulary level is high, if you cover very many of these, which is not what some advocates of communicative approaches, such as Olimpi (2019) recommend. Carlon (2018) mentions 3,000 words as standard for beginners' English courses, but 1,000 as more usual for Latin. *LLPSI* introduces 3,000 words, suggesting that large amounts of vocabulary can be meaningfully introduced to beginners. Even this, however, represents a small percentage of the lexical variety in most texts, and the tension between reading original texts my students need to read, and texts whose vocabulary is not too diverse, remains problematic in a course such as mine. You can, however, use images and other clues to help clarify the vocabulary. Many of these words do have close English derivations, the inclusion of which is recommended in creating tiered texts (see, for example, Sears and Ballestrini 2019). One can easily take just a couple of the riddles (there are many) and create further texts around them in order to reinforce the language (and see Lloyd 2016 on the use of riddles in communicative teaching). The grammatical features are repeated, and so help students to learn about (for example) using genitives to describe nouns in various ways, without having to worry about the technical descriptions of cases. Similar texts were used to teach Latin even in my area. John Harmar, a teacher at Magdalen College School in Oxford, produced a *Praxis Grammatica* in 1623 including short sayings such as:

1. *ego sum hodie apud te pransurus.*
    I am going to eat at yours tomorrow.

2. *tu es liberalis convivator.*
    You are a very generous host.

3. *ille est librorum helluo.*
    He is a glutton for books.

205. *docemur a vobis linguam Latinam.*
    We are taught Latin by you.

(numbers refer to the numbering in the original book)

Harmar 1969; all translations are mine

Not only are these easy to work with for beginners, but they give an insight into the Latin and the teaching approach of the period which my students are studying. Students enjoy these texts, meeting the compelling element of communicative learning, as long as I introduce them carefully enough to meet the comprehensible one. Part of this process has been tiering the texts so that students are led through not only increasingly difficult texts, but increasingly difficult versions of texts (on processes for tiering texts, see Sears and Ballestrini 2019 and Gall 2020). Enabling relevant bespoke Free Voluntary Reading (FVR) is beyond the scope of my course, however desirable; but this does begin to sow the seeds of such a possibility (on FVR and extensive reading, see Patrick 2019 and Olimpi 2019).

The use of *LLPSI* also presents its own challenges here. Where my students' material is compelling but not altogether comprehensible, *LLPSI* stories may be comprehensible, but, in my experience, for the majority of postgraduate students, they are certainly not compelling. The story of the daily lives of naughty children is reminiscent of something akin to a beginners' reading book. This may be of interest to younger students, but it is of far less interest to my mature students so that content hampers rather than promotes motivation. In discussing how to use textbooks, Ramahlo (2019) mentions drawing Sextus falling out of a tree in the Latin coursebook for school students, *Ecce Romani*. The same plotline is used in *LLPSI*. The pedagogical framework may have changed, but the stories often feel very similar, and not appropriate to my students' needs.

At this point, two key factors come in: the nature of classroom activity, and the psychology of the class. The next section of this chapter explores how I have used *LLPSI*, and where I have moved beyond it.

Specific areas of teaching practice

Dictation

When attending Oxford Latinitas classes, I was, for the first time I can remember, asked to take down a Latin dictation. After initiating a Twitter discussion on the topic, I found that this is a relatively common feature in modern foreign languages teaching. Those writing on Comprehensible Input in Latin also discuss its role, especially Piantaggini (2019).

Dictation by itself may not be an obvious part of a communicative classroom; to me it felt like an unexpected task which was not enhancing my Latin but instead testing my ability to hear and transcribe syllables uttered by someone whose accent I might not follow. I therefore decided to explore what part dictation could play in my own communicative teaching.

Pronunciation and orthography

Before considering the pedagogical value of different kinds of dictation, another problem presented itself. Dictation, and indeed reading out loud, raise a further practical challenge. What pronunciation should one use? The Daily Dose of Latin launched in full in 2020. Along with the sister sites for Greek and Hebrew, it offers a verse of the Bible with a screencast translation and commentary. This has decided to use a classical pronunciation over an ecclesiastical one (Daily Dose of Latin n.d.). Classical courses are not entirely consistent, but do often give pronunciation guides, drawing on academic guidance, starting with Allen (2004). Similar guidance was published contemporary with many of the texts my students read, including by Caius in 1574 (Caius and Gable 1968) and Lipsius in 1609 (Lipsius and Moretus 1609). Trying to match a pronunciation to the texts we read can help to make sense of some of the more peculiar spelling conventions, but is unsustainably complicated. My students, however, are studying Latin from a range of centuries, countries, and at different educational levels. Emphasising one pronunciation might enable some kind of common ground in class, but it will not help students access the Latin they need to read, with all the phonological oddities that the original author's pronunciation will have resulted in. Encouraging students to read out loud is important, and phonemic awareness underlies aspects of reading fluency in general (Wegenhart 2015). This need not necessarily be about phonemic awareness for fluency in any kind of historically reconstructed way, although Tunberg discusses some ways to mediate this (Lloyd 2016). It might, however, allow a personal fluency, increased confidence, and a more rounded appreciation of the language. Getting pronunciation 'right' presupposes that there is a 'right' to get, and risks becoming a barrier to learning Latin rather than an aid to understanding.

We therefore need to agree on a compromise which allows us at least to be mutually intelligible, even if not identical. Given my background in Classics, this is broadly the classical Latin pronunciation I learned, influenced by works such as (Allen 2004) and modified by my own further philological study.

Once we have established this compromise, I can begin to work on dictation as a skill. My initial attempts at dictating have been positive. Students made errors over word breaks, but discussions over errors helped clarify the likely forms of Latin words, for example. My students' spelling was remarkably consistent, which suggests good training in tuning in to me as a teacher. Something like dictation, which involves communication only in one direction from teacher to student, also reminds us that although we might be aiming to benefit from the principles of communicative teaching, it does not need to be all or nothing, and building in elements of it, in a hybrid teaching fashion, may in fact be a good way forward in general, but particularly for someone new to the approach (as suggested by Ramahlo 2019, Atkinson 1993 and Lloyd 2016 on the fallacy that 100 per cent immersion is needed to be successful).

Reflecting on these first steps in using dictation, I have investigated further how other language teachers do so. Dictation in pairs, where students dictate to each other and check each other's work, allows students to practise both speaking and listening skills, and to understand problems better as they work on correcting misunderstandings together. Conti recommends a form of delayed dictation, where students wait before writing down what they have heard, which requires them to remember what they have heard, and perhaps start to make more sense of it, rather than acting as automatic scribes (Conti and Smith 2016). Involving a range of skills, dictation used repeatedly, with space for improvement and correction, has the potential to give students a sense of owning the words they are writing on the page, of mastering Latin to some degree. This sense of mastery is itself a good outcome, regardless of whether it fits neatly with communicative approaches.

Student psychology

LLPSI may not contain narrative content which my students find compelling, but it is sufficiently juvenile that I can at least convince them to find it amusing in a more ironic kind of way. This is just one example of how teaching postgraduate students offers me some opportunities to make more use of communicative methods than some of my constraints might suggest. Ash (2019) summarizes that a communicative curriculum needs not only to be compelling and comprehensible, but also caring. To this end, a few further factors are relevant in my group.

Levels of perfectionism among high-achieving students have been shown to be particularly high in adult learners (Griffiths 1992). The classroom therefore needs to be one in which students feel very comfortable about making mistakes at all, and particularly in front of each other. Griffiths (1992) and Patrick (2019) write about students limiting themselves in order to avoid errors, for example. The removal of formal assessment takes away much pressure from the course, and allows the class the flexibility to try out approaches as best suit the individuals in the group. Piazza (2019) suggests, however, that the removal of external motivation does sometimes prevent the students from seeing how much they are learning and increases the pressure they feel on themselves, Sinclair (2018) reports that students can find communicative methods uncomfortable, and therefore it is important to mitigate that. One task I have is to help them set realistic and achievable personal goals.

Although my postgraduate students have a very narrow focus of personal academic interests, they are also drawn from a broad range of universities and courses. Very few of my students were undergraduates at Oxford, and many have come from abroad. Their intellectual curiosity and enthusiastic breadth of academic vision often makes them more open-minded than the more goal-orientated and curriculum-enclosed students at lower levels. They can, however, be much more reticent about new ways of learning, as they are more sure that they know what works for them, and about how they learn languages successfully (Griffiths 1992). I need to convince students to collaborate with me in the teaching methods I use. This means that I am relatively explicit about my methodology and its rationale, as well as the fact that I am capitalizing on the good will generated by tailoring the course to include reading their own texts. When this works, it reduces the levels of frustration that Miller (2018) describes when students are asked to read rather than translate, for example. As Grasha (1984) and Gregorc (1984) both discuss, teaching methods need to be varied to avoid boredom and engage students.

Communicative methods help maintain a level of variety in the classroom, because they are relatively unusual, as noted even by Rouse in the early days of the Direct Method (Stray 1992). In my case, students have the added incentive of reading texts directly relevant to their interests as a result of engaging with the method.

Moving forward

My move away from reliance of *LLPSI*, however, brought with it the need to think carefully about how else I might teach intuitive reading. I have further changed my teaching practice to incorporate elements of pre-reading strategies and tiered readings. As Russell (2018) notes, learning by reading demands highly motivated students who are already motivated in their own language. This is precisely what I do have, which makes the extensive reading recommended in CI very attractive. In incorporating extensive reading as part of a communicative approach, students learn more about reading as a process, bringing us back to communicative methods and their aim for procedural knowledge.

Students have sometimes commented that it is easy when I'm leading them, but without me asking questions, they don't know what to do. I have started to mock up their texts as annotated videos talking through the process of reading which I undergo in Latin, and the bells which ring in my head at various points which give me insights into a text. By showing them thinking and reading in action (without allowing them to dwell too much on my propensity for decoding in keeping with my training as a translator), I hope to model ways in which they can approach their own texts. Part of this includes teaching them to be comfortable with a higher level of uncertainty than even the 90 per cent threshold for effortful reading would incorporate (Carlon 2018; Sears and Ballestrini 2019). Careful discussion about decision-making opened and closed by each word in a Latin sentence helps students learn to read, for example. Taking on board work on learning to read in Latin word order (Russell 2018) and scientific approaches to teaching reading (Wegenhart 2015), I am continuing to develop ranges of pre-reading activities that blend these approaches.

Conclusion

As Richards and Rodgers (2001) noted, the pedagogical influence of Latin waned as modern foreign language instructors improved their own pedagogy. Groups such as HOLLT.net (the History of Language Learning and Teaching Network), founded in 2015, have opened up more potential for dialogue between ancient and modern language pedagogy. In a 2019 lecture, Henry Widdowson, a pioneer of the paradigm shift of CLT, challenged the rhetoric of language teaching being necessarily characterized by a series of new starts and radical departures in teaching style, arguing for something far more blended, overlapping, incremental, and circular (Whyte 2019b). I still use elements of 'formal' grammar teaching, which, as summarized by Hood (1994) can be both communicative and learner-centric, without resorting solely to the 'pop-up' grammar suggested by some of the classical literature, wherein grammar teaching is not planned, but points are explained as they 'pop up' in a text or discussion. Blending communicative approaches with other teaching methods may not be a turnaround in teaching methods, nor an abandonment of method and theory, but a new phase in the development of a student-centric style of teaching.

It is important to compromise between comprehensible and compelling Latin when it comes to groups whose needs are specific, challenging and disparate, such as mine. The lack of an authoritative textbook suitable for older learners brings into focus the importance of collaborating with colleagues in our methods and resources. Teaching older students is inherently challenging, and more work needs to be done on adapting communicative methods for adult education in general, and Higher Education *ab initio* Latin groups in particular.

PART 3
TOTAL IMMERSION IN FORMAL AND INFORMAL SETTINGS

CHAPTER 12
GLOBAL LATIN, ACTIVE LATIN: KENTUCKY AND BEYOND
Milena Minkova and Terence Tunberg

Conventiculum Latinum Lexintoniense (Terence Tunberg)

The *Conventiculum Latinum Lexintoniense* takes place annually in Lexington, Kentucky. It was the first total immersion workshop to be founded in North America since the Second World War to be devoted to Latin as a spoken language, but unconnected to any religious organization and devoid of any religious mission. Before I founded the *Conventiculum Latinum Lexintoniense*, I had become convinced that the effort to produce intelligible extempore Latin discourse in a syntax reasonably close to that of classical Latin texts, and to understand others engaging in the same way with the target language, offered a way to develop an intimate knowledge of Latin more quickly than would be possible from reading and translating alone. I had taken part in Latin immersion gatherings which were celebrated each summer in Germany, Belgium and France. These could trace their origin to the first international congress for living Latin, celebrated in Avignon in 1956. I decided that something similar should be available to the teachers, professors, students and other cultivators of Latin active in North America. But we (I and the group of friends who joined with me to develop the Lexington *Conventicula* in the first years of their existence) wanted to offer a much wider range of activities designed to encourage interaction in the target language than those which we had experienced in the European seminars. In 1996, eleven people attended the first *Conventiculum Lexintoniense*. Within four years, the enrolment was over sixty. And since that time the number of participants each year has consistently ranged from about sixty-five to eighty people. These attendees have come not only from all over North America, but also South America, Mexico, Australia, Japan, several countries in continental Europe, Ireland and the United Kingdom. While we still have much to learn, and we are always looking for ways to enhance the event, the *Conventiculum* already seems to us to be a story of success. To what factors can we attribute this success?

From the very beginning the organizers, a small group of Latin specialists based in Lexington, tried to formulate as accurately as possible what we were trying to do, and we tried to define realistically the limits of what we could do in the week-long format (a period of days that was not only typical of many European events, but also seemed to represent what would be practical for most potential participants in terms of cost and time away from family and work). Our seminars would be designed to add an active and communicative dimension to the Latinity of people who had already acquired at least a passive understanding of the structure of Latin and could read unadapted Latin texts of the simpler kind (even if needing frequent help from a dictionary). But previous experience with Latin as a spoken or communicative language would not be necessary for admission into the *Conventiculum*. Helping people already equipped with a passive knowledge of Latin to attain some ability to use Latin actively, and to develop a more instinctive relationship with this language, seemed to be a viable goal for a space of seven days – whereas teaching all the main language structures from the very beginning level would not be a reasonable goal in such a space of time, however intensive the instruction.

During the seven-day immersion period, we would design a programme aimed at making the most of the time to enable each participant (not all of whom are interested in speaking Latin for purposes that are primarily pedagogical) to enhance their *own* powers of Latin expression and comprehension. Our target would be the participants themselves – people with some passive knowledge of the language, and who therefore could already do some things beginners could not yet do. Teachers, of course, can and do make use of communicative powers and increased fluency gained from the *Conventiculum* in the classroom to complement whatever teaching strategies each one prefers. And, actually, it has turned out that many of the exercises we have designed for participants in the *Conventiculum* also work very well (sometimes with a bit of adaptation) as communicative activities appropriate for the beginning-level classroom.

These were some of our strategies when we founded the *Conventiculum* and they still serve as our basic guidelines. Our motivation arose not from modern language theories and practices relating to communicative approaches, but from personal experience of the effects of Latin immersion among the organizers, and from observation of the progress made by participants at our Conventicula over the years. Nonetheless, it was interesting to see our practices analyzed through a modern language perspective by one of our participants (Lloyd 2017: 204–60). What then goes on in the *Conventicula* and how are they organized?

Everything in the *Conventiculum* happens in Latin. Among the participants, who sign a promise on the first day to use no other language but Latin with each other, there is indeed a Latin universe. People unused to this level of immersion can, of course, find this challenging in the beginning, but there has been almost unanimous agreement among participants over the years that the effort is worthwhile. Each person's dedication to this principle enhances the experience for all who take part.

We strongly urge our participants not to be afraid of making mistakes, and are very careful never to correct people in quotidian interaction during the *Conventiculum*. Of course, everyone's goal is to speak correctly and with a degree of fluency, but no one will progress towards this goal, unless she or he is bold enough in the beginning to make the attempt to speak. To instill this confidence in beginners, we never fail to point out that even the most experienced speakers of Latin make slips on occasion, and that people speaking their native languages make mistakes all the time; when this happens, they typically correct, clarify or change the expression and proceed without a second thought.

The whole body of participants in the *Conventiculum* is usually divided into groups of about six to eight people, in order to maximize the amount of interaction for each individual. The constituency of these groups is changed every day, and sometimes several times per day, so that everyone in the *Conventiculum* has a chance to interact with everyone else. The conversations in each of the groups or *greges* are usually guided by a leader or *dux*. The *duces* are veterans of many previous *Conventicula*, and have learned by experience how such groups operate. They do not function as teachers, but 'facilitators', whose goal is to keep the conversation moving and as inclusive as possible. We encourage everyone in the *Conventiculum*, even the most experienced, to regard themselves as learners.

During the morning sessions, a further division takes place. In these sessions, first-time participants and people new to spoken Latin are separated from those who are more experienced in conversational Latin. The beginners are then introduced to the vocabulary of subjects useful for conversation, such as the weather, salutations, clothing, food; they practise saying aloud simple and grammatically correct sentences appropriate for conversational topics; they build vocabulary by engaging in word games (and new games are introduced every few years). Sometimes they write passages dictated by others – and then answer questions about these passages – in order to get used to hearing and understanding others speaking Latin.

But we also believe that the beginners can benefit from interaction with the more experienced. For this reason, new groups are usually formed for the afternoon sessions, in which beginners and experienced people are mixed. These groups take part in activities in which all levels of speaking experience can participate, and in which the more experienced can act as guides.

We place considerable emphasis on discussion, explanation and interpretation of passages from Latin literature. In each group each person in turn will read aloud a portion of a passage under discussion, and then try to paraphrase it in her or his own extempore Latin. Well before the *Conventiculum*, all participants receive by email six or seven unadapted passages from Latin authors from quite diverse periods (and one of our purposes is to stress the temporal, geographical and ethnic diversity of the Latin patrimony), which they are asked to read carefully before the seminar, so that they are ready to interpret these passages with their fellow participants. And during the seminar, of course, everyone who wishes to search for phrases has access at all times to lexica, phrase books and grammars, either online or in paper format. This *enarratio auctorum* (detailed interpretation of authors) is very important to us, because it is always our hope (for reasons to which we will return) that people in the *Conventiculum*, with all due allowances for errors or lack of experience, will strive in a simple conversational register to model their own Latin as consistently as possible on the usage and syntax of the authors held up as exemplary by the Latin tradition (i.e. the syntax presented as normative in modern handbooks of Latin grammar, such as those by Gildersleeve or Allen and Greenough, which is biased towards the normal prose usage of Caesar, Cicero, Livy and others who followed this usage).

We make extensive use of images in the *Conventiculum*. We use new images every year. They range from paintings (on any conceivable subject) to humorous cartoons without words. Although we treat images in many different ways, the discussion of images always happens in smaller groups (typically of six to eight people). Sometimes images can be the basis for vocabulary or phrase building when people in a group come up with as many synonyms or near-synonyms as possible that fit an entity depicted in an image, or as many phrases as they can to describe an action shown in an image. More creativity is needed when the exercise involves telling a story implied in an image, or series of images.

In every *Conventiculum* some activities include the writing of sentences, short passages, even dialogues. Indeed, we are not just interested in speaking Latin; we also like original Latin composition in writing (i.e. composition that does not involve translation from any other language). In our view, speaking and writing are complementary activities. Both are active and communicative. Each has certain benefits of its own. Speaking trains one to find appropriate words and phrases more quickly. Writing allows the composer to think more about the choice of word or phrase – and the practice of written composition will ultimately enhance the quality of one's extempore oral expression. We introduce new games or activities involving written

Latin composition every few years, or sometimes reuse such activities from earlier *Conventicula*. Composition of very short dialogues about an image, for example, takes places as a communal effort in groups of about six to eight people. The dialogues thus composed are then presented by members of each group to the whole body of *Conventiculum* participants. Sometimes individuals write (anonymously) single sentences relating to a set topic on small cards, which are mixed in a box or jar. Then a number of cards selected at random are read to the whole body of participants at the end of a day. Activities involving written composition are too many to be enumerated here. But one activity which includes written composition has remained a constant feature since the early *Conventicula* – and it typically provides us with a kind of climax and conclusion to each year's event. The participants, divided into groups, compose and perform their own plays about one of the passages assigned for reading before the seminar. All the groups must base their play on the same passage, so its theme will be recognizable to every participant in the seminar. It is enjoyable and enlightening to see how each group creates a drama (nearly always comedy) from the same passage. This exercise combines all the activities that interest us: reading comprehension of a passage; exercise in ex tempore speaking while interpreting the passage and composing the play; exercise in written composition while composing the dialogue; exercise in enunciation, delivery and aural comprehension while the play is being performed.

Immersed in these and similar activities, people live their lives for a week entirely in Latin, and Latin functions as a communicative medium for a contemporary environment. But for us the starting point and frame of reference for usage always remains in the language of the ancient *auctores probati* (esteemed authors) and the *recentiores* (more recent ones) who closely imitated the usage of the ancients. There are good reasons for this stance. First, Latin is a relatively unchanging language. In fact, people have continued to use Latin ever since the time of the Ancient Romans. Of course, new nouns and adjectives are sometimes employed when Latin is applied to modern life (new words have been a necessity throughout the history of Latin – something that Cicero himself knew would be the case: *De finibus*, III, 1–7). But, since the demise of the Western Roman empire, the syntactical and idiomatic norms of correct expression in Latin have not been evolving in the same way as they do in the current national languages. The norms of Latin for all this time have been fixed in texts. For the Middle Ages, the normative texts were the Scriptures and church fathers. Since the Renaissance the standard for prose has been found in the works of Caesar, Cicero, Livy and later writers who followed their usage. Second, Latin is not the language of any one country. The enormous heritage of Latin literature is the Latinists' country. Our reason for developing Latin proficiency is to communicate with that heritage and those who study it. We would argue, based on personal experience and observation of conventiculum participants, that speaking Latin – if the target is the norms of expression found in the canonical tests – can help develop this proficiency. Most people will grasp and appreciate the language more instinctively, if they have to use it. We are convinced that maintaining an active dimension, i.e. speaking, or written composition, or both, if one can manage it, should ideally be an accompaniment to one's reading of Latin and cultivation of Latin for life.

Institutum studiis Latinis provehendis (Milena Minkova)

The success of the summer Lexington Latin seminar *Conventiculum Latinum* naturally led, in 2001, to the establishment at the University of Kentucky of the Graduate Certificate curriculum in Latin Studies, or, as we are accustomed to call it, *Institutum studiis Latinis provehendis*, the 'Institute for Promotion of Latin Studies', or – for brevity – 'the Institute'. At the University of Kentucky, a Graduate Certificate curriculum is an integrated group of courses that is designed to have a clear and focused academic topic or competency as its subject area. The Institute provides a glimpse into the entire Latin tradition in its continuity from antiquity until modern times. The Neo-Latin patrimony, in particular, comprehending Latin works from Petrarch until the present day, is immensely vast, multicultural and interdisciplinary in its very nature, and offers infinite opportunities for study, research and understanding of the classical tradition. Indeed, it pertains to many populations throughout the globe: in Europe, Asia, Africa, South and North America, even Australia. The Neo-Latin patrimony also encompasses a wide range of disciplines: literature in all its genres, history, philosophy, theology, pedagogy, mathematics, physics and astronomy, chemistry, geography, biology, medicine, visual arts, music even sports. Just a few examples, which are mere drops in the ocean: there could be no reason to exclude from the study of the classical patrimony the masterpieces of Erasmus and Thomas More, the various accounts of the explorers of the 'New Worlds' and the first contacts with their indigenous populations, the groundbreaking scientific works of Copernicus and Newton, Kepler's science fiction or Holberg's fictional narrative and the whole tradition of fantastic tales with their multifaceted reflection on the human condition. The other distinctive feature of the Institute is the use of the target language, Latin, as a language of communication, not only with authors who lived centuries before us, but also among students and teachers, in class presentations and discussions, in papers and all written work, as well as outside the classroom. Thus, the Institute has naturally become a place which attracts a variety of people with different backgrounds from all over the globe; in so doing, it has established a vibrant Latin community, a small *res publica litterarum*, 'a republic of letters', in Lexington and beyond, extended to any place in the world to which our alumni depart upon graduation.

Some may be surprised that we trace the origins of our Institute to a concept and a movement that emerged in the second part of the last century. In 1956, the first international congress for living Latin – *Premier congrès international pour le latin vivant* – was celebrated in Avignon, France. Its organizer, Jean Capelle, was an engineer by profession, and the participants of the congress came from everywhere. In some ways, this congress was an attempt to find a common language, literally and figuratively, in the wake of humankind's divisions after the Second World War (Beach 1957). Several societies and Latin discussion circles were subsequently established, the largest of which, *Academia Latinitati Fovendae*, the 'Academy for Promotion of Latin', founded in Rome in 1967, held one of its first conventions in Senegal. A number of full-immersion Latin seminars took place in various locations. Terence Tunberg happened to attend some of the German seminars and returned to the United States with the resolution to found such a seminar in North America. This happened in 1996. The *Conventiculum Lexintoniense* was the first full-immersion Latin seminar in North America that was open to everyone. Inclusion and immersion in the rich and varied Latin tradition became important principles for the Institute as well. In fact, the global character of Latin patrimony makes its study more pertinent in today's global age, and the immersion in the target language more relevant in a time of growing interest toward communicative approaches to Latin teaching and learning.

Students have come to the Institute from all corners of the world – including Brazil, Australia, Italy, France, the Netherlands, the United Kingdom and Malawi – as well as from every part of the United States of America. The institutions which our students have attended before coming to us include Yale University, Harvard University, Cornell University, College of William and Mary, University of Austin, University of Illinois Urbana-Champaign, University of Bologna, the Sorbonne, and Fordham university, and many of these students enrolled in the Institute having already earned an advanced degree (M.A. or Ph.D.) in Medieval Studies, New Testament, Teaching English as a Second Language and Musical Arts. In this way the Bluegrass area, a renowned horse capital of the world, has become a Latin centre as well. Students seek the opportunity to be trained in the continuity of the Latin tradition from ancient to modern times, a tradition that not only expands beyond the first centuries of the Common Era, but also beyond the geographical and conceptual limits of the Roman world. Such students also embrace the opportunity to engage thoroughly with Latin by taking part in the four activities leading to language competence – reading, writing, listening and speaking (ACTFL 2012) – and by fostering a personal, emotional connection with the language.

The students who complete the Graduate Certificate curriculum (approximately three to five each year) typically also earn a Master's degree in Classics, and are able to share credit hours between the degrees. Some students pursue a concurrent degree with the Master's of Teaching World Languages programme also hosted in our Department of Modern and Classical Languages, Literatures and Cultures. Advanced undergraduate students, many of whom are interested in the Institute, have availed themselves of the University Scholars Program, in which undergraduate and graduate studies can be carried out at the same time. Thus, advanced undergraduates can have graduate credit for the graduate classes they are taking. University scholars earn a degree in four or five years. This also provides opportunities for creating a community of graduate and undergraduate students and a beneficial exchange between them. A common factor is their participation in the Institute courses.

Thus, through its active Latin programme, the University of Kentucky is a global destination. At the same time, it is also a point of global departures. Upon graduation students often become teachers or return to teaching, since gaining a broad and deep familiarity with Latin was their reason for coming to us. They teach in private, public and charter schools across the United States. Many students have opted to pursue doctoral studies — they have departed to Brown University, Johns Hopkins University, University of Virginia, New York University, University of Colorado, University of Arizona, University of Minnesota, University of Cádiz and Pontifical Salesian University. Some of the students have already sent us their own students to learn with us, thus initiating a most felicitous circle. Our alumni have gone to teach and study in Europe, South America, Asia and Africa. Some of them have been associated with institutions with which we maintain research ties, including Louvain University, the Ludwig Boltzmann Institute and University College Cork.

Let us return to the programme of study that the students follow while with us. Every student takes a thorough course in Latin Composition. Normally, there is a Latin Composition class conducted mainly in English devoted to simple sentence and coordinate clauses and an Advanced Latin Composition and Reading class conducted mainly in Latin and dedicated to subordinate clauses. We do not conceive of Latin Composition as translation from the vernacular into Latin, as is often the practice in the English-speaking countries, but rather as a process of expression directly in Latin. In our classes, composing originates as a continuation of our reflection on a text. Students give alternative words and constructions in exercises pertaining to the text; they fill in blanks, rewrite sentences and complete sentences for which they have a prompt: there are plenty of exercises of this type in a book that we have created specifically for this purpose (Minkova and Tunberg 2004). In none of these exercises does a student need to pass through English or another vernacular language; the thought process for each exercise should be in Latin. For example, consider the following: after reading Tacitus's passage about the fire at Rome in 64 CE, the students have to complete a dialogue between two Romans about the fire – a dialogue imagined to have taken place quite some time after the event. Some of the sentences in the dialogue are incomplete. Various temporal circumstances are described in parentheses but need to be expressed explicitly. Indeed, the main emphasis here consists of the different ways of expressing temporal circumstances. Thus, the students need to choose an appropriate way to complete each sentence with a temporal construction that would make sense according to Tacitus's account of the fire.

Beyond the Composition classes, each semester we offer a survey of Latin literature of various periods: ancient, late antique, medieval, humanistic and early modern. Sometimes the class is centred around a single author or single work (such as Cicero's *De re publica* or Erasmus's *Stultitiae Laus*), a literary genre (such as *De epistulis*) or a single topic (such as *De optimo genere dicendi* or *De optima re publica*). These classes are conducted entirely in Latin. As in the summer *Conventiculum, enarratio auctorum,* 'detailed interpretation of authors', is an essential part of the class routine. The texts are explained in Latin with paraphrases, alternative constructions and synonyms, or their meaning is elucidated by asking a series of questions in Latin to which the answers need to be given in Latin. Instead of moving back and forth between Latin and a vernacular language, there is a full Latin immersion that allows the students to be thoroughly imbued with the language, think in it, and 'converse' with the authors. Secondary literature relevant to the topic is read in the language in which is published but is discussed in Latin. Assignments are composed in Latin. These might consist of a summary of a text, such as the arguments for the study of Latin in the first preface of Lorenzo Valla's *Elegantiae linguae Latinae*, or an explanation of a poem such as one of Juvenal's *Satires,* given in prose. Another assignment might consist of a typological comparison with another text which is not necessarily written in Latin: for example, various aspects of More's *Utopia* might be compared with aspects of Plato, Bacon, Swift, Zamyatin, Huxley or Orwell. An assignment could require the interpretation of concepts in a text (such as 'the other' in Erasmus and Busbecq's *Epistulae Turcicae*), or the analysis of a text's literary techniques, perhaps even in comparison with other works in similar genres but for different media (such as Kepler's *Somnium* or Holberg's *Nicolai Klimii iter subterraneum* versus *Star Trek*.)

Students have also written their Master's theses in Latin, on a range of subjects. These have included: prose rhythm in Marcus Antonius Muretus; the pedagogical speeches of Muretus; Muretus and Plato; Johann Fux's musical theory; a poem on the 1741 Battle of Cartagena; and the scholastic use of More's *Utopia*.

Since 2001, we have also been conducting additional conversational Latin sessions two or three times a week. In these sessions, we frequently read Neo-Latin scholastic *colloquia*, by Erasmus, Vives, Corderius, Schottenius, Mosellanus, Salazar and others, varying in their scope and language, ranging from simple conversations on everyday topics to polished literary gems. We read, discuss and act out the dialogues contained in them, all in Latin. In other sessions, we read and discuss other texts, such as anecdotes by Valerius Maximus, or love poetry by Catullus, Horace, Ovid, Propertius or Tibullus. As in the summer *conventiculum,* we describe in Latin various images, or a series of images that tell a story. These sessions are conducted in a relaxed and welcoming atmosphere – graduate and undergraduate students, not to mention sometimes even Latin aficionados from the local community, spend time together conversing in Latin. The result is a continuing opportunity to foster familiarization with the Latin language, to make Latin one's own, and to cultivate a community of Latin learners.

These opportunities continue in the weekly Latin lunches, Latin dinners, Latin walks, picnics and outings, as well as a formal Latin lunch at the end of the year in which the Certificates in Latin studies are awarded. Students have even established a *Domus Latina,* a 'Latin House', a location where only Latin is spoken. As one of the world's greatest Latinists, Professor Dirk Sacré of the University of Louvain said when visiting the Institute during the celebration of its tenth anniversary: '*vos Latine vivitis*!' ('You all live in Latin!').

I think that I am correct in affirming that the Classics initiatives at the University of Kentucky have influenced, both in the USA and globally, the way people learn, study and research Latin and Classics. What does the future hold? Currently, the Department of Modern and Classical Languages, Literatures and Cultures at the University of Kentucky is working on an interdisciplinary doctoral programme in World Languages, Cultures and Second Language Acquisition, which would provide students with more research opportunities. The Master's Programme in Classics and the Graduate Certificate in Latin Studies will soon be in a position to offer some of their courses online for easier access by a global audience. For the same purpose of sharing and exchange, these programmes are endeavouring to make available on digital platforms some of the research conducted through them, mainly exploring the enormous Neo-Latin patrimony. At the University of Kentucky, Latin is indeed alive and relevant for our past, present and future, from Perth to Appalachia, from Japan to the Straits of Magellan.

CHAPTER 13
A CONVENTICULUM FOR SPEAKERS OF ANCIENT GREEK: THE LEXINGTON ΣΥΝΟΔΟΣ ἙΛΛΗΝΙΚΗ

R. Stephen Hill

In the discipline of Classics, one is more often obliged to acknowledge Rome's debt to Greece than vice versa. But here I must begin with the relationship of my subject, the Lexington σύνοδος ἑλληνική or Greek Conventiculum, to its illustrious predecessor, Terence Tunberg's *Conventiculum Latinum*. In 1996, Professor Tunberg founded a summer seminar at the University of Kentucky (Minkova and Tunberg, this volume), an event in which participants speak only Latin to each other for one week. Its popularity grew, and today it draws almost 100 people to Lexington each year. When I arrived at the university to study Latin, having already taught summer courses in spoken Ancient Greek, I immediately began to speculate about launching a Greek equivalent of the Latin *Conventiculum* – a concept which, at the time, had no North American precedent. Several years later, in 2017, the first σύνοδος ἑλληνική was held immediately prior to that year's *Conventiculum Latinum*.[1] In what follows, I will address the primary features and basic schedule of the σύνοδος, explain some of its activities and their basis in second language acquisition (SLA) research, and discuss its significance for the growing community of Ancient Greek speakers.

The σύνοδος: An outline

The σύνοδος shares many characteristics with the Latin *conventiculum* on which it is modelled. First of all, it is not designed for beginners: participants must have already acquired a basic knowledge of Greek (at least four university semesters). Often, they have never *spoken* Ancient Greek before. Second, the σύνοδος is not a course or a class designed to impart grammatical knowledge in a systematic way: meaningful communication is the primary focus, and we address questions of grammar or usage incidentally. In other words, the goal is to improve participants' command of Ancient Greek by 'activating' the passive knowledge they already possess, not to teach the elements of the language *ab initio*. Third, in order to accomplish this goal, Ancient Greek is the only language participants and facilitators use to communicate with each other for the entire week. Although many sessions centre on Ancient Greek texts that participants have read in advance, it is the opportunity to discuss those texts *in Ancient Greek* that seems to keep participants coming back year after year.

Anyone interested in attending the σύνοδος for the first time must submit an online application, of which the most important component is three excerpts from Greek texts. Applicants must estimate their understanding of these texts without any aids on a percentage basis. The first paragraph's difficulty is roughly equivalent to the easier narrative passages of the Greek New Testament or *A Greek Boy at Home* (Rouse 1909); anyone who understands less than 90 per cent of this passage is encouraged to wait a year and apply again. The second paragraph usually contains selections from moderately difficult Attic prose, such as Xenophon or Plato's easier dialogues, while the third is designed to identify the advanced readers by offering a more complicated text, such as an excerpt from Plato's *Phaedrus* or Philostratus' *Lives of the Sophists*. The three texts together enable us to gauge a person's receptive ability in Greek. We also ask participants to outline their previous study of Greek and explain why they want to attend (to make sure no one arrives expecting to speak English for the week). Applications are evaluated as they arrive and participants are notified within a few days. Each year's group generally represents a wide variety of backgrounds and careers, although the majority are normally students or faculty in Classics and related disciplines, teachers in secondary schools, or avocational students of Ancient Greek. Facilitators and participants are generally united by a commitment to studying Ancient Greek texts, a desire to read them more fluently, and a conviction that actively using the language is the most effective way to improve one's reading ability.

The σύνοδος officially begins with an evening reception, usually on a Sunday, at which any and all languages are allowed (on these occasions I hear primarily English and Latin, but also – *inter alias* – Ancient Greek, German and Spanish). The following morning, we begin in earnest, forswearing the use of all languages other than Ancient Greek. At this point, participants must choose either the beginning or advanced level; anyone unsure may sample each during the first day before deciding. Some participants who have spoken before choose the beginner group because they have less experience with the language overall, while others without speaking experience may have read Greek for many years already and so feel comfortable in the advanced group. A typical day lasts from 9.15am to 5.10pm and consists of five sessions (διατριβαί) of about an hour each and twenty-minute breaks in between, with an hour and a half for lunch: this works out at 315 minutes of sessions and 180 minutes of breaks per day. Although devoting over a third of the day to breaks may seem excessive, we find that speaking Ancient Greek, especially at first, requires substantial mental effort; twenty minutes of rest between sessions seems to strike an effective balance between efficiency and the weakness of the flesh. (Of course, nothing hinders participants from holding Greek conversations during the breaks as well, and many do.) On Wednesday, we spend the morning outside at a local park. Arranging carpools and giving directions in Ancient Greek creates genuine communicative need, and participants usually appreciate the chance for free and unstructured conversation as we wander among the plants and trees. The last session of the event usually involves speeches in Greek prepared by the advanced group for the edification of all.

I should here address two practical problems that immediately confront those who wish to speak Ancient Greek: pronunciation and dialect. To begin with the less contentious, our standard of reference for the σύνοδος, as for all other Ancient Greek-speaking environments I am aware of, is Attic and literary *Koine* prose. The addition of *Koine* (broadly construed to include authors such as Plutarch) is necessary because the relatively small corpus of classical Attic does not contain sufficient vocabulary for day-to-day conversation, while dialects are avoided because the vast majority of extant Ancient Greek texts use Attic and literary *Koine* for representing in prose the speech of educated language-users.

These principles are relatively uncontroversial. Pronunciation, on the other hand, is often a lightning rod for polemic among speakers of Ancient Greek, some of whom are content with the Erasmian pronunciation, while others vigorously advocate either for so-called restored Attic, Randall Buth's 'Imperial *Koine*', or simply the pronunciation used by modern Greek speakers. This paper is not the place to stake out a position: suffice it to say that participants in the σύνοδος are welcome to use whatever pronunciation they please. Most use some variety of Erasmian, as do the facilitators, though usually one or two have adopted Buth's Imperial *Koine*. Since the majority of Ancient Greek speakers use Erasmian (and consequently most of the few Ancient Greek audio materials currently available are in Erasmian), Imperial *Koine* users benefit from exposure to the dominant pronunciation. Furthermore, since it represents the historical pronunciation of a particular time period, Erasmian users benefit from an improved awareness of what Greek may actually have sounded like around the first century AD.

The σύνοδος and SLA: Research and practice

The facilitators of the σύνοδος endeavour to implement a variety of concepts derived from SLA and language-teaching research, such as comprehensible input, interaction and negotiation, group and pair work, and tasks. The σύνοδος is anchored in the conviction that both input and output are necessary for increasing one's proficiency in a language, and it therefore offers as many opportunities as possible for participants to hear and speak Greek in communicative situations. In this section, I will briefly outline the basis for this conviction in the SLA literature and address a selection of σύνοδος activities that illustrate their practical application. First of all, we must address the notion of comprehensible input and the related problem of explicit and implicit learning, all of which are bound up with the Stephen Krashen's work during the 1980s. Of Krashen's five language-acquisition hypotheses, I will focus here on the acquisition/learning hypothesis and the comprehensible input hypothesis. The former posits an unbridgeable gap between acquisition – what researchers now call 'implicit learning' – and learning – what researchers now call 'explicit learning' (such as grammatical instruction). Krashen subscribes to the no-interface position, according to which explicit learning has no effect at all on implicit learning. It is crucial to note that there is no consensus on the no-interface position among SLA researchers; many argue that explicit learning can indeed contribute to implicit learning: Mitchell et al. (2019) provide a useful overview, while Long (2015) defends the weak interface position, which envisions a limited but not non-existent role for explicit learning. According to Krashen's comprehensible input hypothesis, understandable messages (that is, 'comprehensible input', defined as the learner's current level plus a slight increase in difficulty, or $i + 1$) in the target language are a necessary *and sufficient* condition for implicit learning. While researchers agree that comprehensible input is necessary for implicit learning, it is far from clear that it is also sufficient; and in fact Krashen's claim for sufficiency was already being challenged by Swain in the 1980s and 1990s; her work showed that output also has an important role to play in language-learning (Swain 1985 and 1993). Swain's important corrective to Krashen's view of input underlies the σύνοδος and its commitment to providing not only comprehensible messages in the target language but also opportunities for participants to produce those messages themselves.

It is important to note that Krashen's hypotheses are not objective realities but theoretical constructs that are difficult or impossible to test (not only the notion of $i + 1$ but also other constructs such as the 'affective filter', responsible for a learner's attitude toward the language, and the 'monitor', which purportedly controls a learner's ability to access explicit learning) and as such they are highly problematic (see Gregg 1984 for a devastating critique of Krashen's theory and Jordan 2004 for a more up-to-date account of theory construction in SLA). They are often useful as pedagogical metaphors, but we should be careful not to refer to them even implicitly as realities whose existence has been incontrovertibly established by empirical evidence, since such is not at all the case (it is particularly unfortunate that the term Comprehensible Input or CI – note the capital letters – has become shorthand for a cluster of assumptions both about the findings of SLA research and about second-language pedagogy, which together are often presented incorrectly as a consensus among SLA and language-teaching researchers). The σύνοδος both incorporates Krashen's work and moves beyond it. On one hand, the event is based on Krashen's correct claim that understandable messages in the target language are absolutely necessary for developing learner proficiency. On the other hand, more recent research has shown that language-learners need more than just input: they also need output and interaction, to be discussed below. Additionally, even the explicit discussion of language features can itself become grist for the mill of language-learning when done in the target language, as we do in the σύνοδος.

The activities of the σύνοδος, therefore, also owe much to SLA research in interaction, negotiation, and pair and group work. If output is not optional for developing proficiency in the target language, as Swain showed in the 1980s, then it stands to reason that increasing the amount of time students talk in the classroom will, *ceteris paribus*, benefit their learning. Long and Porter (1985) made the definitive case for pair and group work in the language classroom, arguing from a review of the research that such work improves the quality and quantity of student talk while not contributing to reduced accuracy in student output compared to teacher-fronted work (Long and Porter 1985: 221–2). Additionally, communicating in the language involves *negotiation for meaning*: 'Negative feedback obtained during negotiation work or elsewhere may be facilitative of L2 development, at least for vocabulary, morphology, and language-specific syntax, and essential for learning certain specifiable L1-L2 contrasts' (Long 1996: 414). In other words, when learners encounter communication difficulties, they are forced to solve the problem, often by attending to individual linguistic forms. (For more on the Interaction Hypothesis, of which negotiation for meaning forms a part, see Long 2015: 52–7; for the difference between Focus on Forms – the futile attempt to make students notice all linguistic forms in the input simultaneously – and Focus on Form – the practice of calling students' attention to particular matters of linguistic form only when they become relevant for communication – see Long 2015: 316–21). Naturally, by increasing the quantity of participant talk, pair and group work also increases the quantity of negotiation for meaning and thereby contributes to the development of learner language.

Many σύνοδος activities therefore involve a substantial pair and group work component, which takes various forms depending on the activity in question. As with all pair and group work, it is essential to circle around the groups as they discuss in order to answer questions or provide assistance as the need arises. In its simplest manifestation, a facilitator provides students with copies of an image, often (but not always) depicting an event from classical history or mythology, along with a list of various questions. For beginners, these questions may ask them only to identify objects they see or describe the action portrayed. Instead of or in addition to an image, facilitators often provide a text. For example, I often pair Pseudo-Apollonius' account of Odysseus and the Sirens with John William Waterhouse's (1849–1917) artistic depiction of the same event. Apollonius writes the following (*Epitome* 7.18–19):

παραγενόμενος δὲ [Ὀδυσσεὺς] πρὸς Κίρκην ὑπ' ἐκείνης προπεμφθεὶς ἀνήχθη, καὶ τὴν νῆσον παρέπλει τῶν Σειρήνων. αἱ δὲ Σειρῆνες ἦσαν Ἀχελῴου καὶ Μελπομένης μιᾶς τῶν Μουσῶν θυγατέρες, Πεισινόη Ἀγλαόπη Θελξιέπεια. τούτων ἡ μὲν ἐκιθάριζεν, ἡ δὲ ᾖδεν, ἡ δὲ ηὔλει, καὶ διὰ τούτων ἔπειθον καταμένειν τοὺς παραπλέοντας. εἶχον δὲ ἀπὸ τῶν μηρῶν ὀρνίθων μορφάς. ταύτας παραπλέων Ὀδυσσεύς, τῆς ᾠδῆς βουλόμενος ὑπακοῦσαι, Κίρκης ὑποθεμένης τῶν μὲν ἑταίρων τὰ ὦτα ἔβυσε κηρῷ, ἑαυτὸν δὲ ἐκέλευσε προσδεθῆναι τῷ ἱστῷ. πειθόμενος δὲ ὑπὸ τῶν Σειρήνων καταμένειν ἠξίου λυθῆναι, οἱ δὲ μᾶλλον αὐτὸν ἐδέσμευον, καὶ οὕτω παρέπλει. ἦν δὲ αὐταῖς Σειρῆσι λόγιον τελευτῆσαι νεὼς παρελθούσης. αἱ μὲν οὖν ἐτελεύτων.

Frazer 1921

When Odysseus had come to Circe and had been sent forth by her, he put out to sea and sailed by the island of the Sirens. And the Sirens were the daughters of Achelous and Melpomene, one of the Muses, [and their names were] Peisinoe, Aglaope, and Thelxiepeia. One of them played the cithara, another sang, and another played the flute, and through these means they persuaded those who were sailing by to remain; and from the thigh down they had the shape of birds. As Odysseus sailed by them, wanting to hear their singing, at Circe's behest he stuffed the ears of his companions with wax and ordered himself to be bound to the mast. And being persuaded by the Sirens to stay, he begged to be released, but they bound him all the more, and in this way he sailed past. Now there was an oracle for the Sirens themselves that they would die if a ship sailed past; and so they died.

Author's translation

Although participants have read this text in advance (as part of the reading packet distributed several weeks before the σύνοδος), they always have questions about its grammar and vocabulary. Before discussing those details, however, the beginners discuss the following questions in groups or pairs:

1. Τίνες ἦσαν οἱ τῶν Σειρήνων γονεῖς [ὁ πατὴρ καὶ ἡ μήτηρ] (Who were the Sirens' parents [their father and mother]?)
2. Τίνα ὀνόματα ἦν ταῖς Σειρῆσι; (What were the Sirens' names?)
3. Πῶς ἔπειθον τοὺς παραπλέοντας ναύτας καταμένειν (How did they persuade the sailors who were sailing by to remain?)

After pair and group work, we discuss as a whole group and resolve any remaining difficulties (such as the second sentence, which beginners often find unclear). I then ask two more questions for pair and group discussion:

4. Πῶς ἀπέφυγεν ὁ Ὀδυσσεύς (How did Odysseus escape?)
5. Διὰ τί ἀπέθανον αἱ Σειρῆσι (Why did the Sirens die?)

This usually leads to a discussion of the last two sentences, which often confuse beginners at first glance. After establishing a shared understanding of the text, I provide Waterhouse's painting of Odysseus bound to the mast in the midst of his sailors with their stopped-up ears, to be discussed first in pairs or groups and then all together. The text provides useful scaffolding for discussing the picture; participants now have thematically relevant vocabulary fresh in their minds. Questions on this text for more advanced students are largely similar but employ more complex constructions, such as:

6. Ποῖαι τὴν μορφὴν ἦσαν αἱ Σειρῆνες (Of what shape were the Sirens?)
7. Πῶς ἐκ τοῦ τῶν Σειρήνων κινδύνου διεσώθη ὁ Ὀδυσσεύς (How was Odysseus saved from the danger of the Sirens?)
8. Τίς ταῦτα τῷ Ὀδυσσεῖ παρεκελεύσατο (Who gave this advice to Odysseus?)

I use the same outline with other texts; for advanced σύνοδος groups, favourites have included some of Lucian's shorter pieces, selections from Plato's *Symposium*, and Herodotus 1.30–1 (on Cleobis and Biton). Other activities I use every year include 'Spot the Difference', in which each member of a pair is given a variation on the same picture and required to discover the differences by working together (either by looking at the two images together or by using conversation alone to discover the differences), and jigsaw readings, in which a text is divided into three or four sections and each section is distributed to a group with comprehension questions. After each group has answered the questions, new groups are created (for example, AAA BBB CCC becomes ABC ABC ABC) in which each group participant is responsible for explaining his or her section of the text to the other members (who have not read it). In this second round, the goal is to order the three sections correctly. Eavesdropping on group discussions during these sorts of activities, I hear all sorts of linguistic discussions: debating the meanings of particular words or constructions, searching for new vocabulary, and correcting their own or others' utterances (in the latter case, usually with tact). On such two-way tasks as 'Spot the Difference' and jigsaw readings, each participant has information necessary to accomplish a goal. Research shows that these tasks are superior to one-way tasks, where one participant does not have any necessary information and must extract it from another, in terms of the negotiation for meaning they produce (Long 2015: 242).

The σύνοδος also provides a useful forum for the development of task-based materials for ancient languages. I have dealt with the application of task-based language teaching (TBLT) to ancient languages in more detail elsewhere (Hill, forthcoming); here, I will briefly introduce TBLT and describe a successful task-based σύνοδος activity. Since the 1980s, TBLT has often been misunderstood simply as 'language-learning activities' (Long 2015; 2016), when in fact 'task' in the TBLT sense properly denotes 'the real-world activities people think of when planning, conducting, or recalling their day' (Long 2015: 6). Tasks are selected by identifying what students need to be able to *do* in the target language and then converting these real-world tasks into pedagogic tasks that can be realistically carried out in a classroom. Now, applying such an approach to ancient languages obviously requires adjusting our notion of the 'real world' (see Hill, forthcoming), but to oversimplify, TBLT is valuable to ancient language teachers because it insists on making activities purposeful and relevant to students. In the case of the σύνοδος, it provides the impetus for tasks that result in a product and require collaboration in order to accomplish a goal.

Following (more or less) the principles of TBLT as described in Long (2015), I developed the following task: first, students read a selection of so-called 'sacred laws' or ritual norms. These are inscriptions found at sacred sites all over the Ancient Greek world that prescribe proper behavior for worshippers (Petrovic 2015): for example, Χάρισιν αἶγα οὐ θέμις οὐδὲ χοῖρον (It is not lawful to sacrifice a goat or a pig to the Graces, *LSCG* 114B [Sokolowski 1969]) or Ἀμύητον μὴ εἰσιέναι εἰς τὸ ἱερόν (The uninitiated may not enter the temple, *LSS* 75 [Sokolowski 1962]) (the selections I provide are generally complete in one to ten lines). After a session devoted to explicating the texts, I give participants the following task:

Ἐν τῇ Ἀττικῇ ἱερὸν οἰκοδομεῖται καινόν. γράψατε οὖν πρόγραμμα μετ' ἀλλήλων, ἑπόμενοι τοῖς ἤδη ἀναγνωσθεῖσι, ὥστε πάντας εἰς τὸν καινὸν ἱερὸν ἀφικομένους καὶ τὸ ὑμέτερον πρόγραμμα ἀναγνόντας εἴτε ὁσίους εἰσελθεῖν εἴτε ἔξω μένειν, τοὺς νόμους οὐ παραβαίνοντας. ἐν δὲ τῷ ὑμετέρῳ προγράμματι γραφήσεταί τι περὶ κρέατος, ἐσθῆτος, ὁσιότητος, χρημάτων. ἔξεστι δὲ ὑμῖν ἑλέσθαι τίνος θεοῦ ἔσται τὸ ἱερόν.

In Attica, a new temple is being built. Write a sacred law with each other in accordance with the ones you've already read, so that all who arrive at the new temple can read your law and either enter in piety or remain outside without transgressing the laws. Write something in your law about meat, clothing, piety, and money. You may choose for which god the temple will be.

Participants work together in groups to draft a law which they then present to the rest; not only are their texts often both brilliant and hilarious, the activity also provides ample space for negotiation of meaning and attention to linguistic form, along with the camaraderie that makes collaborative language-learning so enjoyable.

Conclusion

The basic assumption of an event like the σύνοδος is that developing active skills in a language has a beneficial effect on one's receptive skills. This has certainly been the experience of hundreds, if not thousands, of students who flock to communicative ancient language courses year after year, and it was in fact my own motivation for speaking Greek in the first place. After two years of grammar-translation instruction, I could understand hardly anything when I attempted to read authentic Greek – even the easiest New Testament passages required substantial mental effort and help from notes and dictionaries – while after two years of communicative Spanish, I could read authentic texts for pleasure. Although I recognized, of course, that Greek was objectively harder for native English speakers, I suspected that the complete absence of speaking and listening (and the comparatively tiny volume of text actually 'read') must also be responsible. And after taking a four-week course in spoken Ancient Greek with Christophe Rico some years ago, I found (anecdotally and impressionistically) that my reading speed for easy texts had nearly doubled and the mental effort I needed to expend on reading was substantially reduced. Similarly, one 2018 σύνοδος participant, a high-school Latin teacher and Greek enthusiast with no prior speaking experience, wrote the following about his experience:

I'm leaving the σύνοδος feeling like I have seen my future. I simply did not know this was possible. I could continue reading and teaching as I always have, but what I learned this week is that if I go that route, I and my students will read only a small fraction of the Greek that would be possible by learning to speak Greek fluently.

Davidson 2018

This, simply put, is why we hold the σύνοδος every year: to demonstrate that spoken Ancient Greek is far from being a party trick with no relevance to the 'real' work of philology, but can in fact significantly increase one's linguistic proficiency and thereby remove obstacles that hinder us from encountering the ancient texts on their own terms.

Speakers of Ancient Greek have never been as numerous as speakers of Latin, and the modern study of Ancient Greek (unlike Latin) in a monolingual, immersive environment is a relatively recent phenomenon. Events such as the σύνοδος provide the inestimable benefit of bringing members of a small but growing community of language users into contact with each other to form friendships that often outlast the week spent together and are maintained through online interaction. Ever-increasing enrolments in the σύνοδος and immersive summer courses testify that they meet a perceived need among students of Ancient Greek, the same need that drove me and has driven many others to begin speaking the language in a quest for increased reading proficiency. For that, after all, is the reason for such events, whether for Ancient Greek, Latin or any other ancient language: to foster each participant's ability to read ancient texts not as a linguistic code to be broken, but as a language like any other.

Note

1. I cannot express sufficient gratitude to Terence Tunberg, who has fostered the σύνοδος by treating it as a counterpart and indeed a sibling to the Lexington Latin *Conventiculum*. Without his assistance, the σύνοδος ἑλληνική would not exist. I am also most grateful to my co-facilitator, Christophe Rico, who lent his time and expertise to the σύνοδος from the very beginning and bears (at least) equal responsibility for its success. The σύνοδος is a joint venture of Terence Tunberg's organization Humanitas, Inc. and the Polis Institute, Jerusalem.

CHAPTER 14
TEACHING ANCIENT GREEK BY THE POLIS METHOD
Christophe Rico and Michael Kopf

Introduction: Jerusalem, the Polis Institute and the method

The teaching of Ancient Greek in total immersion has been at the heart of the Polis Institute's mission since its foundation in 2011. During this short period of time, teaching methodology and practice have been evolving rapidly, not least through the exchange of ideas with teachers of other immersive language courses offered at the institute (Biblical and Modern Hebrew, Spoken and Modern Standard Arabic, Latin, Syriac and, more recently, Coptic). Total immersion is indeed the cornerstone of the Polis Method: classes make exclusive use of the target language and so translation exercises and the use of any other language, even to explain grammar, are excluded during class time. Following this principle guarantees what for us are certain critical features, such as maximum exposure to the target language. It also befits the institute's multilingual and multicultural environment in Jerusalem, where it occasionally happens that a group of students does not share any common language but the one they are studying.

The other principle at the heart of the Polis Method is that it wants to provide a μέθοδος (*méthodos*, a suppletive verbal noun of μετέρχομαι, cf. ἔξοδος : ἐξέρχομαι) in the literal sense: a going from A to B, a way followed, a predefined route to be taken by the learner in pursuit of a profound understanding of the language. Thus, unlike other more purely communicative approaches to language teaching, the Polis Method does prescribe a universal curriculum as a framework for the individual learner's progress in acquiring the language.

In the following three sections, we want to present a selection of typical classroom situations, much like milestones, which mark the path that leads Polis' Greek students through two years of total-immersion Greek classes.

First steps: Communicating in the *Hic & Nunc*

To someone with a more conventional background in teaching classical languages, total immersion in Ancient Greek may indeed sound outlandish. Amongst other concerns, this impression may arise from the fact that total immersion prohibits a stringent 'grammatical' (that is, typically morphological) layout of the curriculum. From the outset, all communicative needs which emerge in the classroom need to be answered in Greek. This constantly requires grammatical elements which, at first glance, appear to be simply inaccessible to the students; very early on, for instance, we want to be talking about μαθηταὶ καὶ διδάσκαλοι (*students and teachers*) at the same time, even though these nouns have very different morphological profiles. It is because of the semantic connection between these two nouns, and their shared context in the world and in the texts, that we use these words together. In the framework of the Polis Method, we try to look at language in a holistic way, thus conceiving of the students' progression not as merely 'grammatical' in the literal sense. Many words and phrases that seem demanding from the morphological point of view are suitable for beginners because of their conceptual simplicity and relevance, both in the classroom and for the students themselves. Recognizing that every word, phrase or pattern is peculiar with regard to its prosody and pronunciation, its morphology and etymology, its syntax and complementation, as well as its semantic qualities, can yield surprising results, in terms of their overall adequacy for the course group's respective level.

Furthermore, it is necessary to recognize the gradual nature of language acquisition: students are not expected to master every element they encounter in the Greek classroom immediately. Instead, the instructor will define different learning objectives for different lexical items and patterns. This way, some words are to be encountered only once, others should be recognized and possibly reproduced upon request, and some, of course, have to be analyzed, employed and manipulated by the students.

Thus, at the beginning of the very first Greek lesson at the Polis Institute, the teacher will enter the classroom and wait for the students to listen. Once everyone has settled, the teacher starts greeting the students, waving his or her hand, shaking their hands:

Teacher [*To all of the students once:*] Χαίρετε πάντες. (*Good day to all of you!*)
[*To students individually:*] Χαῖρε. Χαῖρε. Χαῖρε. Χαῖρε καὶ σύ, ὦ κυρία. (*Hello! Hello! Hello! And you, madam, good day to you!*)
[*Stops at one student. Slowly:*] Χαῖ-ρε. (*Hel-lo!*)
[*Waits for student's answer. If necessary, elicits an answer through further gestures and repetition.*]
Student Χαῖρε. (*Hello.*)
Teacher [*Very joyous:*] Χαῖρε, χαῖρε πολλά. (*Hello! A very good day to you!*)
[*Proceeds to make every student pronounce the greeting individually.*]

During all these interactions, the teacher signals that meeting the students is a great joy. This is communicated by nonverbal means, positive body language and profuse use of mostly nonlinguistic sounds (such as laughter), but also certain interjections like ὤ (*Oh!*) or βαβαί (*Wow!*). We believe that a lighthearted classroom environment is conducive to learning in many ways, so it is desirable that the instructor be unafraid to exaggerate and make use of a comical register that is suitable for this kind of everyday situation.

As soon as each student has pronounced at least once the simple greeting χαῖρε (literally an imperative: *rejoice!*), the instructor returns to the centre of the classroom and proceeds:

Teacher [*To all of the students, pointing to herself:*] Χαίρετε. Ἐγώ εἰμι Βερνίκη. (*Welcome! I am Berenice.*)
[*To one student, again pointing to herself:*] Ἐγώ εἰμι Βερνίκη. Τίς εἶ σύ; (*I am Berenice. Who are you?*)
Student [*Shrugs his shoulders.*]
Teacher [*Squinting her eyes, as if encountering a difficult question, slowly:*] Ἐγώ Βερνίκη. Καὶ σὺ τίς εἶ; Ἆρ᾽ εἶ Ἰούλιος ἢ Μᾶρκος ἢ Λουκᾶς ἢ Σωκράτης; Τίς εἶ σύ; (*I [am] Berenice. And who are you? Are you Julius, Marcus, Luke, or Socrates? Who are you?*)

Student	*[With hesitation:]* Ἐγὼ John. *(I [am] 'John'.)*
Teacher	*[Very joyous:]* Κάλλιστα. Χαῖρε, ὦ Ἰωάννη. *(Excellent! Hello, Iōánnēs!)*
	[Slowly, perhaps repeatedly:] Ἐγὼ Βερνίκη. Σὺ δὲ «Ἰωάννης» ἢ « John »; *(I [am] Berenice. And you, [are you] "Iōánnēs" or "John"?)*
	[Encourages the student to answer.]
Student	*[Slowly:]* Ἐγὼ Ἰωάννης. *(I [am] Iōánnēs.)*
Teacher	*[Applauds the student:]* Καλῶς εἶπες. Χαῖρε, ὦ Ἰωάννη. *(Well said. Welcome, John!)*
	[Turns to a different student and repeats until all students have introduced themselves.]

These typical first-lesson activities should illustrate that it is indeed possible to start from scratch using nothing but Greek in the classroom. This is mainly achieved through effective use of extralinguistic resources: the students have knowledge and expectations concerning the social situation and protocol (they know what a language course is, they expect some kind of salutation and introduction when they first meet their instructor); it is reasonable to assume that they have knowledge of the world (*Weltwissen*) so that common cultural references can be exploited right from the beginning (they recognize certain proper names like *Socrates* or *Luke*); nonverbal means of communication employed by the instructor are an integral part of this extralinguistic level.

For the rest of this first phase of the curriculum, the instructor will make further use of extralinguistic resources like the physical environment: the classroom itself, props and images brought into the classroom, reenactment of scenes with the students. It is important to note that students will at first mostly be asked to listen to the language and prove that they have understood the input, either by executing actions that are presented to them as imperatives – this mode has largely been inspired by Asher's Total Physical Response (see Asher 1977) methodology – or by identifying objects and images in the classroom, pointing at and naming them.

Building on the experience with this mode of teaching and combining Asher's Total Physical Response (TPR) technique with the insights of François Gouin, a French Latin teacher of the nineteenth century, a team of teachers at Polis has developed a new technique by the name of *Living Sequential Expression* (LSE). This technique aims at mapping regular tasks and events in order to cover, as far as possible, the whole spectrum of frequent activities. We consider that someone who is able to talk about all frequent activities in a specific language will have a certain degree of fluency in that language.

In order to map such usual tasks and events, it seems important to us to proceed systematically. First, a list of daily, weekly, monthly and yearly tasks, as well as rare lifetime events, which map human experience, are established.

Then, for each task and event, it is convenient to develop one or several sequences of four to seven actions, consistently related to one another. Thus, the task 'taking the bus' would entail the following sequence of actions:

1. Walk to the bus stop.
2. Wait for the bus.
3. Enter the bus.
4. Go towards the driver.

5. Buy your ticket.
6. Sit down.
7. Alight from the bus.

We can identify some 150 daily, weekly, monthly, yearly or once-in-a-lifetime activities of this kind, like getting up, washing oneself, going to school, driving, cooking, eating, shopping, etc. Each activity may be divided into two to five different tasks. Each task contains four to seven actions. All this amounts to some 2,500 commands and some 3,500 different words which make up the core vocabulary of any language.

This list of sequences could be expanded with what Gouin called 'themes', in order to encompass activities that will probably never be performed by the learner, but could be quite frequently the object of our conversations: ploughing, sowing, harvesting and collecting fruit. . .; sewing, spinning and knitting.

Based on the preceding lists, a team of Polis teachers is currently working to prepare a series of visual books that will help instructors apply the LSE technique. Later on, a series of texts grounded in the vocabulary of every subset of four to seven actions will help to strengthen the acquisition process. These texts will mainly use the vocabulary that was developed in the different sequences through narrative episodes and short dialogues, in order to provide more comprehensible input for the students.

LSE allows the instructor to combine TPR with storytelling and to practise different verbal forms, which is especially helpful regarding morphology-heavy languages. The following is a possible outline of a teaching session.

- **Sequential TPR.** The session should start with TPR: students are given successive and sequential commands in order to perform a task. This series of commands can be performed several times, possibly with different students, to familiarize learners with the vocabulary.

- **Enhancing through images.** At the second stage, it is advised that teachers repeat the commands while projecting images or illustrations of the sequence on the board (without the text). This will enhance students' retention.

- **Enhancing through text.** At this stage, the illustrations may be projected alongside with text, and the instructor may ask students to work in pairs and give each other the commands.

- **Reporting on what I / you / (s)he is doing / has done.** The teacher can now renew the commands to a student and, after each command and performance of the action, ask her or him to say what (s)he is doing. At the end of the whole process, the teacher can also ask what the student has done. Before the process, the instructor can ask the student what (s)he will do. In a language like Greek, it is possible to practise participles by combining the participle of the last action with the conjugated verb of the new one (Ἦλθον εἰς τὸν σταθμόν. Ἐλθὼν εἰς τὸν σταθμὸν ἀνέμεινα τὸ λεωφορεῖον. Ἀναμείνας εἰς τὸ λεωφορεῖον ἀνέβην . . . I came *to the bus stop*. Having come *to the bus stop I* waited *for the bus*. Having waited *I got into the bus* . . .).

- **Enhancing through comprehensible input.** Finally, the learner may enhance the acquisition process through comprehensible input, reading narrative texts and dialogues grounded in the vocabulary of every subset of four or five actions.

Settling in: Narrating in the past

After the first 120 hours of instruction, which are usually given in the framework of a four-week intensive course, during which students become familiar enough with their immediate Greek environment – in particular the sound and prosody of the language, classroom vocabulary and set phrases, as well as some basic grammatical concepts – the curriculum will lead them out of the *Hic & Nunc* into simple narrative registers. Regarding Greek verbal morphology, the internalization of the indicative and the participles of the aorist tense as the basic past tense are central during this period. At this point, the students already know the imperative and infinitive of the aorist, as well as the indicative of the present tense. A typical way of introducing the new morphological patterns would thus be to assign actions through imperatives, have the students perform and describe the actions in the present tense, and finally add a report on what happened in the aorist tense:

Teacher	Ὦ μαθηταί, ἡ ἑλληνικὴ γλῶσσα δύσκολός ἐστιν, ἢ γάρ; *(Dear students, the Greek language is hard, is it not?)*
Students	[Recognizing the set phrase:] Ναί, δύσκολός ἐστιν. Δύσκολος σφόδρα. *(Yes, it is hard. Very difficult!)*
Teacher	Εἰ γοῦν μὴ μανθάνετε τὸν λόγον τοῦ διδασκάλου, τί ποιεῖτε; Οὐχὶ αἴρετε τὴν χεῖρα; Τί ποιεῖτε, ὦ Θωμᾶ; *(So, if you do not understand what the teacher is saying, what do you do? Don't you raise your hand, Thomas?)*
Thomas	Αἴρομεν τὴν χεῖρα. *(We raise our hand.)*
Teacher	Καλῶς εἶπες. Ὑμεῖς πάντες ἄρατε τὴν χεῖρα. *(Well said. All of you, raise your hand!)*
Students	[They raise their hands and keep stretching their arms upwards, as the teacher encourages them.]
Teacher	Εὖ ποιεῖτε. Τί γὰρ ποιεῖτε; *(Good job. What are you doing?)*
Students	Αἴρομεν τὴν χεῖρα. *(We raise our hand.)*
Teacher	Καὶ σύ, ὦ Κορνηλία, τί πράσσεις; *(And you, Cornelia, what are you doing?)*
Cornelia	Αἴρω τὴν χεῖρα. *(I raise my hand.)*
Teacher	Ὀρθῶς γε. *(Correct.)* [Pointing at two or more students:] Καὶ ἐκεῖνοι, τί ποιοῦσιν; *(And those, what are they doing?)*
Cornelia	Αἴρουσι τὴν χεῖρα. *(They raise their hands.)*
Teacher	Μάλιστα. Καὶ ἐκεῖνοι αἴρουσι τὴν χεῖρα. Ὑμεῖς γὰρ πάντες, ὦ μαθηταί, αἴρετε τὴν χεῖρα. Ἀλλ' οὐχὶ κατάκοποι γίγνεσθε; *(Certainly. Those are raising their hands as well. You all in fact are raising your hands, dear students. But aren't you getting tired?)*
Students	Ναί, κατάκοποί ἐσμεν. *(Yes, we are tired.)*
Teacher	Τί οὖν βούλεσθε ποιεῖν; Τί σὺ βούλει ποιεῖν, ὦ Ἀρίστων; *(So, what do you want to do now? What do you want to do, Aristo?)*
Aristo	Ἐγὼ βούλομαι καθεῖναι τὴν χεῖρα. *(I want to drop my hand.)*
Teacher	Ἀλλὰ κάθες δή. Καὶ ὑμεῖς πάντες κάθετε τὴν χεῖρα. *(Then get to it and drop your hand! All of you, drop your hand!)*
Students	[They drop their hands with relief.]

Teacher	Εὖ γε. Ἀναπαύεσθε γὰρ κατάκοποι. Ἀλλὰ διὰ τί κατάκοποί ἐστε; Μήτι τὸν πόδα ἤρατε; *(This is nice: you rest because you are tired. But why are you tired? You didn't raise your foot, did you?)*
Students	Οὐχί, ἀλλὰ τὴν χεῖρα. Τὴν χεῖρα. *(No, but our hand. Our hand!)*
Teacher	Μάλιστά γε. Τὴν χεῖρα ἤρατε. Καὶ σύ, ὦ Δαυιδ, εἰπέ μοι, εἰ θέλεις, πότερον τὸν πόδα ἢ τὴν χεῖρα ἦρας. *(Certainly. You raised your hand. And you, David, please tell me if you raised your foot or your hand.)*
David	Δηλονότι τὴν χεῖρα, ὦ διδάσκαλε. *(Sir, clearly [I raised] my hand.)*
Teacher	Καλῶς εἶπες, ὦ μαθητά. Σὺ μὲν ἦρας τὴν χεῖρα καὶ ἐγένου κατάκοπος. Ἐγὼ δὲ οὔτ' ἦρα τὴν χεῖρα οὔτε κατάκοπός εἰμι. Σὺ μὲν ἦρας, ἐγὼ δ' οὐκ ἦρα. Τί οὖν; Ἆρ' ἦρα ἐγὼ τὴν χεῖρα; *(Well said, my student. You for one have raised your hand and become tired. I, however, have neither raised my hand, nor become tired. You raised [your hand] and I have not raised [my hand]. So? Did I raise my hand?)*
David	Οὐδαμῶς. Σὺ οὐκ ἦρας τὴν χεῖρα. *(Not at all. You did not raise your hand.)*
Teacher	Καὶ σύ; *(And you?)*
David	Ἐγὼ ἦρα τὴν χεῖρα. *(I raised my hand.)*
Teacher	Ὀρθῶς γε. Σὺ δέ, ὦ Πρίσκιλλα, ἦρας τὴν χεῖρα ὡσαύτως; *(Correct. And you, Priscilla, did you raise your hand as well?)* [Proceeds by addressing different students, then changes into the plural, finally adds the third person.]

This example should illustrate how a new grammatical paradigm can be introduced in dialogue form. The conversation starts with an everyday need (*raising one's hand in class to ask a question*) and develops into a game-like mix of actions performed and commented on. The mode described above still relies heavily on the extralinguistic basis of physical actions. However, as the students progress in this phase, the teacher will gradually replace this extralinguistic basis with and make more use of extant linguistic knowledge, so that new paradigms will be grounded upon previously acquired, more fundamental paradigms.

The two main signposts 'from passive to active' and 'from spoken to written' are indeed almost always present when we think about the students' progression, be it in lesson-planning or in laying out the curriculum as a whole. Thus, with the well-known *Four Basic Language Skills* (Aydogan 2014: 673–5) in mind, the students should first *hear* a word, then *pronounce* it, *read* it in certain exercises and finally *write* it down. These categories are applied not only to single vocabulary items, but also to phrases *mutatis mutandis*, as well as to morphological and syntactic patterns. Another guideline for the curriculum is found in a number of *Modes of Discourse*, which we at Polis have defined ourselves and seen that they too follow a certain progression. They highlight language's different functions and registers, namely (a) *Hic & Nunc*: describing one's present environment, communicating immediate needs; (b) *Narration*: reporting on past events, telling a story; (c) *Deliberation*: speculating about future events, arguing about assumptions and consequences, treating abstract topics; (d) *Poetry*: playing with language, appreciating the form of language, pushing language to its limits. It is important to keep in mind that all of these schemes are very general and tentative in nature: it cannot and should not be avoided that some words will be encountered in their written form first, which requires the students to pronounce the script without any acoustic model. Furthermore, some poetry is very suitable for beginners if one introduces it as one would a nursery rhyme, or a simple song in any modern language: one couplet from the Greek Anthology, i.e. *Anthologia Palatina* xi.152: εἰ βούλει τὸν παῖδα διδάξαι ῥήτορα, Παῦλε, / ὡς οὗτοι πάντες, γράμματα μὴ μαθέτω (If you want, Paulus, to teach your son to be a rhetor like all these, don't let him learn his letters [Paton 1979]) has proven to be exceptionally accessible and useful).

Becoming independent: Reading authentic texts without translating them

By the start of their second year at Polis, students have a very firm basis in all participles and moods of the present and the aorist tense, except the optative. They are at ease in the Greek classroom, ask questions and communicate recurring thoughts with automaticity. They have acquired also a good understanding of text cohesion, especially in the simple narrative register. Furthermore, they have already read a longer authentic text written in low *Koine*, such as the Book of Ruth, one of the gospels or the Epictetean *Enchiridion*.

The final phase of the curriculum mainly aims at enabling the students to read authentic texts independently and to start a reading career that will last a lifetime. The grammar classes focus on the remaining tenses, the optative mood and some issues in nominal morphology. Making use of the students' thorough grasp of the principles and basic elements of Greek inflection, as well as of their knowledge of some hitherto isolated items (such as forms of εἰδέναι [*to know*] regarding the perfect tense), this can be done quite efficiently. The function and expressive potential of the new morphology are demonstrated, furthermore, in a number of more complex texts from different literary genres. Finally, our students who, during hundreds of hours in total immersion, have developed a strong intuition for the prosody of basic Greek morphology, can now meaningfully appreciate stylistic and dialectal differences, such as the common 'missing' augments and contractions in Homer (e.g. Od. 1.3 πολλῶν δ᾽ ἀνθρώπων ἴδεν ἄστεα καὶ νόον ἔγνω, (Many were the men whose cities he saw and whose minds he learned [Murray/Dimock 1998]) cf. the Attic/*Koine* forms εἶδεν, ἄστη, νοῦν).

Our final sample of teaching practices at the Polis institute covers the reading of Isocrates' *Against the Sophists* (κατὰ τῶν σοφιστῶν, Isocr. 13). In this short piece of polemic oratory, the Athenian rhetorician speaks out against the misguided or utterly lacking ethical principles of his competitors, and delineates his own theory of education. Although certainly challenging in its wording, the text's arguments are intrinsically relevant to students and teachers engaged in Ancient Greek culture and erudition.

Confronting the students with the text itself without preamble would certainly mean overloading them. Instead, the instructor will employ pre-reading strategies in order to distribute the conceptual, lexical, and phraseological challenges, over a number of phases. In this instance, it seems appropriate to have a preparation session in which words and phrases from the semantic field of 'education, teaching and learning' are gathered and set in relation to each other. The presentation of these vocabulary items can be extralinguistic (using images and props, or performing verbal actions and little scenes) or linguistic (as for example in a conversation in which the students' twenty-first-century learning environment is contrasted with some basic facts about education in antiquity at large). Ideally, this will familiarize the students with 95 per cent or more of the needed vocabulary in such a way that they can already at least passively recognize it during their first encounter with the text itself.

We shall here present only the opening sentence of the text and exemplify some conversational *reading strategies* which allow us to comprehend meaning without translating the text:

Εἰ πάντες ἤθελον οἱ παιδεύειν ἐπιχειροῦντες ἀληθῆ λέγειν, καὶ μὴ μείζους ποιεῖσθαι τὰς ὑποσχέσεις ὧν ἔμελλον ἐπιτελεῖν, οὐκ ἂν κακῶς ἤκουον ὑπὸ τῶν ἰδιωτῶν· [...]

If all who are engaged in the profession of education were willing to state the facts instead of making greater promises than they can possibly fulfil, they would not be in such bad repute with the lay-public. [...]

trans. Norlin 1929

First, the sentence is read aloud either by the teacher or by a capable student. Initially, the focus can lie solely on the sound of the language: pronunciation, prosody and intonation should be performed with clarity and precision. If convenient, students can be made to echo the teacher. This can be done with parts of the sentence, or with the full sentence. To reduce social tension, all students may imitate the teacher in chorus (allowing for a certain degree of anonymity), or, to engage their attention, individual students may pronounce the sentence with a measure of mock competition.

A basic understanding of the sentence's meaning should, by now, be established. The teacher is, however, still well advised to set aside most of the sentence and focus at first on the apodosis οὐκ ἂν κακῶς ἤκουον ὑπὸ τῶν ἰδωτῶν. The phrase κακῶς ἀκούειν ὑπό τινος (*male audīre ab aliquō, to have a bad reputation with someone*) has been introduced in the pre-reading phase as passive of κακῶς λέγειν τινά (i.e. κακολογεῖν τινα, *maledīcere alicui, to speak ill of someone*). Thus, the teacher will make sure the students know that ἤκουον is a form of the verb ἀκούειν (*to hear*), and resolve the counterfactual negative. Subsequently, (s)he will offer synonyms and paraphrases and use simple interrogatives to make the students divide the sentence into its syntactic elements:

Teacher « Οὐκ ἂν κακῶς ἤκουον », τουτέστιν ὅτι ὄντως κακῶς ἀκούουσιν. Κακολογοῦνται γάρ. Ἀλλὰ τίνες οἱ τοῦτο πάσχοντες; (*'They would not have a bad reputation', which means that they do in fact have a bad reputation. They are being disparaged! But who are those who suffer this?*)

Students [*Looking for a nominative plural prompted by the interrogative τίνες used by the teacher*] Οἱ παιδεύειν ἐπιχειροῦντες. Πάντες οἱ παιδεύειν ἐπιχειροῦντες. (*Those who attempt to educate! All those who attempt to educate!*)

Teacher Ὀρθῶς λέγετε. Τίς δὲ τοῦτο ἔχει λέγειν ἑνὶ λόγῳ τὸ « οἱ παιδεύειν ἐπιχειροῦντες »; Τίνες γάρ εἰσιν; (*Correct. Who can say this in one word, "those who attempt to educate"? Who are they?*)

Student Οὐκοῦν οἱ διδάσκαλοι. (*Surely then the teachers [are those].*)

Teacher Μάλιστά γε. Δηλονότι οἱ διδάσκαλοι παιδεύουσιν. Οἱ δὲ μαθηταὶ παιδεύονται ὑπ' αὐτῶν. Οἱ μὲν οὖν παιδεύειν ἐπιχειροῦντες κακῶς ἀκούουσιν ὑπὸ τῶν ἰδιωτῶν. Τίνες δὲ οὗτοι οἱ ἰδιῶται; Μήτι μωροί εἰσιν; (*Most certainly. Clearly the teachers are educating and the students are being educated by them. So, the ones who attempt to educate have a bad reputation with the laypeople [idiōtai]. But who are these laypeople? They are not just stupid people, are they?*)

Student Ἥκιστά γε. Ἀλλ' ἄτεχνοι, ὥσπερ οἱ πολλοί. *(Surely not. But [they are] untrained in arts and science, like the masses.)*

Teacher Ναί, ὠγαθέ. Οἱ γὰρ πολλοὶ κατεφρόνουν τῶν σοφιστῶν. Περί γε τούτου πᾶς ὁ λόγος οὗτος. Καὶ γὰρ σοφιστὴς ὢν αὐτὸς ὁ Ἰσοκράτης χαλεπῶς ἔφερεν. *(Yes, my good man. The masses despised the sophists. This is very much what this whole speech is about: as Isocrates was actually a sophist himself, he was aggravated [by the situation].)*

This example illustrates how the teacher can spell out, together with the students, not only the general meaning, but also grammatical and stylistic features, by asking the right questions: syntagms can be isolated by simple questions; single words can be explained through synonyms, antonyms and etymology; paraphrases are used to simplify syntax. Furthermore, all of these operations can be put to the students as comprehension checks, to practise morphological or syntactical patterns, or for exam purposes.

As the treatment of any authentic text in class demands considerable amounts of time and energy, its reading should always be followed up with *post-reading* activities. These serve to consolidate the knowledge gained, and can range from a multiple-choice quiz on the contents of the text to different written assignments, such as the composition of a short summary, a comparison to a pertinent text, image or video, or any other more creative and open writing assignment in the target language which relates to the text read. At the very least, a text once successfully treated in class should be regarded as a resource, and frequently referenced in subsequent classes.

Conclusion: Total immersion – a challenge worth accepting

Experience at the Polis Institute has shown that teaching Ancient Greek through total immersion is feasible and rewarding: while reading a text, only students who have reached automaticity regarding the most common characteristics, words and formal patterns of the language, have the capacity to recognize and concentrate on rarer lexical items, morphology or syntax, as well as stylistic features.

Furthermore, as total immersion forces the constant use of synonyms and paraphrases, students acquire a vast and tightly knit mental network of Greek. This, we have observed, enables them to retain more of the texts they read, steadily connecting Greek with Greek, and internalizing not only lexemes and patterns, but the very words and wordings of the ancients in a communicative setting.

CHAPTER 15
GOALS AND METHODS IN TEACHING BIBLICAL LANGUAGES AND EXEGESIS: A VIEW FROM THE SEMINARY
Daniel R. Streett

A little learning is a dang'rous thing;
Drink deep, or taste not the Pierian spring:
There shallow draughts intoxicate the brain,
And drinking largely sobers us again.

Alexander Pope, *An Essay on Criticism* (1711)

Pedagogical goals and their importance

As teachers (and students) of biblical languages – Greek, Hebrew and Aramaic – what should our goals be? What are we aiming to accomplish? What should we be trying to achieve in our courses and curricula? These are very important questions as we set out to discuss and debate the best methods for teaching biblical (or ancient) languages, for if we do not have clear goals in mind, we will have difficulty establishing how we attain them.

Unfortunately, it seems to me, based on numerous discussions with fellow professors and their students, that many Greek and Hebrew classes operate on something like autopilot. Professors use, in many cases, the same textbooks from which they were taught. Declensions are learned, vocabulary glosses memorized, verbs parsed, diagrams drawn, charts filled in. Regular quizzes and tests begin to drive the progress of the semester. Professors, often, are simply trying to 'get through the material', while many students are just trying to survive and keep their heads above water. In the midst of it all, we lose sight of exactly what we are trying to do in the first place. The accidental sage Yogi Berra perhaps put it best: 'If you don't know where you are going, you'll end up someplace else (cf. Berra 2010: 132). It is my contention that most Greek and Hebrew classes end up 'someplace else', because our goals and aims are not clearly defined.

In this chapter, then, I address the question of where we should 'set the bar' for both students and teachers of the biblical languages. I approach this question as one who has taught *Koine* Greek and exegesis for fifteen years at both an undergraduate and graduate (seminary) level. Some years were spent using a traditional grammar-translation method, but most of my teaching employed communicative methods that aimed at immersing students in the biblical language. In what follows, I primarily refer to Biblical Greek, since that is my area, but most of what I say also applies *mutatis mutandis* to my teaching of classical Hebrew and Latin.

The problem of definitions: 'Knowing', 'learning', 'reading'

To an outsider, it may seem obvious that the goal of a Biblical Greek curriculum is for the students to learn Greek. When students graduate from a Greek programme, it seems reasonable to expect that they know Greek well enough to read the Greek New Testament and Old Testament (Septuagint) as well as other Greek texts important to the study of early Christianity, such as literature contemporary to the New Testament, and the Greek Fathers. This, however, highlights a central problem in any discussion about Greek pedagogy and its goals: definitions. What do we mean when we talk about 'learning' Greek, 'knowing' Greek, and 'reading' Greek? I will now share my own interpretations of these terms and explain how they underpin the teaching practices I use with my students.

Goals in modern language education

Consider the teaching of modern languages, where the definitions are rather simple and straightforward. Imagine an American student who wishes to be a diplomat to Russia. She enrols in the language training programme at the Foreign Service Institute (FSI), which trains American diplomats. Her goals are simple: she wants to 'learn' Russian or 'know' Russian well enough that she can relocate to Russia and speak, write, read, and understand spoken Russian of all types. To fulfil her role as diplomat, she must become fluent or proficient in Russian.

The FSI calls this goal 'General Professional Proficiency' (see Interagency Language Roundtable 2011). It is Level 3 on a scale from 0 (no proficiency) to 5 (native proficiency), and includes the ability to read widely at normal speed with a high level of comprehension, participate in all types of conversations at normal speed with almost complete comprehension, and write mostly error-free about a wide range of topics (FSI uses the Interagency Language Roundtable scale (Herzog n.d.) developed in collaboration with the FSI and the American Council on the Teaching of Foreign Languages). In brief, if our would-be diplomat achieves this level of proficiency, she will be able to listen, speak, read and write moderately difficult Russian at a reasonable pace. Most importantly for our purposes, when she reads or listens to Russian, she will not usually be translating from Russian into English in her mind. Rather, she needs to be thinking in Russian – anything less than this level of fluency will simply not allow her to be effective in the diplomatic service.

Pedagogical goals in university modern language programmes

Similarly, undergraduate programmes in modern languages at any major university also aim for students to learn, know and be able to read their target languages. Here again, the terms are defined in the normal way, so that after four years majoring in German, a student should be able to listen, speak, read and write German fluently, to the extent that he could live comfortably in Germany without being hampered by a significant language barrier. The bar, again, is set at a level that we would, in normal parlance, call 'fluency'.

'Learning' Ancient Greek

The situation is entirely different, however, when we examine Ancient Greek courses. Each of the key words – *learn, know, read* – seem to me to be dramatically redefined. *Learning* the language no longer means gaining the ability to communicate in it. Such ability is never aimed at or tested for. Instead, students *learn in English about the Greek language*. Classes are conducted not in Greek, but in English (or whatever the first language of the students happens to be). All description and analysis of the language occurs in English, usually with the goal of 'accurate' or 'precise' translation of the text into English. It should be no surprise, then, that students who complete the course have little to no proficiency (as normally defined for modern languages) in Greek. Those who succeed in such a course will not be proficient in Greek, but they may become highly proficient in *metalanguage* – the terminology of grammatical and syntactical analysis. This is to be expected, since this is the very skill their professors have mastered and modelled to the students.

'Reading' Ancient Greek

Perhaps the most pernicious shift in definitions, though, comes with the term 'reading'. In modern language classes, students who achieve fluency in a second language are expected to read that language much the same way they read in their native tongue, with an immediacy and directness between the words on the page and the thoughts or pictures stimulated in the mind of the reader. The reader is expected to be *thinking* in the language.

In the doublespeak of the Ancient Greek classroom, however, 'reading' is often conceptualized as translation. Based on interviews with a great number of novice students over the years, this translation is the result of a long, slow, grinding and laborious process in which almost every word or ending is looked up in a lexicon or morphological chart. Gone is the immediacy and pleasure of true reading, of thinking the author's thoughts after him or her. Now, to be clear, some students – the most disciplined, driven and skilled at memorizing – seem to thrive in such a setting, at least as far as grades go. They are able to remember the large blocks of translation and long lists of English glosses they need to perform well on their vocabulary and reading tests. Some may even become speed translators who seem to the untrained eye to be reading. The internal experience is different, however, because the speed translator never makes the transition to *thinking* in Greek. As a result, she/he will always lack the immediacy of true reading and will always be 'kissing through the veil', as one poet described translation (Bialik 1935: 1.16).

I believe this is perhaps the most important point in favour of adopting a communicative approach to teaching ancient languages by requiring students to develop oral-aural skills. Advocates of communicative approaches often encounter the objection that because Ancient Hebrew, Greek, and Latin are no longer living languages, there is hardly any point in learning to speak them. Why focus on oral-aural skills when we can cut straight to reading the language? That is (they say) our ultimate goal, after all. Unfortunately, this mindset misses the essential link between oral-aural proficiency and reading proficiency.

Psycholinguistics has established the existence of a *phonological loop* that underpins all reading (Cheetham 2014; Baddeley et al. 1981). This means, in simple terms, that when we read, the words do not go right from the page into our understanding in written form. Our brain is hard-wired for audio – not visual – when it comes to words. As children, we learn to listen and speak before we learn to read and write. Listening is the primal skill (this is a key insight of the natural approach to Second Language Acquisition, as advocated by Krashen 1983, who stresses the role of comprehensible input over production in language acquisition). When our brain perceives the words on the page, then, it activates its phonological retrieval system and converts them into virtual sound so that it can quickly recognize and comprehend them (this is known as subvocalization, or the covert production of auditory verbal imagery; see Perrone-Bertolotti et al. 2012). In other words, reading is dependent on understanding what one hears. Taking the claims of Baddeley et al. (1981) to their logical conclusion, true reading (as opposed to translation into one's first language in order to understand) can only occur, at a neurological level, if the reader has *already* internalized the language in an oral-aural form. So, research suggests, unless we achieve a basic level of speaking and listening ability in the second language, in which the production of auditory verbal imagery becomes automatic, we may never be able to think in the language and thus enjoy reading fluency. There is simply no shortcut.

The goals of Ancient Greek classes: The status quo

Now, returning to the topic of pedagogical goals, it seems clear to me that when we equivocate on the meaning of key terms like learning, knowing and reading, our goals are shaped accordingly. Basic Greek classes in seminary typically aim at having students memorize and use metalanguage, translate texts into English and memorize English glosses for isolated Greek words. This is what the assignments consist of, and this is what is assessed. Advanced Greek classes are more of the same, focusing on even more detailed linguistic analysis and perhaps requiring longer blocks of text to be translated.

To gain a sense of what Greek professors require, I have surveyed numerous course syllabi from undergraduate ancient language programmes, seminaries, PhD programmes in religion, and classics departments. I also looked at numerous modern language department course syllabi. Where is the bar being set?

Modern language syllabi

We can begin with a typical modern language syllabus for a second-year German class at a large state university. In this course, students are expected to:

- write six pages of essays in German;
- give a ten-minute class presentation (spoken) in German;
- participate outside of class in coffee hours and club activities where German is exclusively spoken, as well as watch German films and listen to a student-produced German radio show;
- complete laboratory assignments that include speaking, listening, writing and reading components;
- read around forty pages of German text per week and answer (in German) reading comprehension questions.

Of course, in addition to all this, classes are conducted entirely in German. Other modern language classes have similar expectations. For example, a third-year German course at the same university gives students two weeks to read a 220-page book by Gotthold Lessing, after which they must be prepared to discuss the work in class and compose response essays – all in German. That is what language education looks like when the bar is set at fluency.

Biblical language syllabi

Greek courses, to be blunt, simply pale in comparison. Consider a representative syllabus from a third-year Greek course on the New Testament Book of Acts at a rather large graduate programme in theology:

- class is conducted entirely in English. No composition, speaking or listening in Greek is required. No laboratory time is required.
- emphasis is placed on detailed linguistic analysis of the Greek text using English linguistics terminology.
- over the course of the sixteen-week semester, the class will 'read' (that is, write out an English translation) ten chapters of Acts (around 28 pages). To put that in perspective, that is fewer than two pages per week, and less than 2 per cent of what the third-year German class requires.

In my collection of advanced Greek syllabi, there was one standout, a course called 'Advanced Greek Reading' taught at one of the largest evangelical seminaries in the United States. In terms of weekly reading, it was the most demanding of any Greek course I examined, as it required an average of about 100 verses a week, equivalent to about eight pages. This is still only 7 per cent of what the German class requires, and it should be remembered that this course is taught entirely in English and that the reading – in reality, translating – is the only requirement, in contrast to the German course, which also requires papers, language laboratories and extensive communicative work outside class – all in German.

It would appear, then, that we are setting the bar quite low in our ancient language classes when it comes to standards of reading fluency. This is not to claim that Greek classes are easy – far from it. Indeed, the bar is set very high in terms of memorizing, understanding and applying linguistic metalanguage. As a result, students who would have no problem acquiring fluency in a second language find themselves failing miserably in Greek classes that resemble a maths or engineering course more than a language laboratory. One example from my own teaching comes to mind: a student who had native fluency in French and Swahili and near-native fluency in English, but after failing courses in Greek and Hebrew was told by his professors that he was simply not smart enough to learn those languages.

The way forward

[A]How, then, can the situation be improved? My proposal, which is hardly unique to me (see, for example, Miller 2019), is to stop thinking that because Greek and Hebrew are 'dead' languages, they must be taught in a wholly different manner from modern languages. Taking our cues from modern language teaching and drawing on insights from applied linguistics (especially the study of second language acquisition), we must embrace more natural approaches that help our students internalize and enjoy the language rather than see it as an ancient code to be analyzed, dissected and deciphered into English. If we create living language-learning environments where students are immersed in the language (as modern language laboratories do), then there is no reason that we should aim for anything less than fluency or communicative proficiency in our pedagogy (my own experience teaching Greek using a living language approach is described in Streett (2010); cf. the numerous related blog posts at Streett (n.d.)).

Theological seminaries (especially in the Protestant tradition) have historically aspired to train church leaders whose responsibilities, in large measure, revolve around the study, teaching and explanation of the church's sacred texts. A typical Master of Divinity (MDiv) programme is designed to be completed in three years. Is it too much to expect, then, for seminaries to allow motivated students to pursue a three-year sequence in Greek or Hebrew that is comparable in methods and goals to a three-year university course in German?

An even stronger case could be made for seminary students who seek a career in the academy teaching theology, biblical studies or biblical languages. These students will spend the next thirty or forty years teaching language and exegesis courses. Their studies will typically involve three years of MDiv courses, two years of PhD coursework and the production of a dissertation (during which time they will often begin teaching part-time). Given the time involved and the centrality of the biblical languages to such pursuits, it is reasonable to expect these students to gain genuine fluency in the biblical languages.

Practical challenges

There are, of course, enormous practical challenges to this. To begin with, the time required to achieve fluency is substantial. The FSI estimates that one needs 600–1,100 hours of immersive guided training in the language to reach a reasonable level of proficiency (see US Department of State n.d.). Modern language programmes in universities typically require four hours per week of class, plus language laboratory work, communication-based homework and immersive extracurricular experiences, such as residence halls where the target language is spoken exclusively. They also offer summer travel programmes and years abroad that allow students to live in the foreign language and enhance their fluency. In this way, a student can easily gain the exposure and training needed to become fluent.

In contrast, seminaries have virtually no infrastructure to support biblical language education at that level, and, as much theological education moves online, the picture looks even bleaker. Many institutions have opted to lower the bar even more, by adopting a 'tools' approach to biblical language training. On this method, the student is taught how to use Bible software that can parse, diagram and gloss every word as an aid to exegesis. In one sense, this is the logical outworking of the traditional grammar-translation approach to biblical languages, as it accomplishes the goal of the traditional approach – to equip the student to analyze, label, translate and 'exegete' – in a much more efficient way. In the end, however, both the traditional approach and the new digitally based tools method foster in students the deeply unhealthy illusion that one has learned a language and is now able to read it and speak authoritatively about it.

The challenge of exegesis in the communicative classroom

When I discuss the issue with other Greek teachers, one of the most common questions that comes up is: what about exegesis? Most seminary biblical language courses have as their ultimate goal to equip students to do exegesis of biblical texts. The premise of the question seems to be that a communicative approach to biblical languages might teach students how to order coffee in Greek or Hebrew, but it would not prepare them to do the deep exegetical analysis valued by biblical scholars.

The question, it seems to me, usually presupposes a concept of, and approach to, exegesis that is profoundly problematic. When seminary professors teach 'exegesis', too often what is in view is the close – frequently atomistic – analysis of a very short text or *pericope*, perhaps no more than a few lines. For many, to do 'exegesis' is to engage in careful grammatical dissection of the text, detailed word studies to determine the meaning of the key terms or their best English equivalents, and syntactical analysis of the logical relationships between the propositions in the text. Then, as the crowning achievement, one produces a meaning-based or paraphrastic translation of the text into English accompanied by a commentary. Indeed, it seems that much of what passes for 'exegesis' in biblical language classes is in fact artificial, atomistic over analysis of little bits of texts which were originally intended to be heard complete. Can there be any doubt that the grammar-translation method of teaching Greek contributes significantly to the problem?

This all seems rather strange to scholars who study literature. Indeed, if we use Google Books to search for the term 'exegesis', we will find that every book on the first ten pages of results is a biblical studies book. Literary critics do not typically speak in terms of exegesis, nor do classicists. They speak of reading, interpretation, hermeneutics and context, but not 'exegesis'. Their focus is on a close reading of texts in their literary, social, and historical contexts – a much more beneficial approach than the microanalysis of grammar and syntax that is often taught to students in biblical language classes.

In short, I find that that the question, 'What about exegesis?' often assumes that to interpret a text, we must be able to label, diagram and translate it into another language. But, when we read and discuss English literature, we do not usually analyze syntax or diagram sentences, nor do we label each element using linguistic metalanguage. Rather we discuss meaning, themes and characterization. We summarize, paraphrase and make connections with other parts of the text, teasing out logical implications and examining elements of literary artistry. All of this can be done – indeed, is best done – in the same language in which the text itself was composed.

Two exegetical examples

Some brief examples may be helpful for illustrating how this works in a communicative classroom where class is conducted in the target language as much as possible. In the first example, the text to be discussed is John 3. The class begins by reading the text aloud in Greek, and perhaps acting out the narrative with assigned roles. Attention is given to reading expressively, with the correct pacing, phrasing and intonation. Any unfamiliar words are explained a) through definitions in the target language, b) by showing pictures of the action or item, or c) through a quick English gloss. For example, τὰ ἐπουράνια in John 3:12 can be glossed as τὰ ἐν τῷ οὐρανῷ.

In acting out the scene, students are encouraged to rephrase and paraphrase the text, or to bring up questions of meaning or syntax. For instance, the question arises regarding v. 2: ἵνα τί ἔρχεται Νικόδημος νυκτός (Why does Nicodemus come [to Jesus] at nighttime?). Students should be asked to propose possible reasons (e.g., ἔρχεται κρυφῇ, He is coming in secret; or, οὐ θέλει ἀνθρώπους ἰδεῖν αὐτόν, He doesn't want anyone to see him). The professor might also ask students what Jesus means by 'seeing' (ἰδεῖν) the kingdom of God: τί σημαίνει τὸ ἰδεῖν; (What does 'seeing' mean?), and offering some options, such as εἰσέρχεσθαι or πνεματικῶς καταλαμβάνειν (see Cramer 1844 for examples of patristic discussion of the Greek New Testament in Greek). The grammar, too, can be discussed in Greek (not English), employing the terminology used by ancient Greek grammarians, instead of English linguistic metalanguage (see Dickey 2007 for terminology).

In my conversations with other Greek teachers, they often bring up Paul's use of πίστις Χριστοῦ (faith of/in Christ, e.g. in Rom 3:22 and Gal 2:16) as an example of an issue they can hardly imagine being able to discuss in an immersive classroom. This phrase, they explain, must be presented to students in terms of the various uses of the genitive case, with special attention to the difference between the subjective genitive (i.e., depicting Christ as the one who believes or is faithful) and the objective genitive (i.e., belief in, or faithfulness to Christ). While I certainly agree that aspiring biblical scholars should be made aware of current academic debates and the terminology used (such as 'objective' or 'subjective' genitive), the issue can be discussed in Greek quite easily without resorting to English metalanguage. The professor can simply ask the students to produce a paraphrase, so that they must choose whether to depict Christ as the object or subject of faith (i.e. ὁ Χριστὸς ὑπακούει τῷ θεῷ or Χριστιανοὶ πιστεύουσιν τῷ Χριστῷ). Indeed, when people opposed to communicative pedagogy use this example, it indicates to me that they tend to view Greek pedagogy more in terms of providing students with the ability to read and understand academic commentaries on Scripture, and less in terms of actually acquiring facility in the language. These are not mutually exclusive, but only one can rightly be called 'learning' a language.

Conclusion

Language training in seminaries and theological academies is in crisis, as institutions eliminate language requirements from their curricula or adopt a 'tools' approach that involves little more than software training and a rudimentary introduction to linguistic terminology. The fault lies largely with language professors who continue to perpetuate a discredited pedagogy (grammar-translation) that had its heyday in the mid-nineteenth century (see Eyckmans et al. (2016: 223), who describe the grammar-translation method as 'irretrievably discredited' by the 1940s, while Richards and Rodgers (2001: 7), state that in current language pedagogy, the method 'has no advocates'). In a course dominated by grammar-translation, 'reading' is actually translation and 'learning' a language has little to do with acquiring proficiency in the language itself and more to do with becoming fluent in the metalanguage of linguistic analysis (i.e. speaking *about* the language rather than speaking the language). Students typically gain no exposure to the language beyond a single corpus (i.e. the New Testament), and thus struggle to develop a feel for the language. Students are taught to exegete by labelling, analyzing and translating, as if this will enable them to make judicious decisions about the meaning of these ancient texts.

In my opinion, the way forward requires that we draw on the insights of contemporary second language acquisition research, which demonstrates that communicative proficiency (especially aural skill) underlies fluent reading. I believe that there is no shortcut to such proficiency, as it requires hundreds of hours of guided immersion in the language. Perhaps the most important step is to set the bar high and then sort out exactly what methods and techniques will get students there most efficiently. In setting our goals, it is helpful to look at the level of fluency modern language training programmes expect of their students. In comparison, the bar is set shockingly low in biblical language training.

The current volume is one of many voices advocating for pedagogical reform. Perhaps in ten to twenty years there will be seminary classrooms in which the New Testament, Josephus and the Greek Fathers are read for pleasure and 'exegetical' papers are written and discussed entirely in Greek. For too long, we have contented ourselves with teaching about Greek, rather than teaching Greek, with translating rather than truly reading, with linguistic analysis instead of literary appreciation. We have set the bar far too low, allowing our students to get a 'little learning', which, as Alexander Pope reminds us, is 'a dang'rous thing'. It is time for us to raise the bar and aim for true fluency, to urge our students to 'Drink deep, or taste not the Pierian spring'.

CHAPTER 16
LATIN TEACHING IN POLAND: A NEW RENAISSANCE WITH COMMUNICATIVE APPROACHES?

Sebastian Domagała, Marcin Loch and Katarzyna Ochman

Introduction

Latin was the second language spoken in Poland for many centuries, allowing educated people whose native tongue was so different from other Western languages to communicate effectively with the rest of the world and to participate on equal terms in the international cultural exchange. The use of Latin among Poles faded away significantly later than in other European countries. It is significant that Polish national identity has been concisely expressed with the phrase *eques Polonus sum, Latine loquor* (I am a Polish gentleman, I speak Latin).

In the nineteenth, twentieth and twenty-first centuries, classical education in Poland shared a similar fate to that of the rest of the Western world, with the most rapid decline occurring over the past thirty years. These lamentable changes have been described in detail by many researchers (e.g. Brzuska 1990, 2016, 2019; Czetwertyńska 2014; Malinowski 2016; Popiak 2005; Ryba 2015). This chapter results primarily from the three authors' experience of teaching Latin in Poland at high-school and university level, as well as from their own experiences learning ancient and modern languages using a variety of methods. It aims to offer the reader a ray of hope that not everything is lost for the descendants of such eminent Latinists as Ioannes Kochanovius, Martinus Cromerus and Matthias Casimirus Sarbievius. We strongly believe that the return to the use of communicative methods in teaching ancient languages, which has been recently observed worldwide, is capable of bringing back Latin as the third – after Polish and English – language of the modern *equites Poloni* who wish to become members of the emerging international *res publica litterarum*. In order for this to happen, we need to create many more opportunities to learn Latin and to produce a new generation of teachers not only equipped with updated skills, but also representing a different mindset.

The chapter is divided into three main sections. In the first part we present some didactic innovations that preceded the current growing movement of so-called 'spoken Latin' in Poland, as well as describing the transformations happening in the organization which can currently be considered the institutional heart of this movement: the University of Wrocław. The second part is focused on the teaching techniques applied during the Latin and Greek Summer Schools that take place in Poznań. The third part explains the educational context of these undertakings: the striking discrepancies between the teaching of modern and ancient languages in the Polish educational system and the professional training of teachers of these two groups of languages. We trust that the endeavours described in Parts 1 and 2 can be an effective way of gradually reducing the gap between ancient and modern language pedagogies evident in Part 3.

Part 1

Innovations in teaching Latin in Poland in the twentieth and twenty-first centuries

The contemporary reality of teaching Latin in Poland dates back to at least the turn of the twentieth century, when the classical languages curriculum was limited: the number of hours was gradually reduced from about 2,000 in an eight-year-long cycle in most schools in the early 1900s to 240 hours in a three-year-long cycle available in only a few schools at the end of the twentieth century. Low efficacy of the grammar-translation method (henceforth, GT) quickly became apparent to many educators, and was under discussion together with other school reforms in many countries (Viëtor 1882; Rosenthal 1924; Tacke 1923).

A debate over curricular changes in Poland had gained momentum by the 1930s, in the context of the Educational Reform of 1932 (Malinowski 2016; Loch 2015). Publications from that period criticized the reforms (in particular, shortening of the classical languages curriculum) and were filled with longing for the paradise lost, such as eight-year classical secondary schools (*gimnazja klasyczne*). Juliusz Krzyżanowski was one of the few scholars in Poland who emphasized the importance of changes in teaching methodology (Krzyżanowski 1936, 1937a, 1937b; *cf. etiam* Lenkowski 1937). On several occasions he took part in the Summer Schools organized in the UK from 1911 by the Association for the Reform of Latin Teaching. He also attempted to popularize in Poland the methods developed there by W. H D. Rouse (see, for example, Stray 1992 on the Direct Method). Unfortunately, his proposals were misunderstood and criticized by Polish teachers of classical languages; nevertheless, his voice re-initiated the discussion on teaching those languages, which was in turn interrupted by the outbreak of the Second World War. Krzyżanowski died in 1950 (as a professor at the University of Wrocław), and thus did not play any major role in the history of classical languages didactics in post-war Poland.

After the Second World War, Poland was located behind the Iron Curtain and heavily influenced by the USSR, which significantly limited the exchange of ideas and new publications with the Western world. However, when Hans Ørberg published his innovative handbook *Lingua Latina secundum naturae rationem explicata* (today in its final form known as *Lingua Latina per se illustrata* (Ørberg 2011, 2017), or *LLPSI* for short), Jan Horowski, a university professor from Poznań, who was interested in CLT (communicative language teaching), went to great lengths to prepare the ground for introducing *LLPSI*. He argued, inter alia, that the book had been particularly well received by Soviet scholars (Horowski 1972). Thanks to his efforts, during the 1970s Ørberg's handbook became the standard handbook for Classics students in Poznań and remained so until the mid 80s. Unfortunately, though, CLT-oriented teachers stopped teaching at Poznań, and use of the book was set aside for almost thirty years.

The beginning of institutional changes: University of Wrocław

The 'natural method' returned to Poland in 2007 after the Institute of Classical, Mediterranean and Oriental Studies at the University of Wrocław needed to design a Classics curriculum for candidates who – due to the drastically reduced number of high schools offering Latin (Malinowski 2016: 71–3) – wished to start Classical Studies, but had no previous knowledge of Latin. The authorities of the Institute concluded that traditional GT techniques alone were no longer effective at the university level and decided to search for alternatives. The legacy of Professor Krzyżanowski and the fact that *LLPSI* had been used in Poznań in the 70s were forgotten or unknown to the lecturers in Wrocław; however, by chance one of them found Ørberg's series online and wrote a review which appeared in *Classica Wratislaviensia* more than fifty years after the original publication of the textbook (Poznański 2009). In this review it was not assumed that *LLPSI* would be used as a CLT textbook, but by a happy coincidence, around the same time a group of newly arrived PhD students founded the *Circulus Latine Loquentium Wratislaviensis* (Wrocław Latin Speaking Club). The original members of the *Circulus* were Ałła Brzozowska, Kamila Bober-Wysłucha, Agnieszka Franczyk-Cegła, Antoine Haaker, Katarzyna Ochman and Adam Poznański. The *Circulus* also stayed in contact with father Jan Ożóg SI, who had studied Classics at the University of Wrocław in the early 1960s and even at that time was the only student fluent in spoken Latin (which he had learned previously while in the seminary). Because of this, the respected Jesuit became an honorary member of the *Circulus* and was bestowed with the unofficial title *Ultimus Wratislaviensis Latine Loquens* (the last Latin-speaking inhabitant of Wrocław). He did not, however, remain the last one for long. In 2009 Ørberg's *Familia Romana* was introduced as the official textbook for first-year students of Classics and has been in use ever since. Understandably, not all members of the Institute are equally enthusiastic about speaking Latin in the classroom (not to mention the lecture hall), but at least some diversity has been implemented: the students have been given an opportunity to participate in courses held entirely or partially in Latin, both at the introductory level and in later semesters, when 'real' Latin authors are read.

Today, ten years after *LLPSI* was introduced in Wrocław, some results of this 'experiment' (as it was initially named) can already be assessed. Because of the small number of students and the varying level of their initial knowledge of Latin, there is not enough data to investigate statistical differences in the results before and after the introduction of the new textbook. However, the classes have consistently received positive reviews from students, especially from those who could compare them with the GT courses of Latin which they had previously attended.

The new approach has also received positive opinions from several language acquisition specialists. One of them decided to personally take part in 180 hours of Latin classes together with the students of Classics and compared it with her own GT experience from several years before. She wrote:

> The effect of this system is a very good understanding of the contents – certainly not worse than that achieved with the grammar-translation method. The understanding of the text in this case does not consist in translating it into the native language, but in comprehending the concepts included in the text. Writing them down in Polish, when needed, does not pose any problem either.
>
> *Małgorzata Bieszczanin, expert opinion from 25 April 2012, private communication. The author is a lecturer in the field of teaching English as a foreign language at the Philological School of Higher Education in Wrocław.*

In the estimation of the authors of this chapter, the very fact that both students and instructors are visibly more enthusiastic and engaged in the teaching process in comparison with the GT-only groups is enough to judge the experiment a success. There is, however, one more tangible result: a new generation of teachers has emerged. These graduates are happy to not only teach their own students according to the new method, but also to investigate it, promote it and even creatively develop their own communicative teaching practices. Some of them are researching active Latin teaching techniques as a part of their doctoral research. The opportunities to teach Latin at the high-school level are very scarce: as of 2018, only four of Wrocław's fifty-eight high schools offered Latin (of which two used *LLPSI*). Therefore, the young instructors from Wrocław, together with some undergraduate students, have been gaining experience by tutoring private students, teaching at the *Schola Aestiva* (Summer School) courses, organizing various events directed at the general public, as well as visiting primary and secondary schools and holding spoken Latin workshops. Since 2017, some of the doctoral candidates have started to offer extra-curricular Latin classes conducted in Latin for undergraduate students of Classics and other subjects at the University of Wrocław.

In 2014 *LLPSI* was also re-introduced at the Adam Mickiewicz University in Poznań, where it is used as the main textbook for first-year students of Classics; it is, however, currently taught as a reading course. In 2018 a group of students at the Jagiellonian University in Cracow, who had previously attended the *Schola Aestiva*, requested an extra-curricular class where they could read *LLPSI* and learn to speak Latin. Ørberg's materials, combined with innovative teaching methods, are gaining increasing acceptance in Poland. Requests have been made to make *LLPSI* available on the local publishing market, because at the moment it can only be purchased directly from the publisher or from booksellers abroad.

Part 2

Schola Aestiva as a teaching lab

A good place for both teachers and learners to try out communicative innovations in the field of Latin pedagogy are the Summer Schools for Latin and Greek (*Scholae Aestivae Posnanienses*), which have been taking place for twenty years now at the Institute of Classical Philology at the Adam Mickiewicz University in Poznań. Initially these courses were aimed at Classics students, who learned Latin through GT, and who wanted additionally to develop their oral-aural skills (such as listening comprehension or spontaneous speech production) as well as to learn to read and understand texts without extensive dictionary work and translation into their mother tongue. With time, the Schools gained in popularity (with a growing demand for beginner and intermediate courses), which resulted in the offer being enriched. The last three years have seen a growing number of participants in particular: the annual event which for many years used to gather one or two dozen enthusiasts suddenly attracted sixty-five people in 2017, seventy-five in 2018 and 130 in 2019! Typically, about half of them are Polish, and the other half come from various European countries, and even from other continents.

At present both Greek and Latin are taught, and students are divided into several proficiency groups. Each course comprises forty hours of formal practical workshops. Besides these, leisure time is organized informally with the expectation that Latin (or sometimes Greek) will be used as the language of everyday communication. Activities include having meals together, going for a walk or sightseeing with a Latin language guide. The authors have observed that spending time together while speaking Latin in informal situations contributes to learning effectiveness. Our present Latin courses are available at six proficiency levels, and Ancient Greek courses at three. The first four Latin courses (*Tirones* I–II–III–IV) are based on Ørberg's *Familia Romana*. Each group reads ten chapters of the handbook and uses Latin as the language of communication throughout classes. The more advanced groups (*Tirones provectiores* and *Veterani*) work with materials prepared by the teachers as well as with Latin literary texts, again discussing everything in Latin.

Though *LLPSI* is the focus of our introductory courses, classes also include a variety of other activities. It is important to underscore that almost none of these activities focus on teaching what might be called 'contemporary Latin'. It is only natural that some modern Latin words (such as *computatorium,* computer) might occasionally be introduced, as they are part of classroom equipment, but the majority of teacher–student communication revolves around the ancient (or timeless) reality presented in the textbook and in the literary sources. The following are just a few examples of the varied activities that take place in a *Tirones I* class:

Speaking practice

For example, after reading *Colloquium II* in *Colloquia Personarum* as well as watching other students performing it in a short play available on YouTube (Llewellyn 2008), students are able to answer such questions as:

1. *quis est Libanus?* (Who is Libanus?)
2. *suntne multi liberi in familia Cornelii?* (Are there many children in Cornelius' family?)
3. *suntne multi servi in familia Iulii?* (Are there many slaves in Julius' family?)

We find it useful to give students the questions in a written form on a handout before playing the video. Once students have watched it, the teacher asks them questions orally, eliciting answers and more details if a vague or general answer is the only one given (for a video recording of a sample lesson, see Loch 2018b). Such a dialogue might take one of the following forms:

Example 1

Teacher *quis est Libanus? estne dominus?* (Who is Libanus? Is he a master?)
Student *non, servus est.* (No, he is a slave.)
Teacher *cuius servus est? estne servus Iulii?* (Whose slave is he? Is he Julius' slave?)
Student *non. servus Cornelii est.* (No. He is Cornelius' slave.)

Example 2

Teacher *suntne multi liberi in familia Cornelii?* (Are there many children in Cornelius' family?)
Student *non sunt.* (There are not [many].)
Teacher *optime! quot sunt? duo filii et una filia?* (Excellent! How many are there? Two sons and one daughter?)
Student *non. unus filius et una filia.* (No. One son and one daughter.)
Teacher *quid nomen filii est? estne Quintus?* (What is the son's name? Is it Quintus?)
Student *non, Sextus est.* (No, it is Sextus.)

Communicative Approaches for Ancient Languages

Handouts and visual aids

The aim of this exercise is to prepare students for reading Ørberg Chapter 5 by introducing new vocabulary using the Magister Craft podcast. The teacher distributes to the students a handout including the plan shown in Figure 16.1. The plan shows the names of the parts of the villa and household objects: *taberna, ianua, fauces, atrium, impluvium, compluvium, cubiculum, ala, lararium, tablinum, peristylum, triclinium, culina, latrina, cella*. At the beginning of the exercise, the teacher reads aloud these words. He does not explain the meaning of these words but prepares the students for hearing them in the podcast. The teacher then plays the video *Villa Romana* from the Divus Magister Craft YouTube channel (Craft 2016), where, in very simple Latin, a Minecraft homunculus shows the students around a Roman villa and names its parts, recapitulating the vocabulary that the teacher read to them earlier. Now they have been introduced to everything that they need in order to complete the Roman villa handout by labelling the places and objects associated with the Latin words.

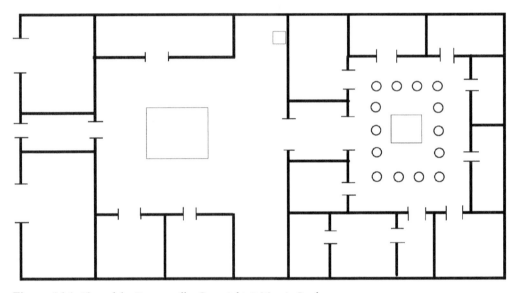

Figure 16.1 Plan of the Roman villa. Copyright © Marcin Loch.

After the students have watched the podcast and completed the plan, the teacher asks simple questions about the location of the house parts (he can draw the plan on the board or use the projector), e.g. *quid est hoc?* (What is this?), answer: *est ostium* (It is a door); *estne hoc atrium?* (Is this an atrium?), answer: *non, peristylum est* (No it is a peristyle) etc. A similar exercise can be done working with the *Forum Romanum* podcast (Craft 2017).

Reading original texts for gist

After Chapter 8 or so of *LLPSI Famlia Romana*, beginners can start to read Catullus' *Carmen III – de passere mortuo*. We give students the original unsimplified text and then explain it in Latin in a simple way. First, we want students to get the gist of the text. We do this by using words and grammatical structures learned by students as well as with appropriate pictures.

One example is the activity designed by Marcin Loch, which can be seen online (Loch 2018a). The instructor distributes a copy of the poem *de passere* by Catullus to students. After reading the text, he asks the following questions while showing pictures and demonstrating meanings of words and expressions. This may take the following form:

The teacher says	Illustrations used
quid est passer? (What is a sparrow?) *ecce passer!* (This is a sparrow!)	A picture of a sparrow.
ecce Catullus, Gaius Valerius Catullus, poeta Romanus primi saeculi a.Ch.n. et ecce Lesbia. Catullus Lesbiam amat, sed Lesbia non amat Catullum. (This is Catullus, Gaius Valerius Catullus, a Roman poet of the first century BC. And this is Lesbia. Catullus loves Lesbia, but Lesbia does not love Catullus.)	An illustration presents Catullus and the period where he lived. Next to it there is a picture of Lesbia. On Catullus' side, there are little hearts. Lesbia is turning her back on Catullus, and turning her face towards the sparrow (cf. *A Difference of Opinion*, Lawrence Alma-Tadema, 1896).
amor eorum mutuus non est. ecce amor mutuus. (Their love is not mutual. This is mutual love.)	A picture of two people between whom there are little hearts and a two-sided arrow.
Lesbia non amat Catullum, Lesbia passerem amat. (Lesbia does not love Catullus, Lesbia loves the sparrow.)	A picture of Catullus crossed out. Next to it is a picture of the sparrow.
cur Lesbia passerem amat? quia mellitus est, id est dulcis ut mel. (Why does Lesbia love the sparrow? Because it is honey-sweet, it is as sweet as honey.)	A picture of a honeycomb, sugar and sweets.
sedet in eius gremio – ecce puella sedet in gremio matris. (It is sitting on her lap – here is a girl sitting on her mother's lap.)	A picture of a little girl sitting on her mother's lap.
et circumsilit. quid est? passer non ambulat ut Iulius et Aemilia et Catullus, passer salit. circumsilit. (And it is hopping around. A sparrow does not walk like Iulius and Aemilia, and Catullus; a sparrow jumps. It hops around.)	A short animation of a jumping sparrow. The teacher may also demonstrate how a sparrow walks (jumps).
et pipiat. (And it is chirping.)	A picture of a bird singing (for example, surrounded by musical notes or with musical notes within a speech bubble coming out of its beak).
passer optimus est! sed . . . passer mortuus est. (The sparrow is the best! But . . . The sparrow is dead.)	A picture of a dead bird with the caption 'R.I.P.'.

Communicative Approaches for Ancient Languages

The teacher says	Illustrations used
estne Lesbia laeta? minime! Lesbia plorat. plorat, id est luget. (Is Lesbia happy? Not at all! She is weeping. She is weeping, that is: she is in mourning.)	A picture of Lesbia crying.
ecce Lesbia, oculi eius magni sunt, id est turgiduli. (This is Lesbia; her eyes are big, that is: swollen.)	A picture of swollen, tearful eyes.
solane luget Lesbia? (Is she weeping alone?)	
minime! etiam Venus, et Cupidines et omnes homines lugent. . (Not at all! Venus and Cupid are too; all people are weeping.)	A picture of Venus, Cupid and a group of people.

We can also sing the poem as a song (see below) and do a number of exercises with questions to the text. This way, we help our students to get the gist of the literary piece *without* having to translate it word by word. Students get a lot of satisfaction from contact with an original Latin text just a few days into the course.

Role-playing

In Chapter 8 of *LLPSI*, the material in the book can be augmented by numerals and basic phrases related to haggling and shopping. We organize a shop selling various products, each of which has a tag indicating its name. We invite someone from an advanced group to run the shop; therefore, the seller conducts transactions with a high degree of fluency. Each student receives 100 coins (*nummi*) and is supposed to buy as many products as possible (or alternatively everything from their shopping list) at the lowest price possible. The player with the biggest savings against tag prices wins.

Singing

Alessandro Conti has released a CD entitled *Carmina Latina Per Se Illustrata* with songs matching the vocabulary of the first thirteen chapters of the Ørberg's textbook (Conti 2019). After listening to each of them a few times, we can perform individual songs with students and thus consolidate the material.

During the Catullus class, we can teach students to sing *Carmen III* to the melody composed by the group Tyrtarion. The music is written and performed in such a way that it helps students to feel and correctly produce the rhythm (metric structure) of the Latin verse (recording available on YouTube: Tyrtarion 2010).

At the end of the *Tirones I* course, we can sing songs related to Ovid's *Tristia* (Tyrtarion 2011) as well as read and analyze the text: students may underline words that they understand or can put into categories, e.g. verbs, pronouns, etc. Next, we can try to 'decipher the text': the teacher guides the students (partly in their mother tongue) to the meaning of individual words or phrases. The purpose of this exercise is to show students how many new things they have learnt during a two-week course, and how much they can already understand. This exercise helps to challenge the stereotype that all literary texts are difficult. As a result, we find that students overcome their fear of new texts.

Tirones provectiores, the fifth group, is intended primarily for participants who have already studied Latin (mainly through GT), but have never had the opportunity to work with other methods – this is the most challenging group from the teachers' perspective as they must design activities that will help all the members of a very heterogeneous group to progress. The main purpose of these classes is to activate the participants' passive knowledge, and transform it into actual language skills that can be used communicatively. Therefore, various tasks are used in this group to activate and broaden participants' lexical repertoire. Some of these include:

Text-based exercises

A typical task will require students to take a single story, such as one of *Fabulae Syrae* (Miraglia 2010), read it section by section and discuss it in Latin. Alternatively, the teacher reads a story aloud while students try to understand as much as possible aurally. On a different day, students use Latin to describe a picture and attempt to guess what mythical story hides behind it. They might also be asked to come up with alternative endings, again discussing and producing everything in Latin.

Yet another way of working with a text is the 'Messenger' (a game proposed by Małgorzata Bieszczanin). Students are split into several teams, each of which receives a piece of text. Each team sends a messenger to the other teams. The messenger has to share their team's piece of the story as well as find out about the other pieces. Finally, each team tries to reconstruct the whole story.

A text might also provide a starting-point for other creative and output-oriented activities in groups. These might take the form of dialogues (for example, a conversation between the jealous Juno and Jupiter), role-playing or discussions (such as taking on the role of gods discussing whether it is right for Ganymedes to stay in Olympus). Discussions in Latin are used frequently, and they do not always result from reading a text. In our experience, students are usually very active when defending or attacking views which have been allocated to them, especially if they are controversial. For instance, we have had a very lively debate about the death penalty. Students are required to present randomly assigned specific views, rather than their personal opinions, which helps to avoid conflicts, and promotes critical thinking as well as active language use.

Functional language

To teach functional language, the teachers prepare their own materials, which in the case of everyday life may include polite language, describing people, everyday routines, telling the time, talking about emotions, seasons and the weather. Students practise this material speaking in pairs and small groups; after that, they might be asked to write down their answers and read them aloud to the class. In order to promote communication in Latin also *scholis peractis* (after the course), students are provided not only with functional vocabulary but also with useful grammatical structures. Special attention is paid to these structures which are notorious for their difficulty such as *accusativus cum infinitivo*, *nominativus cum infinitivo* and impersonal verbs such as *taedet me*.

To give an example, a class on describing people might consist of the following stages:

1. warm-up and activation of prior knowledge. Students in small groups recall from memory all the body parts they know in Latin and they compile a written list.

2. presentation. Each list is read out and the teacher collates all the words on the board. He or she also adds any important missing items.

3. practice. One student comes up in front of the whiteboard. This student's task is to draw an accurate depiction of a person described to her by the rest. The teacher asks questions such as *estne homo statura magna? quales oculos habet?* (Is it a man of large build? What sort of eyes does he have?) to elicit what the given character looks like while the students who sit at their desks use their imagination to create a funny character. When the group is satisfied with the outcome, another student comes up to the board and uses the others students' cues to draw another character. Finally, the teacher elicits information concerning the character's personality and daily habits.

4. production. The students create a 'chain story' with these two characters. Each student makes one sentence, and the next student adds a logical continuation.

Describing pictures

Students work in pairs. One student describes their picture to another while the other draws it. Next, both the pictures are presented to the class. Everybody participates in finding differences and comparing the pictures (again using Latin throughout).

Total Physical Response (TPR) and Teaching Proficiency through Reading and Storytelling (TPRS)

Activities which involve movement and repetition work very well both at introductory levels and with 'false beginners' (i.e. students in a beginners' class who have actually studied Latin before) who need to put known vocabulary into practice. Basic verbs and commands (*surge!* (Stand up!); *veni huc!* (Come here!); *conside in mensa!* (Sit on the table!)) are especially relevant for *Tirones I*, but it is important to understand that also the grammatical forms which are traditionally considered 'difficult' (such as the imperative of deponent verbs) should not be avoided, because they are perfectly clear from the context. This is particularly the case when the teacher tries to make as many combinations as possible with the very few words known so far to the students; it often leads to a comic effect, which greatly facilitates remembering: *osculare ianuam!* (Kiss the door!); *amplectare mensam!* (Hug the table!), etc. *Tirones provectiores*, on the other hand, often confess that only through the means of such basic exercises were they finally able to grasp the meaning of the grammatical forms they had previously studied.

The sixth group, *Veterani*, works with an extended original text, either in prose or verse. The focus of the class is listening comprehension, speaking and mediation (i.e. reprocessing and reformulating texts in various ways). The teacher reads out a text sentence by sentence while the students, who do not have copies of the text, attempt to understand it aurally. They are asked to answer the teacher's questions about the content of the section of text that has just been read or to create a summary or paraphrase an excerpt with their own words. This procedure not only encourages the students to listen carefully and attentively, but also aims to activate their language knowledge and broaden their lexico-grammatical repertoire.

Additionally, the students of all the groups sing songs (classical poetry with modern arrangements, such as *Carmina Burana*, or songs by Tyrtarion), play various board and card games (e.g. *Versipelles/Latrones* (The Mafia, literally 'Transformers'/'Assassins'), or *Dicere nefas* (Taboo, literally 'It's forbidden to say'), or participate in lectures and workshops: they might be taught, for example, to write metric poetry (these classes are led in Latin by Martin Freundorfer, a Latin poet from Vienna), or to recite metric poetry with a reconstructed classical pronunciation. In 2019, a class in Latin and Greek calligraphy was introduced as an experiment and proved to be a huge success.

We have been organizing Ancient Greek language classes for four years, and we are still trying out various ways of doing this. In 2019 our Greek courses comprised, as already mentioned, three levels: *Tirones I* for those who had never studied Greek; *Tirones medii* for intermediate learners; and *Veterani* for those who were most advanced.

The classes in the *Veterani* group were conducted using similar techniques to those for Latin veterans. They were based on a text that we read, explained, commented on and summarized – all in Greek! – as well as various text-related exercises such as developing a thread of a story, writing an answer to a letter or inventing alternative story endings.

To date, with *Tirones I* we have used the textbooks *Athenaze* (Balme et al. 2008, 2013), *Alexandros* (Ávila 2014), *Polis* (Rico 2015) and *Dialogos* (Martínez 2014). We managed to cover a substantial portion of the material in *Polis* – we completed the first eight chapters, including exercises, within forty hours. However, we found that the material was too simple for students who had already had some contact with Ancient Greek; at the same time, the level expected of the advanced group proved to be too challenging for some students, even though they had some previous knowledge of Greek. Therefore, in 2019 we introduced a third, intermediate group: *Tirones medii*, the syllabus for which is based on *Alexandros* (Ávila 2014) and *Athenaze* (Balme et al. 2008, 2013).

To conduct classes in our *scholae* we invite both teachers experienced in working with the methods described above and less experienced (often younger) instructors. The latter have a unique opportunity to put into practice their innovative ideas. We provide them with professional support, advice and guidance based on our own experience. In our environment, they can grow as teachers and enrich the repertoire of their teaching techniques and methods.

Summer schools are slowly beginning to influence the academic environment. On the one hand, there are teachers who learn new methods and activities and apply them in their regular classes; on the other hand, the high-school students and Classics students who come to us get an insight into modern-day communicative approaches to the teaching of classical languages, and increasingly expect the same from their teachers and tutors at school or and university. However, the most important effect seems to be the creation of a community which not only participates in speaking Latin, but, first and foremost, sustains the continuity of an international Latin-speaking tradition that has lasted for thousands of years. This longevity is what clearly distinguishes Latin speakers from any other language group in the world.

Part 3

The place of Latin in the Polish educational system

As noted in the introduction, a new Renaissance would mean a fundamental change not only in the methods ancient languages are taught (as discussed in Part 2), but also in their accessibility as well as in teachers' attitude to language teaching. In short, we are convinced that giving ancient language teachers the knowledge, skills and teaching time similar to those enjoyed by modern languages teachers would make it possible to bring their students to a level of linguistic competence comparable with that of modern languages. The sheer scale of this task can best be understood by investigating the gap between teaching modern and ancient languages in Poland. These differences concern students' access to languages as well as teachers' attitudes, which are discussed in the first and second part of this section.

Access to ancient languages can be described quantitatively and qualitatively. Consequently, this section will explore the number of institutions offering ancient languages, contact hours and the amount of available teaching material, as they affect *the number* of students learning these languages. Next, the quality of access will be outlined in terms of variety and goals of courses and teaching materials, as they determine what *kinds* of learners can be reached and what potentially they can achieve.

The number of schools offering ancient languages to pupils aged seven to nineteen has decreased dramatically. Ancient Greek has all but disappeared from the curriculum; Latin, on the other hand, is available, but in a small number of institutions. For example, the Polish Philological Society (*Polskie Towarzystwo Filologiczne*), a national organization concerned with classical languages, has listed on its website about 270 schools offering Latin (PTF 2017; this list may not be comprehensive). Given that there are about 35,000 schools in Poland, that means Latin is available in less than 1 per cent of schools. It should also be noted that out of these 270 schools, most offer very short courses: in most schools where Latin is taught, teaching time can range from thirty hours at worst, up to 120 hours in some places; in just twenty-five schools are 240 hours offered. Moreover, it is telling that out of 247,230 students taking the end-of-school exam in 2019 only 141 (or 0.06 per cent) took Latin, whereas all of them had to take one modern language (see Figure 16.2 below; these data come from CKE 2019). In addition, Latin in state-run schools is taught at a very late stage of education, at high school (ages sixteen to nineteen). Latin is an optional course, and according to the common opinion among Latin teachers (explained in detail by Ryba 2019), the design of the National Curriculum discourages students from selecting it. It is not perceived as something useful, because it is not necessary in order to gain admittance to any university course, while success in other examination subjects does open up a number of higher education opportunities. In our opinion, the low number of contact hours make it impossible to develop linguistic competence, which is reflected in the number of students willing to test their skills in exams. In fact, very few schools offer the 240 hours during three years that are required to meet the goals set by the National Curriculum for Latin as well as the national exam.

The difficulties students may have in accessing Latin in Poland become all too clear when the number of contact hours for modern languages is compared with those for Latin. One modern language is compulsory from primary school (ages seven to fifteen) to the very end of high school (age nineteen). Normally, a student can have 990–1,440 hours for modern languages, while Latin is restricted to from fifteen to 240 (but see the caveats above).

	Modern languages	Latin
Total number of students taking the high school national exam in 2019	247,230 students	141 students
Total number of in-class hours during 12 years	990–1,440 hours	15–240 hours

Figure 16.2 Latin and modern languages in state-run schools in Poland. Copyright © Sebastian Domagała, Marcin Loch and Katarzyna Ochman.

In our view, the number of Latin language lessons must be increased in order to give students a chance of mastering at least basic grammar and vocabulary and achieving minimal reading fluency.

Moreover, the situation at universities is lamentable. For generations Latin (and earlier also Ancient Greek) played an important role in the curricula of such courses as Law, Medicine, Theology, History or Linguistics. Nowadays, however, a growing number of institutions is either removing it completely or reducing it (this is our observation, as this problem has not been researched yet). In practice, only a small number of universities offer at least an elementary Latin course, and the teaching time varies between fifteen and 240 hours. In contrast, every university student is expected to take a four-semester modern language course and pass an upper-intermediate exam (B2 according to the Common European Framework of Reference for Languages (CEFR) (2011), a document designed by the Council of Europe to describe students' achievements at progressive proficiency levels).

Furthermore, the Polish publishing market offers only a handful of Latin language handbooks. All of them were written in line with a GT methodology; most of them have no pictures and an old-fashioned black-and-white design, while the exercises are usually translations and contextless inflections. In most cases there are no audio, video, comics, games or online materials. One recent important exception is *Homo Romanus,* a very well prepared and beautifully edited textbook by Janusz Ryba, Elżbieta Wolanin and Aleksandra Klęczar (2017, 2019), which has been used by many teachers; however, it does not facilitate CLT. Foreign textbooks must therefore be imported, which drastically increases their price. On the other hand, materials for modern languages are offered by both local and foreign publishers, with a wide range of prices and auxiliary materials.

From a student's perspective, access to a language also translates into a variety of courses and teaching materials. At present, the teaching of Latin seems to take a similar form in most institutions. State-run schools are obliged to meet the demands of the national curriculum, where Latin is not grouped with other languages but instead regarded as part of *artistic* education (Strycharczyk 2014). In fact, the full name of the subject used by the ministry is 'Latin Language and Ancient Culture'. Ancient culture is normally studied using Polish as the teaching language, while Latin is taught by means of GT. Students learn declensions from charts, parse words and translate short paragraphs word-by-word: all lessons are conducted in Polish. The final goal of the course, reflected in the final exam design, is to translate a passage from Latin and write an essay in Polish where some knowledge of the ancient world can be demonstrated. The knowledge of Latin appears to be narrowed down to a mastery of inflections and syntax, and little attention appears to be paid to vocabulary acquisition. It seems that many students are discouraged from studying Latin due to the tedious work that is usually associated with parsing and translation (Osipowicz 2003). The means and goals seem to be very similar in private schools and at universities. Dedicated students may enjoy such courses, but in our opinion, most prospective Latin students do not find this approach attractive and many of them probably perceive Latin as a waste of time.

On the other hand, the goals and methods of modern language teaching differ considerably. In state-run schools, at the end of high school, every student is expected to reach B1+/B2 (intermediate+/upper-intermediate) in receptive skills as described by the CEFR. It means they are supposed to be able to 'understand the main ideas of complex text on both concrete and abstract topics, including technical discussions in his/her field of specialisation' as well as 'deal with most situations likely to arise whilst travelling in an area where the language is spoken … produce simple connected text on topics which are familiar or of personal interest … describe experiences and events, dreams, hopes and ambitions and briefly give reasons and explanations for opinions and plans'. The goals of modern language instruction are based on the CEFR, hence their practical, communicative, task-based nature. Classes are meant to teach practical skills of reading, listening, writing, speaking and mediation. The national exams reflect this approach, and their design is very similar to the Cambridge English as a Second Language exams. However, teachers have the freedom to choose the methods they find most effective in a given situation; in consequence, even though technically and formally communication-oriented, classes may range from having a focus on learning grammar and translation to communicative-language-teaching-style with no translation and emphasis on interaction in the target language.

In comparison with modern languages, Latin teaching can be characterized by a considerably smaller number of hours and educational institutions, the focus on grammatical analysis and translation rather than communicative goals, a preference for learning and not acquisition, dominance of a single method (GT), scarcity and obsolescence of learning materials, and low popularity with students.

The vast majority of high-school and university students have no access to Latin, and even if some of them do, their courses are very short. To make things worse, the market offers only a few handbooks, most of which are very old fashioned, unattractive and based on just one methodology. It seems that the current system is withdrawing from teaching Classics and nothing can reverse the course. In our opinion, a comprehensive revival of Classics is possible only if the curricula are expanded and made much more diversified and attractive products are made available. But how can students and educational administrations be persuaded that teaching Classics through ancient languages is worth time and money?

We strongly believe that teachers are the key to a renaissance of Classics. It is through them that a reform can be brought about. In our view, however, a new mindset is indispensable – methods need to change, to be sure, but so do teachers' educational backgrounds and their ideas about language and language-learning. In short, receiving an education more similar to modern language teachers and holding onto similar values – which are, incidentally, similar to those of the international *res publica litterarum* from the Renaissance – could help to build a bridge between Classics and modern students. Figure 16.3 below summarizes some of the differences between approaches, means and ends of modern language teachers, GT teachers and communication-oriented Latin/Ancient Greek teachers.

	Modern languages	Latin in state-run schools	Latin and Ancient Greek in summer courses
General goals	Effective international communication	Knowledge of grammar, ancient culture and its influence	Reading original texts and communicating with Latin/Ancient Greek speakers
Knowledge	All languages systems with focus on functional and situational language; elements of target language culture	Morphology, syntax; ancient culture and its heritage	All language systems; Latin language culture until today and Ancient Greek culture in antiquity and middle ages
Skills	Reception, production, interaction, mediation	Mediation in the form of translation	Reception, production, interaction, mediation
Assessment	Informal in class and formal in national exams	Informal in class and formal in a national exam	Informal in class
Approaches and methods	The communicative approach	Grammar-translation	The communicative approach (grammar discussed in the target language)
Materials	Ministry-approved handbooks and authentic materials	Ministry-approved handbooks, simplified and authentic passages	*LLPSI*; Polis, Athenaze, Dialogos, Alexandros; authentic texts
Source texts	Mostly press articles, radio broadcasts, videos	Literary texts	Literary texts
Language perception	Tool for communication	A formal system of signs governed by grammatical rules	Tool for communication
Teacher's role	Organizes class activities and facilitates communication	Provides and explains grammar rules; dominates in the classroom	Organizes class activities and facilitates communication
Student's role	Reads, listens, communicates with others and expresses themselves	Memorizes grammar rules and produces translations	Reads, listens, communicates with others and expresses themselves

Figure 16.3 Comparison of languages teaching. Copyright © Sebastian Domagała, Marcin Loch and Katarzyna Ochman.

Modern language teachers want to prepare their students for international communication by means of the communicative approach. Market demand is very high, so they are eager to constantly develop professionally and find new ways to connect with their students. For example, they want to use modern technologies in class. Moreover, in Poland they have usually attended university courses not only on grammar and literature but also on teaching pedagogy, psychology, Second Language Acquisition (SLA) theories, discourse analysis, conversation analysis, psycholinguistics, sociolinguistics, translation theory and corpus linguistics. In their eyes, language is a means of communication in social context, a tool to fulfil several functions, defined, among others, by grammar, lexis, pragmatics, discourse and semantics (Komorowska 2005). They will use a wide array of teaching tools to engage their students. Within the communicative approach, their role is to facilitate students' self-expression.

Conversely, Polish teachers of Latin are likely to have received an education based on a curriculum which has not changed much since the nineteenth century. The focus of their studies is usually grammar analysis, literature study and ancient culture. The pedagogical courses specifically designed for ancient language teachers are very limited – if present at all. The most recent handbook of Latin language pedagogy on the Polish market is forty years old (Ostrowski 1981). Graduates will usually have little knowledge of modern linguistics or translation theory, and usually no knowledge of second-language development theories whatsoever. They will often see language through the lens of nineteenth-century philologists, for whom language is lexis (codified in a dictionary) and a set of grammar rules codified in a prescriptive grammar book (cf. Richards and Rodgers 2001; Stern 1983). They may perceive Latin and Ancient Greek as dead languages embodied in texts that are only to be translated. The other unusual aspect of a classical language syllabus is its focus on literary texts, which are almost completely absent from modern languages syllabi in early years. Any attempts to communicate in ancient languages and create new texts may seem to many GT teachers to be eccentric, if not ridiculous (for instance, the attempts to change the perception of Latin as a dead language were described by the Americans Ball and Ellsworth (1997) as a 'bizarre idea').

Our proposal

Studying ancient languages takes a totally different shape in the summer schools, from the point of view of students and teachers alike. All the participants are well motivated and have some interest in ancient culture. They have about forty formal lessons in one course, but if they progress from *Tirones* to *Veterani*, the time will amount to 240 hours; however, the total time will include also additional optional activities outside class and the chance to adopt ancient languages as a means of everyday conversation in every hour of the two-week event. Even though grammar is taught in classes (through the medium of Latin), equal or greater attention is devoted to mastering vocabulary and pronunciation. The students read and discuss texts in Latin, but also speak, write and listen to the language. Most lessons are conducted entirely in Latin or Ancient Greek respectively. Moreover, many classes involve communicative games. In fact, such classes are similar to modern language classes in state-run schools. An important contrast with modern languages is the focus on Latin and Ancient Greek literature from early in the course, as opposed to discussing practical details of everyday life. For example, the teacher will not practise buying a train ticket in Latin; she will, instead, engage students in a role-play concerning ancient sea travel, which is a reality that can be actually found in original Latin texts. The idea is to prepare students to read independently without dictionaries and grammar books, and to develop a community of people willing to read literature and discuss it in its original tongues.

Conclusions

Several scholars (Herman 2016, Malinowski 2016, Czetwertyńska 2014) regret that we live in the days when knowledge of Latin is diminishing with every passing day. Since the end of the Second World War, its importance has been drastically reduced. That Latin was an official language of the Kingdom of Poland, that a great wealth of texts in Latin were written by the citizens of our country (and a vast majority of them have not yet been translated), that quotes, paraphrases and allusions to ancient literature have been present in Polish literature since the Middle Ages until the present day, that elements of ancient culture are to be found in virtually all areas of Polish and European art, not to mention its role in law, medicine, the Catholic church, or science – awareness of these facts is fading away. With such a small number of students having any form of contact with Latin in schools, it is unlikely that the situation will improve in the near future.

However, we do hope that our informal and communicative ways of studying Latin and Ancient Greek at the *Schola Aestiva* as well as training new Latin-speaking teachers at the University of Wrocław may rekindle the interest of Polish students and others who join us. We present the ancient languages in an attractive form with a focus on the student and his or her practical skills. If these students enjoy being taught with communicative approaches and demand changes in their state-run schools and in the government guidelines, it can be hoped that Latin and Ancient Greek will return from the shadows back to schools and the society, and provide a broader variety of students with the opportunity to come into contact with ancient culture and thereby understand aspects of their own culture more deeply and from a wider perspective. In this way the study of ancient languages and cultures could be enlivened by – and in fact be kept alive by – the seeds of innovation sown in Poznań and in Wrocław.

Postscript

The final version of this paper was prepared during the Covid-19 pandemic. The amount of high-quality online materials produced amid this difficult time by the international Latin-speaking community is overwhelming. The fact that you can now simultaneously follow several dozen independent courses and podcasts about Latin language and literature – in Latin! – without even leaving your bedroom corroborates our hope that the next Renaissance has actually already begun. This is, however, a topic for another chapter and book.

CHAPTER 17
STUDENT-LED INITIATIVES AT OXFORD AND CAMBRIDGE
Iván Parga Ornelas and Josey Parker

The Oxford Latinitas Project (Iván Parga Ornelas)

The Oxford Latinitas Project (OLP) was formed by a group of students from the University of Oxford and other British universities in collaboration with members and former students of the *Accademia Vivarium Novum*. The approach to ancient languages and literature of the *Vivarium Novum*, which combines an active and effective language-learning methodology with a rigorous study of the classical authors, was an inspiration for students who are now part of the society. The realization, moreover, that such an approach could be implemented with great advantage in the environment of the British universities, led to the creation of the OLP.

I believe that Classics faculties all over the world could benefit from the active use of ancient languages, mainly because this style of learning provides an accelerated way to approach the classical texts, learning the grammatical rules from original authors while simultaneously practising and memorizing them through active use, thus reducing the amount of time that needs to be spent in pure grammatical study (Miraglia 2009: 64–74). It has been argued that this may prove a more enjoyable experience for students than traditional passive learning methods (Letts 2019) – and indeed my own personal experience bears this out. Furthermore, members of our society claim that achieving fluency in spoken Latin not only leads to fluency in reading Latin, but also helps us to understand certain nuances and subtleties of the language with greater precision. Lastly, the habit of speaking Latin, of reading and understanding a text without the need to translate it in our heads, of writing in Latin trying to imitate the style and prosody of ancient writers, of thinking and living, so to speak, in Latin, seems to be a powerful tool to better understand the texts and authors that occupy us as scholars.

We also take inspiration, in certain respects, from the classicists of the Renaissance. Our society aims to be modelled after the *cenacula* of the humanists, such as the one formed by Erasmus of Rotterdam, Thomas More and John Colet. Indeed, they often gathered in Oxford and joined innovative philosophical and philological investigations with a sincere interest in the formation of the well-rounded human being through literature, liberal arts, and through an engagement with the questions raised and explored in times and places very different from our own (Hogrefe 1959; Seebohm 1867). Another principle we take from such humanistic circles is the concept of the res publica litterarum, a commonwealth of knowledge and culture that joins together people from different parts of the globe and from different historical moments through their shared possession of these invisible goods. We have found that having Latin as a common language — which is not the first language of any individual — naturally diversifies our membership. Since its foundation in 2017, for instance, committee members have come from Italy, the UK, Saudi Arabia, the United States, Mexico, the Czech Republic, Russia, India and Latvia. There is also great diversity in the areas of study of our members, who come from various areas of the humanities, and also from scientific disciplines such as mathematics, chemistry and physics.

At the core of our society are its weekly activities that range from Latin and Greek language classes for beginners through to seminars where students aim to read and analyse entire works of ancient literature. These sessions, held mostly in Oxford colleges but independent from the university curriculum, are open to anyone interested and not only to students of the university.

They take place once a week and attendees are divided into two or three groups with different levels of proficiency. The most important aspect of these sessions is that they are conducted entirely in Latin. This may sound unfeasible in a group of complete beginners, but it is not impossible if the moderators stick to the most basic elements in the first sessions and save the more complicated explanations for later (Miraglia 2009: 95–6). In my personal case, I started learning Latin at the *Accademia Vivarium Novum* – without any previous knowledge of Latin – with a Czech teacher who did not know one word of my native language, and with whom, to this date, I have never spoken a word in any other language than Latin. The session may start with the instructor looking directly to one student and saying '*salve!*' ('Hello!') while waving her hand, then turning to the rest of the group and saying '*salvete!*' ('Hello!' – plural form). She may add '*quo modo te habes?* bene' ('How are you today? fine?') – while smiling and giving a thumbs up – or '*an male?*' ('Or bad?') – while frowning and giving a thumbs down. Most students will understand everything that has been said, and additionally, they may start to lose the dread and awe that 'dead languages' tend to inspire. The book that we use both in the Oxford project and the *Academia, Lingua Latina per se Illustrata* by Ørberg, (2018) facilitates this task by offering a text entirely in Latin that begins with sentences that can be easily understood by inference – like '*Roma in Italia est*' ('Rome is in Italy') – and gradually increases in complexity, but never uses modern languages for explanations or definitions. Comprehension is aided by maps and pictures labelled in Latin (Miraglia 2009: 47–57).

Another practice that distinguishes our Oxford Project sessions, and which makes exercises like the one briefly outlined above much easier, is that they are conducted simultaneously by two instructors. This facilitates the work by allowing the leaders to support each other and ensures that the lesson runs smoothly. For instance, while one of the instructors explains a grammatical rule (in Latin), the other may write the paradigm on the board; or while one explains the passage that is being read (again always in Latin), the other may write up the new vocabulary or certain figures of speech worth analyzing in more detail. We have found that sessions work better when there is a good rapport between the two instructors: this may lead to improvised conversations or jokes, which helps to create a relaxed learning environment, and we have found that comical or unexpected situation help the concepts being learned to be fixed in the memory of the student (Banas *et al*. 2011: 132–4; Miraglia 2009: 116–17).

Among the most important activities of the OLP are the sessions called '*lumen litterarum*'. These are attended by students who already have a good grasp of the language but wish to work on their fluency in speaking and reading, or by others, including faculty members (who have now started to join the original student group), who simply wish to read classical texts and discuss them in Latin. These sessions are led by a member of the Project who chooses the text, introduces its context if necessary, clarifies difficult passages and moderates the discussion, all of which is done in Latin, unless a specific piece of information needs clarification in English. The attendees are encouraged to participate as much as possible in the discussion. To this end, the moderator may ask someone to paraphrase a passage or explain it in his own words. She or he may also propose more engaging questions (again all questions and answers are in Latin): What are the opinions and ideas implicit or explicit in the text? What do these ideas tell us about the culture in which they were produced? Are they relevant for our time, or how may they be adapted in order to be useful to the modern reader? Another goal of these sessions is to offer a wider perspective of Latin literature than is provided in most courses. We do this by treating authors from different periods. Apart from selections of classical authors like Cicero and Ovid, we have read late antique writers like Boethius or Venantius Fortunatus, medieval authors like Hildegard of Bingen, Othlo of Sankt Emmeram or the Correspondence between Héloïse and Abelard, or Renaissance and early modern writers like Petrarch, Laura Cereta or Erasmus of Rotterdam. In addition to *'lumen litterarum'* sessions, we always hold one or more reading groups, in which the participants read one entire work of Latin or Greek literature and discuss it in the language of the text. These sessions do not have a moderator; instead all participants rely on each other to progress through the work. One of the goals of these sessions is to read the original texts and not critical scholarly material or translations. The most popular of these are the *'lectiones Vergilianae'*, or Vergilian readings, weekly term-time sessions which aim to read the entire Aeneid.

Apart from our weekly activities, we organize regular events that make our activities and methods accessible by the wider community. At least once a term we host a *'dies Latinus'*, a study day devoted to readings from various authors, discussion, rhetorical exercises and singing Latin poems. We start the day with words of welcome in Latin and English, and the rest of the day is conducted in Latin. The students are divided into small groups, which allows the moderators to pay attention to each one of the participants and encourage them all to take part and speak Latin. The first session is dedicated to conversational Latin. This is followed by one or two reading sessions, and we close the day by gathering all the participants to sing and read classical and medieval poetry. Singing Latin poetry, like the rest of the activities, has a didactic goal, which is for the metre of the poem to be expressed through the rhythm of the music and not simply by scansion. We also find that the music makes the poem and its metre more easily memorized.

These study days provide an experience of different ways and levels on which a communicative approach to Latin may be put into practice. They also serve the important purpose of renewing the friendship and relationship with students, professors and teachers, who attend this event from universities and schools within the UK and from other parts of the world.

The *'septimana Latina'* or 'Latin week' is the major annual event organized by the OLP, a one-week programme of Latin full-immersion at the *Accademia Vivarium Novum* in Rome, in which forty students and teachers from different British universities are able to experience the benefits of spending an entire week speaking, reading and writing only in Latin. The programme consists of conversational Latin sessions, *'lumen litterarum'* (see above), poetry and prose composition, and rhetoric classes. We also organize a trip to the ancient city of Tusculum, a place mentioned frequently in *Lingua Latina per se Illustrata*. This lies just a short walk from the campus of the Academy. We also visit one other archaeological site such as the Roman Forum, Ostia or the Villa Hadriana. These trips are not only for leisure, but they provide an important occasion to learn directly from the classical authors about aspects of Roman life in the locations in which they lived, or simply to read important or beautiful passages of Latin literature in fitting places. The tour of the sites is conducted in Latin, and we read extracts from classical authors in relevant spots. For instance, in the sepulchral monuments outside of Ostia we read Catullus's elegy to his dead brother (Catull. 101). In the *thermae* (baths) we read extracts from Seneca's letter 56, where he complains about the fact that he lives too close to the Roman baths, and then vividly describes the activities that went on in there. In the Villa Hadriana we read and sing the beautiful composition that the emperor Hadrian himself wrote to his own dying soul (*Hist. Aug., Had.* 25,9). This is a practice inspired by the *Accademia Vivarium Novum* who have been conducting such trips for several years.

Participants of the '*septimana Latina*' have expressed very favourable opinions about it. Dr Melinda Letts, tutor in ancient languages at Jesus College, Oxford said: 'Ideally every Latin student should do a *septimana Latina*, worth many weeks of traditional teaching. The human contacts were great, and I was struck by the strong sense of community.' A Classics postgraduate student commented: 'The week at the *Accademia* provided me not only with an excellent opportunity to improve my Latin, but also made me realize the value and joy of the humanities. *Vivarium* seems to be as concerned with teaching the students wisdom as with teaching the language.' Likewise a chemistry undergraduate student from Oxford wrote that the Septimana provided: 'A wonderful opportunity that allowed me (an undergraduate in science) to progress with my Latin, find new friends, and to develop my understanding of the world – of the ancient and modern worlds, and the world that is within called the soul' (*Testimonies*, 2018–19).

Beyond these scholarly activities, the OLP retains the spirit of its origins as a circle of friends and a community of scholars who share the persuasion that literature and the arts may help us to better understand ourselves and our world. For this reason, our informal gatherings to discuss any aspect of our studies, to read together a text and help each other understand it better, or our supper parties, where there is always a bit of poetry and discussion on classical studies, are as important as any of our more formal sessions.

All our activities require that the leading members of the Project are fluent in Latin. Finding enough people who have the ability to conduct a lesson, explain a text or moderate a discussion entirely in Latin, who share with us the persuasions that drive us, and are willing to spend a great amount of time into fostering our initiative without financial reward, is one of the greatest challenges in establishing a student association such as ours. We were lucky enough to have a good number of fluent Latinists to start our activities, but most of the leaders and instructors in the following years started as students in our classes. This is a great joy, for it demonstrates at the same time the success of our classes and assures us that the Project can persist even if the founding members cannot always be involved. Moreover, we have also been fortunate to have a wide network of friends in sister organizations around the world. We advise that activities such as ours are always conducted in conjunction with other organizations already established.

Our next step is to demonstrate the value of implementing the communicative approach in the formal teaching of universities themselves. The potential rewards to scholarship are considerable: the speed with which students can develop their skills in grammar, syntax and vocabulary, and the enhanced ability to interrogate the works of ancient authors that ensues, together constitute a powerful foundation for excellence (Letts 2019). The success and growth of our project demonstrates not just the hunger that exists for fluency in reading ancient languages but also the benefits which that fluency offers to excellence in research and scholarship.

Circulus Latinus Cantabrigiensis (Josey Parker)

The *Circulus Latinus Cantabrigiensis* (CLC) was founded in October of 2017 in a small pub in Cambridge called The Mill. A group of three students, who had attended the *Accademia Vivarium Novum*'s summer Latin immersion programme together in 2016, reconnected in Cambridge to found a small reading group to practise speaking Latin together. Our experience at the *Accademia* demonstrated the impact which two months of language immersion can provide for fluency, which we wished to continue to develop by meeting on a regular basis. Initially, the group gathered weekly to chat and discuss short texts in Latin. After meeting for one term, however, and seeing the progress which the Oxford Latinitas Project (OLP) had made at establishing a larger spoken Latin society within their university, our group decided to formally found the society, associate it with the university, and apply for Arts and Humanities Research Council funding. In early January, the newly created *Circulus* sent out emails to the Classics, History and English Faculties at Cambridge, inviting anyone with an interest in spoken Latin to an initial taster session.

With the help of a research fellow at Peterhouse, Cambridge, who had spent six months at the *Accademia Vivarium Novum*, we planned to run two parallel classes using the textbook *Lingua Latina Per Se Illustrata* by Ørberg. One class would cater for Classicists and those already adept at reading and writing Latin (*peritiores*), the other to novices (*tirones*). The response to the initial invitation emails was overwhelming. We had initially booked a room in the History Faculty anticipating twenty people attending, but over forty undergraduate and graduate students arrived for the first sessions, forcing the *Circulus* to expand into the room next door. However, after a few meetings, we quickly realized that our society had many key differences from the OLP which forced us to rethink the content and structure of our sessions. First, our more advanced members, though passionate about spoken Latin, were less experienced with speaking Latin than many of those in Oxford who had attended the year-long Latin immersion programme at the *Accademia Vivarium Novum* and other such institutions. Second, most of the students who attended our sessions were classicists or historians who could already read Latin at an advanced level, meaning that the *Lingua Latina* curriculum was too basic for most of us. Third, organizing our society like a class allowed for less participation by individual members and therefore less actual experience speaking and discussing texts in Latin, which was what most of our members wanted.

In the Michaelmas term of 2018, our committee decided to radically re-organize the *Circulus*. Instead of providing classes as the OLP did, we structured our meetings as reading groups, led by different individuals each week, either students from within the *Circulus Cantabrigiensis* or guests from other universities. For the past year, the *Circulus* meetings have been structured as follows: the leader (*dux*) of the week chooses a text, usually with which the leader has a personal research interest, and guides the group through the text in Latin. Seated in a circle, each person reads a sentence or two, rephrasing the Latin with some help from the leader if necessary. This practice not only allows us to become more familiar with Latin as a language to be spoken and heard aloud, but also to adjust to actively using the language to construct new sentences. Afterwards, the leader might introduce questions about the text for discussion or present a game or exercise to practise spoken Latin. This format has allowed the *Circulus* to share leadership and responsibility while engaging members with new and interesting Latin texts, such as Bartolomeo Platina's fifteenth-century Latin cookbook *De honesta voluptate*, the anonymous fourth-century *Historia Augusta*, and faux textual criticism by 'Martinus Scriblerus' (the pseudonym of Alexander Pope and Johnathan Swift), as well as classical authors like Seneca, Cicero and Catullus. The shared responsibility of the *Circulus* has also created an encouraging and forgiving environment in which members can speak without fear of judgment for their mistakes. Although our lack of experienced leaders has presented a major challenge for the *Circulus*, reorganizing our sessions as member-led discussion groups has been a promising solution.

The goal of the Circulus Latinus Cantabrigiensis continues to be the cultivation of fluency in reading, writing and speaking Latin. We attendees believe that the familiarity with Latin that we develop through speech gives us the ability to better understand Latin texts, whether they be classical, medieval or Neo-Latin. We look to the example of the ancients themselves, as well as modern language learners, who have developed fluency not by reading, writing, and translation alone, but also by speaking. By discussing our experiences of Latin learning together we have found that those of us who have learned Latin in whole or part by immersion often share the belief that communicative methodology helps us to read and understand texts without the need for translation, allowing us to approach Latin in a mindset closer to that of the ancient reader, eliminating the need for English as an intermediary language. The ultimate goal of the Circulus is not eloquence in oratory, but facility in reading, as we believe that the value and beauty of Latin is primarily found in the wisdom, eloquence, and truth contained in texts written over millennia in Latin. Through Latin we can approach Cicero, Augustine, Erasmus, and so many other great minds on their own terms; it unlocks a world of writing which has shaped and moulded much of modern civilisation and from which there is still much to learn. Cambridge has long been associated with new communicative approaches for learning Latin, beginning with Rouse's work to advocate the use of the Direct Method of teaching Latin and Greek at the Perse School in the first half of the twentieth century (Stray 1992). The Circulus hopes to reclaim this association by providing a space where spoken Latin and the humanities more broadly conceived can flourish within the University of Cambridge.

Many of our current members had never tried speaking Latin before coming to the *Circulus*. Undergraduate Classicist Joe Ross-Biddles writes that he has found attending meetings while at university to be a truly transformative experience:

> I first heard about the *Circulus Latinus Cantabrigiensis* before I ever arrived at university, and knew immediately that I had to join it. Having attended regularly ever since my first meeting, I can say that its effect on my capability in Latin has been profound: it is difficult to get a true feeling for how a language works without ever using it, and the *Circulus* offers excellent opportunities to experience spoken Latin both for beginners and for those with extensive prior knowledge of the language. In composing Latin, particularly in composing verse, I depend heavily on the experience of speaking Latin, which also contributes greatly to the ability to sight-read and fluently translate the language. The value of the insight into Latin that spoken Latin provides cannot be overstated. I have had the privilege of learning to speak Latin conversationally with many very talented people from whom I've learned a great deal.

Max Hardy, a third-year undergraduate reading Classics, and vice-president of the *Circulus* from 2019 to 2020, was also introduced to spoken Latin through the *CLC*:

Joining the *CLC* in my first year was a daunting and exciting decision – I had not ever spoken Latin before! I swiftly found it to be a fun and engaging way of practising a language that I had otherwise only used in writing. Speaking Latin has been a useful pastime: it has given me a firmer grasp on grammar and syntax, and conversation about everyday affairs has raised me a rich stock of rare vocabulary. The *CLC* is a brilliant institution for its own reasons too. Our invited lectures and social events have introduced me to all kinds of fellow enthusiasts, and our member-led discussion groups have acquainted me with a dazzling variety of texts and authors, such as I might never have discovered otherwise.

Various guests from other universities, such as Dr Jason Harris from University College Cork and Dr Christian Laes from the University of Manchester, have given longer, more formal lectures at *Circulus* meetings on topics such as the language of kissing in Catullus and current disagreement about methodology among modern Latin speakers. These lectures have attracted novices who were interested in each of their topics and listening to an extended academic talk in Latin, while also allowing regular members a chance to engage with more fluent Latin speakers. Dr David Butterfield from the University of Cambridge has also given two talks for the *Circulus* on prose and verse composition at Cambridge, and has become the faculty sponsor for the *Circulus* as of March 2019. Though the society continues to be student-led, having a member of the Classics faculty who is enthusiastic about spoken Latin has proved a valuable asset for the *Circulus*; we now are able to book rooms within the Classics faculty and advertise more easily. Additionally, in coming years, after the current committee has graduated, some degree of continuity will be ensured for the *Circulus*, which is key for the continued success of the society.

In 2019, we have tried to increase our number of meetings and events each week. In addition to our regular Wednesday afternoon meetings, we have created a breakfast and verse composition group which meets on Thursday mornings. This new group gathers to compose hexameter and elegiac poetry in Latin, both original compositions and translation from various English sources, ranging from nursery rhymes to spam emails. While this group has remained small, it has attracted a few students who had not previously attended *Circulus* events and who were perhaps more motivated to attend because of their interest in composition rather than conversation. As well as these regular groups, we have organized a few socials throughout the term, pub nights (*Tabernae Latinae*) and a formal dinner (*Cena Latina*), to encourage casual Latin conversation in a more relaxed setting. These social events usually attracted larger numbers than our weekly reading groups, due in part to an increased amount of advertising and in part to the more social nature of these gatherings.

Many challenges still remain for our *Circulus* to overcome. Our biggest concern is how to attract and retain new members, specifically those who are completely new to spoken Latin. Novices often find complete immersion somewhat overwhelming, especially since the level of participation within our society is particularly high; during our meetings, one is expected to actively engage with texts in Latin, which, for beginners, can be daunting. Given that our meetings are designed for those with a firm grasp of Latin grammar and vocabulary, accommodating those who haven't studied Latin before university has been a challenge and has resulted in a few students attending once or twice before deciding that the level at which our group operates was too advanced. It is exceedingly difficult to strike a balance between engaging advanced speakers and accommodating beginners, since splitting into two separate groups is logistically unfeasible at the present date. We hope in the future to find a way to accommodate beginners as well as more advanced Latinists.

Another challenge we are currently facing is replacing administrative leadership within the *Circulus*. Most of our current organizers are set to graduate in a year's time, which will create a vacuum for the society. In light of this, gaining and engaging new members who can take over when the time comes is of vital importance for the continued life of the society. We are hopeful that the enthusiasm of Dr Butterfield as well as other, younger members of the *Circulus* will allow it to flourish for years to come.

Today, many people study Latin and Greek for years and yet, when the opportunity arises, struggle to hold a simple conversation in the languages and to read any extended text without painstakingly slow translation (see Carr 1930 as an example of the long-standing nature of this problem). There is a true need for a dramatic shift in methodology. This shift, however, need not only be driven by teachers. Collaboration between students can lead to societies like those which have been established at Oxford and Cambridge. Although establishing a society which promotes communicative approaches to Latin and Greek is not without some difficulty, students can drive change just as much as staff, and in some cases, even more so. We hope that the examples which have been set at Oxford and Cambridge will lead other students at universities around the world to create societies which breathe new life into ancient languages, which foster collaboration and serious scholarship, which cause the worldwide community of Classicists to take notice.

PART 4
VARIED APPROACHES IN UNUSUAL SETTINGS

CHAPTER 18
NEW APPROACHES TO ANCIENT LANGUAGES: THE PAIDEIA INSTITUTE'S PEDAGOGY
Marco Romani Mistretta and Jason Pedicone

Introduction

This chapter describes the Paideia Institute's 'Living Latin' method, a holistic approach to ancient language teaching that blends innovative communicative approaches with both new technologies and time-honored teaching methods.

For its language courses, the Paideia Institute draws upon a diverse and variegated pool of instructors, each with their own teaching style and methods. Thus, while it seems hard to talk about a specific 'Paideia method', this article will focus on a number of communicative approaches used by Paideia instructors, and the way in which such pedagogical approaches may benefit from being combined with reading-based practices.

Telepaideia: communicative approaches and new technologies

The opportunity of learning Latin communicatively has been more accessible than ever with the advent of audio-visual communication via the Internet. In 2016, the Paideia Institute saw the potential of applying the new technologies to ancient language pedagogy and developed *Telepaideia*, a suite of language courses taught through online communication platforms (such as Google Meet). As Lloyd's (2017) experience shows, *Telepaideia* played a pioneering role in promoting communicative approaches to Latin teaching through technology.

Telepaideia courses comprise up to three one-hour sessions per week, taught over a period of one or two semesters. Despite being held entirely online, all *Telepaideia* classes are taught in small groups, usually capped at five students. This is because Paideia instructors believe that smaller sections facilitate learning through a 'tutoring' relationship, which brings students and teachers closer to each other despite the obvious online physical distance (see, for example, Walden 2019).

Intensive Latin classes are among *Telepaideia*'s most popular courses. These classes are designed to prepare beginners to read original Latin texts at an intermediate level through spoken Latin techniques. Instructors typically start by teaching Latin greetings and basic conversational phrases, such as *salve, quid agis?* (Hello! How are you?), then gradually move towards on-the-spot English-to-Latin translation, such as *quomodo dicitur Latine . . . ?* (How do you say in Latin . . . ?) before starting to communicate directly in Latin with students. In-class exercises also feature Latin dictation, story time in Latin, and explicating Latin texts in simpler Latin, an activity which has been particularly well received by students. Sometimes, Total Physical Response-style 'Latin charades' are played: a student (or the instructor) acts out the action described by a Latin verb in front of the video camera, while other students are asked to guess what the verb is from the actions. The *Telepaideia* experiment has shown to us that limiting the use of technology to the traditional teaching and learning of grammar and vocabulary, as has often been done in the past (see, for example, Daugherty 1998; Latousek 1998; Goodhew 2003; White 2015; Chadwick 2019), is a missed opportunity, and that communicative approaches can thrive when combined with online teaching.

In what follows, we shall outline the Paideia Institute's use of communicative approaches in physical classes as well, with a brief illustration of the Paideia approach's roots in Reginald Foster's Latin pedagogy.

Fostering a Living Latin approach

Father Reginald Foster, the Vatican Latinist who famously taught a summer Latin programme in Rome for over twenty years, was known for speaking Latin. To us, he is no doubt one of the best Latin speakers alive. However, anyone who walked into his classroom would find it very different to Latin classes which used communicative approaches today. Foster almost never spoke Latin extemporaneously. Instead, his spoken Latin group resembled an on-the-fly prose composition class. Students would translate headlines from the Italian newspaper *Corriere della Sera* into Latin, or Foster would make up English sentences based on some funny anecdote or recent event in the news for them to translate into the target language. While Foster – unlike many of today's Latin educators – never operated with a fully fledged theory of second language acquisition, his pedagogical tenets are made crystal clear not just by his teaching practices, but also by his published work. In 2014, he was asked to offer 'A Comment on Speaking Latin', in which he outlined the two main principles underlying his approach to Latin pedagogy. Here is an important excerpt from that piece:

1) In order to speak, converse in any kind of Latin, one simply has need of very much, long practice of some living Latin language – just as foreigners for a certain period of time in a new country's language – such active Latin is found in numberless examples from the past 2,400 years just waiting to be imitated, absorbed, personalized.

2) In order to understand, comprehend accurately any real Latin literature of any past or present age – in oratory or poetry, in treatises or correspondence – one simply has need of very much, abundant knowledge of the concrete language and its infinite subtleties throughout the centuries.

Foster, 2014

In his decades-long teaching activity, Foster has paid tribute to these principles by introducing his students not only to the language and literature of Roman antiquity, but also to the Latin of authors like Hrosvitha, Aquinas, Erasmus, Galileo, Descartes, Newton, Linné and Pascoli. The fact that Latin ceased to be a 'natural' language after antiquity does not imply, according to Foster, that it also ceased to be a 'living' or communicative language. On the contrary, the breadth of medieval, early modern and modern Latin literature shows, in his view, that Latin continued historically to be a language of (learned) communication long after antiquity, and that there is a virtually inexhaustible kaleidoscope of styles to choose from when it comes to introducing students to the nuances of Latin prose, poetry and conversation. It is particularly significant that, in our excerpt, Foster mentions '*some* living Latin language' (emphasis added): according to him, Living Latin is by no means a monolith equated with a single, univocal understanding of the language – such as, say, 'classical' Latin or 'church' Latin. Rather, Foster's notion of Living Latin challenges old-fashioned views and provocatively puts the works of Cicero and Virgil on equal footing with the writings of Héloïse and Linacre, insofar as their pedagogical value in familiarizing students with Latin communication is concerned.

In Foster's summer course, Latin conversation took place in the context of informal, optional gatherings 'under the trees' (*sub arboribus*) in the garden of his monastery. He encouraged memorization and dramatic performance: in fact, he would pay students 20,000 lire to recite a passage of Livy or a few lines of Ovid in front of the class. Students also sang Gregorian hymns, and re-read Latin passages they had just translated together. In other words, Foster brought Latin to life while not using a 'communicative' approach in the modern sense. However, in what follows, we shall show how Paideia's teaching method incorporates communicative approaches while ultimately staying true to Foster's pedagogical legacy.

Paideia's flagship course: *Living Latin in Rome*

The Paideia Institute's pedagogical approach is largely derived from the way Foster taught Latin. Similar to Foster's summer Latin experience (*Aestiva Romae Latinitas*), Paideia's *Living Latin in Rome* programme incorporates both active Latin communication and more traditional philological activities in a very particular kind of communicative approach.

In the Paideia classroom, Latin comes alive through being spoken. Teachers and students cultivate Latin as an active language of conversation. During *Living Latin in Rome*, many of the sessions are conducted almost entirely in Latin. By activating Latin in this way, we believe students are enabled to read more fluently and to comprehend texts more meaningfully. Depending on the instructor's assessment of what is best for each particular group of students, many traditional tasks are often carried out in the target language: grammar instruction might be delivered entirely in Latin, or translation activities can be from one version of Latin to another, helping to practise synonyms or alternative constructions (see for example, Hunt *et al.* 2018). But one thing remains paramount: rather than having students read textbooks or other material explicitly designed for instruction, the primary focus of the Paideia classroom, like Foster's classroom, is direct encounter with original texts.

On the other side of the spectrum, *Living Latin* in Rome importantly features full-immersion experiences, in which students must communicate only in Latin for a set period of time. Some of those experiences follow an explicit lesson plan designed to improve fluency on targeted topics. These include the Foster-inspired *sub arboribus* sessions, which meet in the courtyard of the Vincentian monastery-turned-study-abroad-centre where the programme takes place. In these conversation sessions, teachers often incorporate Latin games designed as an enjoyable practice of active Latin. Students might play *quis sum?* (Who am I? or Twenty Questions), a game in which each player asks the others a number of questions in Latin to guess the identity of a mystery figure from Roman history. For instance, one student realized that her mystery figure was 'Agrippina' when she received an affirmative answer to the question: '*sumne mater Neronis?*'. This particular activity can also be performed in a 'flipped' variant, whereby one student chooses a well-known figure from antiquity to impersonate and talks about their own *res gestae* (accomplishments) in

Latin, while other students have to guess who the historical figure is. Similar games include *Latin Speed Dating* (completing two-minute conversations with each other to practise greetings and introductions), and *vinco* (Bingo) to practise numbers. There are also specific occasions reserved for free Latin conversation. At least once a week students participate in a *Cena Latina* (Latin Meal), where all conversation is in Latin. Here students do most of the talking, but instructors are present to model linguistic constructions and assist with vocabulary. Immersion experiences also take place with visits to archaeological sites. For instance, when our group visits Pompeii, everyone pledges to speak *tantum Latine* (only Latin) from the time we cross the threshold of the site into the ancient ruins. Speaking Latin on location literally seems to bring the past to life, and provides students with an unforgettable experience. We use the word 'experience' advisedly. This was a term that Foster used for all of his classes. For us it points to a larger pedagogical principle: we want to create learning situations which will remain memorable for students, which they can describe not only as classes but *experiences*. Speaking Latin in Pompeii is an *experience*. One of the ways such experiences are created in Paideia's course is through a technique playfully dubbed *Loci in Locis* (Passages in their Places), where students encounter texts in the actual locations that the texts are describing, and communicate with one another in the language in the very places were that language was used by native speakers for centuries. Rome is the course's classroom. The curriculum explores connections between the Latin language and physical spaces in and around Rome. Students do this both by using Latin to communicate on site (and *about* the site) and by preparing for site visits with extended Latin readings in classroom sessions. Visiting the physical spaces deepens their experiences of texts, while using the language communicatively allows them to connect more meaningfully with the locations and archaeological monuments they visit. As they read and speak Latin, they examine whose voices are heard and what perspectives may be obscured. As they explore the many physical layers of Rome, they always engage with the many layers of interpretation, reception, and re-invention that the city, its monuments and its people have undergone. For example, when they visit the Palatine Hill, they sit in the section of the Frangipani Gardens not far from where Augustus' house stood, and there they read the section of Suetonius' *Twelve Caesars* that describes Augustus' breakfast routine. Students also read and recite the *Odes* of Horace in the Auditorium of Maecenas. During our trip to Naples, they read Pliny's letter about the eruption of Vesuvius while on the edge of the crater of the mountain itself! Even though Paideia's reading methodology is largely based on a grammar-translation model, the inspirational effect of sitting in the very place described in the text that the students are reading brings antiquity to life. In fact, the effect is often so overwhelming that there is usually at least one student who is having the best day of their life on any given day of the programme. 'I've dreamed about doing this ever since I was in fifth grade,' said one young woman as we walked down the Via Appia reading Seneca's *De Brevitate Vitae*. 'I never really had any emotional reaction to Aquinas until today,' another student said after reading an eyewitness account of his death in the room where it happened. 'Now I want to read everything he wrote.' When the class visits the Colosseum, students are divided into two groups for a debate exercise in Latin. Based on the ancient literary sources they have read on gladiatorial games, one group is asked to argue (*tantum Latine*) in favour of *ludi gladiatorii* (gladiatorial games) while the other group argues against them. The debate typically benefits from rhetorical practice carried out during the *sub arboribus* sessions, which often feature *progymnasmata*: exercises in various different genres of Latin oratory. After the course, one student reported, 'I feel like I improved greatly in my spoken Latin ability.'

The programme also features extensive memorization and recitation of original Latin texts, and combines both with the *Loci in Locis* principle. Memorization, however, is never understood as an end in and of itself, but as a means towards performance. Theatrical performance, in turn, is viewed as both a form of communication and a way of internalizing texts and taking ownership of them. In the first week of the programme, students memorize and act out a scene from Plautus' *Pseudolus*. But to make it a truly memorable experience, they perform it in the ancient theater at Ostia. Similar events within our programme take advantage of the backdrop of the city of Rome. In the final week, our group divides Cicero's *Third Catilinarian* into thirty segments, each of which is assigned to one student. The group then heads to the steps of the Temple of Concord in the northwestern corner of the Roman Forum, where Cicero gave that speech. The students stand in a circle and each of them comes into the middle to recite his or her portion of the speech. In the end, the entire oration is recited *in toto* in the very place where Cicero delivered it over two millennia ago. Students are thereby enabled to follow the story in Latin, but the event also has the quality of a ritual of sorts, with each student embodying a different version of Cicero on the dais.

While some students dread the task of memorization, it often empowers those whose conversational Latin may not be as strong: one year we had a student who was facing the challenge of a summer immersed in Latin, English and Italian – three foreign languages for her. But when she stood up there in the Roman Forum, you could sense how completely she had come to inhabit the role of the ancient orator. For some of the students, when they deliver their part of the speech, Cicero is portrayed as being pompous and overstated; for others he is wry and sarcastic; for yet others he is dignified and noble. Some have Cicero shout into the crowd; others let him go slowly, making the audience hang on the periodic sentence structure. But they all seem to learn one thing: oratory is meant to be experienced aloud. It is just as important to recite rhetoric as it is important that drama be staged. In our view, text memorization helps students build language skills towards developing a genuinely communicative approach by ensuring that they have a reservoir of beautifully constructed Latin to draw on when communicating amongst themselves or with their instructor. Through theatrical performance, they rehearse self-expression by delivering what they have memorized while placing themselves in the position of the author or character whose words they are reciting and by focusing on conveying their meaning with real expression.

Alongside the Ciceronian recitation, there are many other such experiences: at Cumae, students are given Latin prophecies written in hexameters in fragmentary form, which they have to put back together using their knowledge of the metre. As one student observed at the end of the course: 'The programme allowed me to maintain my Latin skills over the summer from the combination of classes, site visits, and *ludi*. I felt comfortable and even confident in my spoken Latin abilities for the first time in my years of studying the language. This program has been an invaluable experience for me with unbelievable sights and unforgettable people.'

Conclusion

In sum, Paideia's Latin courses are designed to reach a balance between communication-based and philological models. This holistic approach is augmented by an imaginative approach which always asks, 'How can we make this not only a reading or recitation, but an *experience* that students can talk about decades later?' In this we believe that we are not only offering our students a chance to gain knowledge but a chance to experience true *studium* (learning) – the zeal and passion which is awakened by amazing experiences in amazing places.

In our view, nothing in Latin pedagogy can replace a diuturnal interaction with historical Latin texts. This is why, in Paideia's *Living Latin* programme, our aim is to produce students who are better readers of Latin but, more importantly, to foster their passion for Latin so much and to offer them such memorable experiences that Latin truly becomes a part of who they are, and they develop their own reading habits, which are bound to last for the rest of their lives. We strongly hope that our illustration of the Paideia Institute's pedagogical methods will stimulate further discussion in the burgeoning field of new approaches to ancient language teaching in the years to come.

The authors wish to thank Nancy Vander Veer, John B. Kuhner and Jonathan Meyer for their invaluable suggestions and contributions to this chapter.

CHAPTER 19
THE *LATINITIUM* PROJECT
Daniel Pettersson and Amelie Rosengren

Background

Latinitium.com is a growing online organization for the promotion, encouragement and facilitation of the study of Latin. It was launched as a project in 2016 by Latinist, Daniel Pettersson and historian, Amelie Rosengren. From its inception, the principal occupation of the project has been to create new and interesting resources online for learners and teachers of Latin and to attract more interest to the study of Latin across the world. These resources include videos, recordings, books, guides, online dictionaries and a digital anthology of Latin prose. During the period from October 2016 to October 2019, it's user base grew to around 20,000 unique visitors each month.

Underlying the launch of the project was the conviction that there was a need for new types of learning material that would appeal to modern students and that could be used successfully in conjunction with a variety of teaching approaches, from traditional grammar-translation to communicative approaches, in order to make learning more enjoyable and efficient.

The aim of this chapter is twofold: first, to present some of the project's contributions to didactic materials for teaching and learning Latin using a variety of approaches including communicative approaches; and second, to discuss the challenges and the possible effect of the materials. To attain these two goals, we will first briefly outline the background to why we deemed there was a need for new learning materials. Next, we will detail the nature of the principal materials of the project, ending with a brief discussion on challenges and lessons learned throughout the four-year period. This will be done through the analysis of user statistics and feedback.

Materials adapted for the modern age

Teaching students to read Latin has, through the centuries, been accomplished in various ways with a focus on competencies guided by the needs and language-learning theories of the times. Today, the primary goal of most Latin-learning endeavours is to acquire the ability to read and understand Latin literature within any relevant time constraints (Carpenter 2000). For some years, Latin learning and teaching has been done according to the so-called Grammar Translation method (GT), a method mainly consisting of memorization of morphology, grammatical analysis and careful translation (Richards and Rodgers 2014: 4–8). Common to the method is also the focus on reading literary texts from an early stage.

We believe all these aspects can be useful, and indeed necessary to some extent, in learning Latin, but GT can often lead to lessons wholly focused on the syntactical analysis and translation of classical texts, often so difficult that the learner understands the meaning of the Latin text only through the medium of a translation. In our experience, employing other methods – or elements of them – such as speaking Latin or extensive reading of easy texts can greatly benefit the students in their learning process. They also offer greater possibility for adaptation to the changing nature of learning and students' expectations and preferences.

In Pettersson's years of teaching Latin (mostly to younger adults), he has seen how these expectations, biases and preferences impact the students' learning process. Students have expectations when they step into the classroom or decide to become autodidacts and learn Latin at home. Some expectations are unconscious and are a product of the time in which we live, while others are more conscious expectations of how language and Latin perhaps in particular are 'supposed' to be taught and learned. These expectations vary from student to student, and also from teacher to teacher. Some expect to translate texts, others expect to be able to hold a short conversation after the first few lessons, while still others expect 'drill' exercises, and some long sections of grammar explanation. Students may also bring with them ideas about how they themselves learn best. No matter what the research says or how much evidence is presented, many are adamant that they learn languages in a certain way. This view, we have found, is especially prevalent in students who have experience with learning a second language in school. Furthermore, students find different ways of enjoying studying. Spoken Latin, for instance, is very popular with some, whereas other students find great pleasure in translating difficult texts with the help of grammars and dictionaries.

The changing way in which students and people in general engage in learning online also impacts expectations and preferences. Many middle schools and high schools incorporate audio-visual and computer aided interactive aspects in teaching and learning (Hunt 2016 and 2020). Indeed, students often grow up and live in a digital world where varied, stimulating audio-visuals and interaction is everywhere – and available at their leisure (for examples, see Anderson and Jiang 2018). We have observed that, when learning about a subject or skill, students often go on YouTube first and only subsequently turn to books and courses for more in-depth studies (see also Chau 2010). Today, many universities also offer on-demand video courses online, and the number of learning platforms offering video courses in almost any subject (e.g. Udemy, LinkedIn Learning and Skillshare) testifies to a change in demand from learners. As such, interaction with course content is no longer scheduled but is regularly done asynchronously when the users have the time. In essence, learners are in control of their learning as never before. In light of this development, we have found that many students bring to the classroom expectations or preferences for audio-visuals and interaction. Whatever we teachers think of these changes, the learning students' experience online stands in stark contrast to the traditional methods of Latin learning.

All of these aspects are important to consider when teaching and when creating materials for teachers or for students who are teaching themselves. One type of resource might have strong research evidence supporting its use but, if a student does not like it, or does not feel comfortable with it, the student is less likely to continue studying and thus may not learn Latin.

The *Latinitium* project has therefore attempted to provide a wide array of materials for difference learner preferences, expectations and methods.

Latinitium's resources

The primary goals we set for the project were to create materials that would facilitate the learning of the Latin language, while also promoting the study of Latin's rich literature from antiquity and beyond. Drawing on our own teaching and learning experience, and with a view to the changing nature of learning and the new possibilities offered by technology, we sought to create material that would render learning Latin more enjoyable and efficient for the modern student. Consequently, we decided from the launch of the project that *Latinitium* should provide both video and audio of different kinds that could be used in several ways across a variety of approaches including more traditional approaches as well as those based in reading and communicating. In addition, *Latinitium* provides digitized dictionaries, guides explaining grammar and tips and techniques for learning, as well as articles by scholars presenting aspects of their research, in an attempt to bring recent philological research to a broader audience. The following pages, however, will focus on the material produced by *Latinitium* relevant for communicative approaches: audio-visuals and materials in easy Latin.

We want to underscore here that the materials discussed below are not meant to replace the study of authors such as Cicero and Virgil, but to supplement and prepare students for them. In the creation of our materials, our guiding principle has been to make them interesting for students of various ages, while still making sure, to the best of our abilities, that the Latin we use should be in line with attested usage in classical Latin, as that is what most Latin programmes base their study on.

We established audio and video as a cornerstone of *Latinitium*'s resources for several reasons: first, audio (including, of course, the audio track of videos) has the benefit of being accessible virtually anywhere and anytime as long as the learner has access to a smartphone or computer. Consequently, a learner can listen to the text repeatedly before or after class, and thus start to acquire the language used. Second, continuous audio in Latin encourages the learner to try to understand Latin as communication of thought in real time and in Latin word order; they cannot look at the previous word or look ahead in search for the verb. Thus, they become accustomed to taking in and understanding the text by dealing with words in the order in which they were written and at conversational speed.

Video has all these benefits but also two additional advantages: increased familiarity with the medium and comprehensibility through additional non-verbal information. As mentioned above, video today is a central part of how people obtain and share information online. A good number of students coming to the study of Latin are thus used to this visual format. In addition to this familiarity, videos are typically more engaging and more comprehensible than mere text (or even audio) due to the speaker's facial expressions, gestures and visual aids, such as images of the action and on-screen text (Hunt 2016).

Our audio-visual resources were created to be used both in self-study and for learners in classroom settings. With both the audio and the videos, a central goal was that they could provide a framework for classroom activities where students could first work through the recorded text, reading and listening to it, or watch the video and then engage in communicative activities with the text or video as the context. The audio – and more specifically, the videos – are meant to function as a precursor to communication, providing a subject and vocabulary necessary to discuss it.

The videos produced during the period 2016 to 2019 were all in Latin and fell into two major formats: (1) mini-documentaries; and (2) video lessons.

In the first category, some videos are focused on literary and historical topics, such as the life and works of Petronius or Terence, while others treat more fictional topics, such as ghost stories, the myth of Atlantis and the sea monsters of Norse mythology. Other videos are filmed in locations pertaining to the classical world, an example of which is a guided tour through Herculaneum showing the architecture while discussing the destruction of the city. These videos are geared towards the intermediate/advanced student, but to facilitate comprehension, most of them utilize a large number of images, and some also have Latin and/or English subtitles.

The second category of videos is a series entitled *Loci et locutiones* (Passages and expressions). In this series, Pettersson selects Latin words or expressions and explains the meaning and usage, using quotes from literature and imagery drawn on a whiteboard. In other videos, he takes a short passage from a text and explains the meaning, using paraphrasing. These videos are all exclusively in Latin. The purpose of this series is to provide a resource that will help in developing vocabulary knowledge as well as showing that it is not always necessary to explain a text in the vernacular language but that it is possible to use Latin only. The Latin used is geared towards intermediate and advanced students, but it is spoken naturally and avoids any long Ciceronian sentences and overly convoluted expressions. As such, these videos complement the study of literary texts.

To support study of Latin literature we also recorded a large number of texts. This audio produced for *Latinitium* falls into three categories: (1) short passages from literature and textbooks; (2) short stories written in easy Latin; and (3) full-length Latin audiobooks.

For the first category, we selected interesting passages from a variety of authors, such as Ennius, Cato, Cicero, Suetonius and Sallust. We endeavoured to showcase not only a wide range of authors but also the plethora of subjects treated in Latin literature, from major historical events to more personal everyday subjects treated in letters. With the recordings, we always include the transcript on the website, and this is frequently accompanied by a list of key vocabulary and expressions. These texts, being literary in nature, are, of course, more suitable to intermediate and advanced students of Latin rather than beginners. The need for more accessible materials was made clear by many requests of easier Latin texts we received from users. In 2019, we therefore created a new category of texts and recordings geared towards beginners and lower-intermediate students.

This beginner/lower-intermediate category consists of simple stories that we wrote ourselves based on myths, legends, fairy tales and folk tales dating from antiquity and beyond. These stories are between four to ten minutes in length and are written using a small number of vocabulary words and constructions, and are largely told using the present tense. To ensure comprehension and make their use in classrooms as easy as possible, each story comes with a transcription, English translation, and a Latin–English word list of the most important words.

The third category of audio is full-length audiobooks in Latin. During the period 2017–19, we recorded and published two audiobooks: the 1927 textbook *Ad Alpes: A Story of Roman Life*, by H. C. Nutting; and our own easier Latin novella, *Pugio Bruti: A Crime story in Easy Latin*. The *Pugio Bruti* audiobook is part of a suite of resources created for the book, which will be treated below. These audiobooks were meant to provide learners with extensive listening in Latin as a supplement to reading and other activities. We deemed this an important supplement to the input students receive in the communicative classroom or as the central audio input in traditional methods.

Pugio Bruti: A Crime Story in Easy Latin

In an effort to combine level-appropriate material with audio, video and communicative aspects, we launched the *Pugio Bruti* project. The centre of the project is a crime story written in easy classicizing Latin set in ancient Rome. It was conceived of as a resource for both autodidacts and students in classroom settings using it as a tool and context for communication. The project took eighteen months to complete and resulted in a suite of resources consisting of a paperback, audiobook and a comprehensive video course.

The impetus for this project was that we observed a growing interest and need from users and students for easy and interesting Latin books written for modern learners. The book is a novella of 100 pages written entirely in Latin using only 350 unique headwords while not avoiding the use of a wide array of grammatical constructions such as ablative absolutes and *cum* clauses. Great care was taken to make sure that the text would not only be easily understood but that it would feel as authentically Roman as possible. It was meant to prepare students for the study of classical literature by providing language that would be easy but lexically and stylistically similar to that used in Roman authors. For instance, we set out to only use words, expressions and collocations attested in literature from ancient Rome. For this reason, dozens of hours were spent on stylistics and corpus research verifying proper context for words and expressions. To facilitate teaching and learning, a Latin–English vocabulary was included in the book, and a list of expressions along with a full glossary was made available on *Latinitium.com*, where a study guide was also made public. In addition, we took care to make the surroundings and the historical context as accurate as possible, to add to the feeling that it was an easy Latin book in Roman garb.

Next, to help students with repetition outside the classroom, we created an audiobook version. This would also allow students to develop their ability to understand Latin as a language in real-time and at their leisure.

Finally, the video course was intended to provide a communicative aspect for students who were autodidacts or where communicative approaches were not generally used in their classrooms. The course consists of a multitude of materials, such as reading and listening comprehension exercises, realia, full grammatical commentary and, most importantly, video lessons on each chapter. In these, Pettersson teaches each chapter of the book, explaining challenging aspects and posing questions to the viewer, who is then prompted to respond in Latin to the questions. Of course, due to the one-way nature of video, students responding to the questions are not engaging in real interaction. Nevertheless, it is a way to get students speaking in a safe environment and perhaps provide suggestions for teachers wanting to adopt communicative Latin approaches in their class.

Resource usage and feedback

The nature of *Latinitium* as an online platform has revealed one particular difficulty: understanding how the materials are received and used in learning and teaching. The data we have to rely on for determining this are user statistics and user-generated feedback. Whereas statistics provide the number of visitors, views, and downloads – but without any real-world context – the user feedback provides more information on manner of usage.

The statistics show a positive picture of the interest in Latin in that the number of monthly unique visitors grew to about 20,000 in 2019, with users from all over the world. The largest user groups came from the United States, the United Kingdom, Spain and Italy. These statistics, however, do not necessarily correspond to interest in active Latin and communicative use of the language in the classroom, since Latinitium also provides popular traditional resources such as Latin dictionaries. Nevertheless, our videos, audio archive and *Pugio Bruti* project have all seen steady growth in the number of page views and downloads. The user-generated feedback and the increasing number of unique visitors point to an upward trend for the interest in this type of resource.

The user feedback from 2016 to 2019, consisting of e-mails, comments, conversations and product reviews, has been highly positive but is not extensive because we did not conduct any in-depth surveys of the usage. Nevertheless, according to the available feedback, the Latin videos and the *Pugio Bruti* project was the most popular with teachers using Latin for communication in their classrooms. Teachers from high schools and universities from many countries reported that they were building their classes around them, using the videos or book chapters as the topic of the lesson and providing vocabulary and questions pertaining to the videos. Others reported that they used the *Pugio Bruti* online course in the classroom, watching the videos with the students, and using them to facilitate communication. The project seemed to be especially useful when teachers desired to introduce the use of spoken Latin in the classroom. The wide array of resources available for *Pugio Bruti* seems to have been instrumental in making it accessible to many students and teachers. The reviews of the *Pugio Bruti* project have been very positive, with a rating averaging 4.7 out of 5 (according to statistics collected from Goodreads.com, Lulu.com and the reviews of the Pugio Bruti audiobook on *Latinitium.com*).

One recurring request has been the demand for translations of the book. We were hesitant to create a translation since the aim was that the book be understood in Latin, perhaps mediated through a teacher's explanations. This stance might be a point for reconsideration in the future, as it would undoubtedly make it accessible to more students who do not have the help of a teacher.

The most explicit data we have on interest in using Latin communicatively comes not from video, audio or from *Pugio Bruti* users, but from an e-mail mini-course produced during May 2018. We mention it here briefly as it illustrates a few essential points, and it is by far the most popular of the e-mails we have sent out, thereby providing the project with the most feedback of all its materials. As of October 2019, it had been sent to over 3,200 Latin learners. In the four-part series, we outlined a method for getting started in writing letters in Latin, in terms of finding a topic, writing aids and correspondents.

The interest in this particular type of communicative activity can probably be attributed to the fact that it can be easier and less stressful to write than to speak, since you are afforded as much time as you need and can have recourse to dictionaries and grammars, something which is naturally not possible when having a conversation. The same applies when learners read someone else's letter, as they do not have to understand everything at once but can consult dictionaries at their leisure. We suspect that the existence of letter-writing as literary genre popular throughout history (for examples, see Cicero, Pliny, Héloïse, Abelard and Erasmus) adds weight and legitimacy to the active use of Latin in written communication.

The letter writing series shows that many students are open to active communication, new ideas and new approaches. Although, the quantity of user-generated feedback is limited and provide too little information on classroom usage for generalized conclusions, it does suggest that audio-visual resources and communicative activities are a welcome contribution for teachers and learners wanting to adopt the active use of Latin in the teaching and learning process.

Challenges

The central challenge for *Latinitium* has been to know exactly what teaching and learning resources to create. The lack of the type of real-time feedback from students that teachers get in the classroom while teaching, makes adapting materials much more complicated and required us to try to create a wide range of materials to meet various needs and expectations. This difficulty could perhaps be mitigated by asking teachers to respond to surveys on materials, but this brings with it other challenges; such surveys would take away from the already limited time many teachers have, and it is often difficult to get an accurate picture of how students feel about materials if time passes between their use of them and completion of the survey.

Another challenge has been the achievement of a balance in the materials so that they appeal to both learners and teachers – a balance between the familiar and the new. Our experience and the feedback we have received suggest that in settings where Latin is used actively for communication – to whatever extent – many students have an epiphany, realizing that Latin is not as inaccessible as it may have seemed at first and that it is indeed a language that they can use and learn. However, as mentioned earlier, many students and teachers bring with them expectations about how Latin and language is supposed to be learned and may prefer not using it actively, or at least not solely. These expectations also extend to the materials to be used in class, since many teachers have reported to us that they want to use only so-called authentic Latin, while others require only texts from the canon of classical authors excluding later epochs. For this reason, we tried to combine both our own audio-visual materials with a multitude of passages from Latin literature.

Another challenge for us has been to attend to each level of Latin learners and provide materials across the spectrum from beginners to advanced learners. Here, the project struggled during its first years with too narrow a focus on the higher-level Latin students, a mistake that was corrected with the publication of the *Pugio Bruti* project. During the final year of the period discussed here, creating materials for beginners became a priority for the project, leading to the launch of a series of stories in easy Latin.

Lessons learned

After four years of creating resources online for learners and teachers, two essential lessons deserve attention. First, as mentioned earlier, the absence of real-time feedback in response to the materials being used in the classroom renders adaptation and improvement much more difficult. The only remedy for this is to seek more direct student feedback through surveys and perhaps interviews. Second, a variety of materials useable in different contexts seems to be of great importance. When producing Latin learning materials, a smorgasbord approach seems judicial, providing a wide range of material – from easy to advanced, new and old texts, translations, books, articles, grammar, commentaries side by side with videos, animations, illustrations and audio. Learners are individuals and have different ideas and views on how they learn, on what works and what does not, on what they should read, and what to avoid. Most are open to new ideas, but may still go back to what they are comfortable with or what they have always done. By making sure a resource can be used in many ways, it opens up the door to teachers and learners to use them in any way they wish – be it in an active, communicative approach or grammar-translation or a combination of both. It also enables students to choose their own path: they can listen to *Latinitium's* and other's recommendations, read research about how to learn a language most efficiently, but in the end have the option to choose material and activities (or several in combination) that will actually motivate them to do the work. The importance of this adaptability of resources for various learning settings was exemplified by one of our users who wrote in May 2019: 'I have used the novel [*Pugio Bruti*] and [online] course for my own enrichment, in a reading group with other Latin teachers, and with a small class of advanced high school students.'

In the end, providing material and activities that are varied including everything and anything from conversation, and animated videos and easy texts to translation and letter writing seems to be a good way to attract as many students as possible to the study of Latin and give teachers and learners the opportunity to select from a number of options and try to find what suits them as individuals. The downside to creating such a wide range of materials is the enormous amount of work necessary to produce it.

Conclusion

In this chapter, we have focused mainly on the production of resources in order to facilitate Latin learning and teaching. The *Latinitium* project's ambition was set very high: to facilitate Latin learning, and promote and encourage the study of it. In several ways, it has been successful: teachers and learners, in both high schools and universities, use *Latinitium's* resources daily, but there is difficulty in knowing how they are being used and received in the classroom. The steadily increasing number of users suggests that there is a growing interest in the study of Latin, especially among autodidacts. Even if enrolment numbers in Latin classes in many countries might be dropping, the interest in the language and its literature seems to be alive and well on the internet. In the coming years, we will draw on the experience and lessons we have learned during these four years, and continue to create adaptable materials and to promote the active use of Latin as well as sustaining more traditional approaches to serve as many teachers and learners as possible in the study of the Latin language and its vast literature.

CHAPTER 20
PRIMARY LANGUAGE ACQUISITION OF LATIN IN BILINGUAL CHILDREN: A CASE STUDY
Mallory Ann Hayes and Patrick M. Owens

Introduction

One significant challenge in applying communicative Latin pedagogy is the absence of studies documenting primary-language (L1) acquisition patterns in Latin. Such studies in other languages help clarify educators' predictions regarding the sequencing and hierarchies for students learning that language in a second-language acquisition setting. The lack of case studies on primary Latin acquisition has meant that claims about how children might learn L1 Latin in a natural setting have been highly speculative. This type of hypothesizing has tended toward an assumption that standard literary Latin is too complicated to be understood or acquired by infants and young children as a first language. More people than expected, even Latin teachers, evince incredulity that children can learn the language as an L1. The goal of this case study then is to demonstrate not only that children can learn Latin in a natural setting, but also how language milestones and natural order of acquisition in L1 Latin compare with other L1 languages.

Previous studies of L1 development propose that a universal grammar or language acquisition instinct predisposes children to learn a first language with almost certain ultimate success, at a fast rate, and with a uniformity in acquisition (Meisel 2011: 22). The same research indicates children around the world follow a general pattern of language milestones, from babbling to single-word utterances to sentences. We do not have detailed records of childhood linguistic development for ancient Romans, but both Quintilian (*Inst. Orat. I.1*) and Augustine (*Conf. 1.23*) comment on the optimal way to introduce infants to Greek and Latin and reference many of the same language milestones, so child language development was clearly of interest to some ancients. For the purpose of this case study, the general patterns of natural acquisition will be considered to evaluate how Latin functions as an L1 in children in light of recent modern language research, especially in other highly inflected languages, such as German and Russian.

Linguistic environment

This case study concentrates on the first five years of language development of two children raised from birth in a bilingual English–Latin environment. They were born just over four-and-a-half years apart in 2000 and 2005 respectively; the older child (Child A) is female and the younger (Child B) is male. Their stay-at-home primary caregiving mother followed a pattern of communicating in Latin in the home while alone with the children and in English at most other times, in order to provide an opportunity for simultaneous acquisition of two primary languages.

The children also heard Latin at religious services and occasionally spent time interacting with other Latin speakers besides their mother. Much of this additional exposure came from attending the *Conventiculum Lexintoniense* gathering each year from age three. At this week-long conference, the children interacted in Latin with adults and sometimes even with other children in a variety of social situations. All adults in the children's lives were supportive of their learning Latin, which enjoyed a high-status in their immediate social community. The primary motivation for attempting to raise the children speaking Latin was to facilitate their eventual ability to read authentic Latin from the corpus easily and fluently, with a secondary motivation to observe how children develop Latin when it is encountered as a natural part of the environment.

While speaking Latin, the mother tended to use 'Motherese' techniques, including repetitions and reformulations of grammatical forms as well as variation sets such as saying in a sing-song voice *ego te video et tu me vides* (I see you, and you see me). After about age three, the children occasionally received direct explanations or corrections of both lexical and grammatical forms; for instance, when addressing a group of Latin speakers for the first time, explaining in Latin that *salve* (hello) becomes *salvete* in the plural. The Latin language development for Child A was recorded by the mother weekly on a detailed checklist for typical English speech and language milestones (Gard, Gilman and Gorman 1993) as well as in regular journal entries including verbatim quotes of new vocabulary and grammar. Child B's language was recorded in similar narrative assessments in a journal format. Specific language examples in this chapter refer to data recorded at the time it occurred. Language production in both children tended to lag far behind their comprehension, as is common with many learners (Clark 2009: 120). This was demonstrated by toddlers pointing to pictures and following commands in Latin before they were speaking more than a few words in either language.

Latin language milestones

Throughout the early years, each child met universal language milestones in Latin at the expected time for monolingual speakers as found on the Speech and Language Milestone checklist (Gard, Gilman and Gorman 1993), although milestones were generally met slightly earlier for English. After babbling, single words began at the usual ages. Child A said *uvae* (grapes) as a first Latin word at sixteen months, by eighteen months used ten different Latin words, and by her second birthday had 140 active Latin words. Child B spoke Latin younger, beginning with *lac* (milk) at eleven months. By twenty-one months, he used seventy-two Latin words. These numbers, while representing only the Latin portion of the children's language, are nonetheless average word counts for monolingual English-speaking children (Gard, Gilman and Gorman 1993). Most of these words were nouns, and often specific lexical items reflected either ease of pronunciation (e.g., *uvae* which contains primarily vowel sounds) or time of year (e.g., *cucurbita* (pumpkin) used near Hallowe'en).

The next stage of language development involved using one word to express a question or demand about items not present, as opposed to stating an utterance as a fact. Each child began this stage a few months after initial Latin words started. By eighteen months, Child A asked *area*? (playground?) in order to go to the playground while Child B demanded *lac*! when thirsty. Between eighteen months and two years, the frequency of combined two-word utterances increased although these combinations did not yet consistently reflect Latin noun terminations, and the children tended to use nominative forms. For example, at eighteen months Child A said *amo Mama!* rather than *amo Mamam!* (I love Mummy). At the same age, Child B shouted *volo lac* (I want milk) and at twenty-one months, *plus aqua* instead of the grammatically correct *plus aquae* (more water). At this early stage, the children also showed some awareness of the importance of Latin word order even when case terminations were not used. In this way, at twenty months Child A used *auto<raeda> Mama* for *auto<raeda> Mamae* (Mummy's car) which was in contrast to her English phrase 'Grandma car' and indicates a recognition that in possessive phrases typical Latin word order differs from English.

Looking specifically at inflection, research across multiple languages finds children develop case markers gradually in a three-phase process: a premorphological phase, a protomorphological phase and an adult-like morphology phase (Eisenbeiss, Narasimhan and Voeikova 2008: 380). Child learners begin with a premorphological stage using base forms which may have correct grammatical terminations but which are memorized rather than constructed by the speakers with an understanding of the significance of the terminations. For example, Child A used *si placet* (please) as a rote phrase at 23 months, while Child B used *volo plus* (I want more) in the same way.

Persons and numbers of verbs also developed during the age range expected for monolingual child speakers of an inflected language (Eisenbeiss, Narasimhan and Voeikova 2008: 381–2). At twenty-three months, Child A used *est* (it is) and *ambulat* (he walks) only with singular subjects. Using verb forms other than the third person singular took longer. While *ascendit* (she climbs) was used from twenty-four months, it was three months later that *ascendo* (I climb) occurred as a first-person singular. Perhaps because the Latin-speaking in the home had notably improved by the time Child B was a toddler, he was able to correctly use more varied verb forms earlier; at twenty-one months, he distinguished his usage between *volo* (I want) and *vis* (you want) as well as between *est* (he is) and *sunt* (they are).

Around age two, the children entered the protomorphological phase for noun inflections and verb tenses. This type of utterance shows occasional accurate use of grammatical terminations, but only for some cases or words (Eisenbeiss, Narasimhan and Voeikova 2008: 381). For Child A this happened at twenty-three months, when plural nouns developed, and she distinguished between *murus/muri* (wall/walls) in speech and counted aloud on her own *duo autocarri* (two trucks). She expanded plurals to a variety of words by twenty-six months, including *dens/dentes* (tooth/teeth) and *digitus/digiti* (finger/fingers). Having experienced improved Latin input in the family, Child B was using plural nominatives at twenty-one months including *nummus/nummi* (coin/coins) and *puella/puellae* (girl/girls). Accusatives appeared almost as soon as nominatives. At twenty-three months, Child A said *navem rubrum* (red ship). Although the adjective lacks the appropriate feminine grammatical gender, this phrase was one of the earliest examples of matching cases in the accusative as well as another indication of Latinate adjective word order. By twenty-seven months, Child A was regularly using the ablative singular in full sentences including *ludo cum cane meo* (I am playing with my dog), which was her response to a request for a her to repeat in Latin what she had just said in English. When prompted by *Latine* (in Latin), she switched the position of the *meo* to a more typical Latin position in the process of changing languages. Child B was again a little younger when these protomorphological milestones were reached. He counted *duae puellae* (two girls) at twenty-one months, matching gender, number and case. At the same age, he observed *luna in caelo est* (the moon is in the sky) using an ablative correctly with the preposition. Child B also added adverbs earlier. At twenty-one months he was combining *amo quoque* (I love also) and *abest nunc* (it is gone now). Verb tenses developed contemporaneously with case markers. Both children used present tense first, beginning with third person singulars at around eighteen months old. By twenty-seven months, Child A was using other present terminations such as *capimus novos libros* (we are getting new books) about a trip to the library. By thirty months, both *cepit* (he took) and *fecit* (she did/made) were in regular use in the perfect tense, and at thirty-three months she consistently used the imperfect.

Finally, the milestones of conjunction and subordination occurred. Child B used a typical subordinating conjunction when he argued at 24 months, *quia volo*! (because I want to). By age thirty months, Child A regularly used the conjugations *et, sed, quia, ut* and *dum* (and, but, because, so that and while) while Child B favoured *et, quia* and *sed* (and, because and but). The earliest example of the final adult-like morphology phase occurred with Child A at twenty-seven months: *gigas monstrum habet caudam longam* (The giant monster has a long tail). This phase includes complete paradigms but only of frequent words and still including errors (Eisenbeiss, Narasimhan and Voeikova 2008: 381). At thirty-three months, Child A made a conjecture about a dog-groomer including a relative pronoun: *fortasse est puella quae <canem> lavat* (Maybe she is the girl who washes <the dog>). A typical use of adult-like morphology occurred at forty-two months when Child A commented about another family: *nunc habent novam caniculam quia alius <alter> canis fugit* (Now they have a new puppy because another <the other> dog ran away).

The order of the natural acquisition of nouns for both Child A and Child B are summarized in Figure 20.1 with singular and plural forms recorded separately since gaps of up to six months occurred between a child using the singular and adding its plural.

Both children began with nominatives and accusatives before producing ablatives, genitives and datives, which is similar to the general tendencies seen in the acquisition of case in modern infected languages (Eisenbeiss, Narasimhan and Voeikova 2008: 280). Due to changes in family circumstances, Child A's data for verbs from ages two-and-a-half onwards are more complete than Child B's, thus Figures 20.2 and 20.3 reflect the natural order of acquisition of tense and mood for Child A only.

Case	Age of first usage Child A	Age of first usage Child B
Nominative singular	16 months	11 months
Nominative plural	23 months	21 months
Accusative singular	23 months	21 months
Ablative singular	23 months	21 months
Accusative plural	26 months	21 months
Genitive singular	27 months	27 months
Ablative plural	30 months	30 months
Dative singular	30 months	30 months
Genitive	30 months	30 months
Dative	36 months	36 months

Figure 20.1 Nominal case acquisition order. Copyright © Mallory Ann Hayes and Patrick M. Owens.

Tense	Age of first usage Child A	Examples
Present singular	18 months	*habet, porto,*
Present plural	27 months	*sunt, capimus*
Perfect	30 months	*fecit, cepi*
Imperfect	33 months	*ambulabam, temptabamus*
Future	38 months	*veniet*
Pluperfect	~4 years	*habuerat*
Future perfect	~9 years old	*venerit*

Figure 20.2 Verb tense acquisition order. Copyright © Mallory Ann Hayes and Patrick. M. Owens.

Mood	Age of first usage Child A	Examples
Indicative	18 months	*amo, volo*
Imperative	24 months	*veni! abi! desiste!*
Infinitive	27 months	*volo ire!* *licetne mihi* + infinitives
Participle	32 months	*sum hic edens cibum.*
Subjunctive	33 months	*. . . ut possint videre* *nescio ubi sit.*
Gerund	33 months	*pugnando (abl.)*
Supine	~8 years old	*horribile visu!*
Gerundive (oblique)	~11 years old	*ad libros capiendos*

Figure 20.3 Mood acquisition order. Copyright © Mallory Ann Hayes and Patrick M. Owens.

Tense usage ranged from present singular verbs at around eighteen months, e.g. *habet* (it has), to future perfects at around nine years old, e.g. *venerit* (he will have come). Combining tenses was common for both children after three years old, for instance from Child A at thirty-nine months: *movi sellam et nunc in ea sedeo* (I moved the chair and now am sitting in it). Mood production in speech proceeded from indicatives at eighteen months through gerundives at around eleven years old. At first Child A only used *ut* (so that) or *ne* (lest) with the subjunctive forms of the verbs *esse* (to be) and *posse* (to be able), as in the clause *ut homines possint videre dum in navibus effugiunt* (so that the people are able to see while they flee in ships) at thirty-four months old. It was not until Child A was forty-three months old that she replaced the English-influenced *ut possit* (so that she is able) construction with verbs directly in the subjunctive, such as when she stated about an animal: v*enit ad arborem ut videat folia* (he is coming to the tree so that he can see the leaves).

Between ages two and three, error patterns arose which showed an internalization of Latin grammar, for example in forms like *capites* for *capita* (heads) or *facuit* for *fecit* (made/did).

Such mistakes were not heard in the environment but instead show the common error of overgeneralizing a grammatical pattern just as English-speaking children do with 'runned' as the past tense of run or 'mans' as the plural of man. In contrast, neither child tried to put noun terminations on verbs or vice versa which validates the degree to which Latin was being learned as a primary language since first-language learners do not tend to make such mistakes, though second-language learners often do.

There were other indications that the children were truly learning Latin as a simultaneous L1 in this case study despite the relative strength of their English. As is typical for bilingual children, they often mixed languages, especially around two years old, with phrases including *anas* (duck) walking, under *mensa* (table) and every parent's least favourite, No *te amo* (I <don't> love you). Linguists postulate that children learning two or more languages simultaneously from birth share certain characteristics: they can distinguish the two systems early, proceed through the same stages as monolinguals at roughly the same pace, and are assumed to be able to achieve native competence (Meisel 2011: 212). The children in this study clearly fulfill the first two criteria. Before age two, both Child A and Child B were able to distinguish and name the language used by a speaker as well as interpret words or phrases between languages when asked. In addition, Child A and Child B not only reached all the universal language milestones for Latin on schedule but also demonstrated the expected patterns for inflected languages. The final criterion, however, begins to hint at what is an almost unique problem for Latin. Neither child has achieved native proficiency, nor have many, if any, adult speakers of Latin today. This is not surprising given that no community currently relies on Latin as an L1, and the children were learning from non-native speakers.

In this case study, the intention behind speaking Latin was directed toward literacy in Latin, so a brief overview of the development of the children's reading and writing may be helpful. The children had access to around 100 Latin-language children's books, which they regularly encountered at story times and looked at themselves for pleasure. With a few notable exceptions (Terence Tunberg's *Cattus Petasatus* was a favourite of Child B for several months, and both children enjoyed the Latin *Asterix* series), most of these books were not published in Latin but were actually children's books in which the mother had manually attached Latin text to cover the English. The Latin-language books ranged from board books with labelled images to complex mythology and science story books. Both children began to sound out and read easy Latin and English words around their third birthdays: Child A a few months before age three, and Child B a month after. Each was reading simple stories well by age four in both English and Latin.

When attempting to write on their own, both children frequently used English phonics to approximate Latin words. For instance, at age three Child A drew a cat and labelled it *falais* rather than *feles* (cat) and at three-and-a-half, wrote *faycit* for *fecit*. At age four, she wrote in a story *ollem errat canis* (Once there was a dog) and *nunk dormit* (now he's sleeping) when she intended *olim erat canis* and *nunc dormit*. These types of spelling attempts suggest the children were relying on English phonics to write both languages. With words composed of simpler phonemes, the children performed better. For example, at age three Child B easily labelled a drawing *apis* (bee). Child A was a prolific storywriter in both languages, and between ages three and six years old regularly wrote stories in Latin using a variety of tenses, cases and genders.

Conclusions

What can this case study of two children suggest about Latin language-learning which can be of use in teaching 'adult' students aged twelve and over? Most importantly, this study is a crucial step in gathering empirical evidence that Latin can be learned in the same was as other L1 languages. Indeed, the primary language acquisition of Latin in the bilingual children in this case study followed all the normal childhood milestones at the expected ages and patterns of modern inflected languages. This suggests Latin can and does function in a communicative way as a normal language.

In addition, the study demonstrates that children can certainly learn authentic Latin, even when learning from non-native speakers. If a speaker uses supines, purpose clauses or indirect statements regularly and correctly, the language-learner will eventually understand them and actively use them. From age three, both children in this study engaged in conversations with pre-eminent adult Latinists from around the world. These speakers used various Latin pronunciations, differing regional accents, periodic sentence structure and complex grammar. Nonetheless, the children could understand and respond to them. The study also supports the position that comprehension for learners of communicative Latin greatly precedes and exceeds correct production and usage. For instance, Child A could point to sixteen body parts when asked to do so in Latin before saying even one Latin word.

Another important finding is that memorized forms, even when combined in novel ways, are not the same as internalizing morphologies. In the same way the children in the study said *quaeso* (please) or *eamus* (let's go) but did not extend person or mood to other verbs at the time, students in our classrooms do not necessarily understand case or mood morphology just because they are using *gratias tibi ago* (thank you) or *oremus* (let us pray). Additionally, the study indicates that rare forms are unlikely to be learned only by speaking or even reading but may require direct instruction. In this study, such constructions included future perfects, gerundives other than the nominative and accusative supines. This is not unexpected since even primary-language learners often require direct grammatical teaching to produce constructions found in advanced literature, such as the subjunctive or relative pronouns in literary English.

Finally, this case study indicates that the quality of language input does have a significant effect on learners. All spoken Latin input is not created equal. A baby can apparently learn even with an imperfect model, but as the children grew older, their Latin production reflected the teacher's incorrect constructions, vocabulary errors, and general lack of Latinity. For instance, though both children in this study understood and occasionally even used the passive spontaneously, they did not use the passive as frequently as it is represented in the literary corpus. This is likely because the primary caregiver did not reflect adequate Latinity in using the passive herself since her speech patterns were influenced by interference from her English L1. The same weaknesses in the children's productive language (i.e. speech and writing) were seen in verb placement, sequence of tenses and other aspects of Latin which differ substantially from English. A similar dilemma faces teachers who want to teach Latin communicatively in the classroom. On one hand, ensuring as much exposure to Latin as possible for learners is crucial. On the other hand, maintaining accepted standards of authentic Latinity is necessary in order to make the Latin which is acquired more useful for reading authentic literature, translating according to the expectations of school exams, and composing Latin consistent with classical norms. Perhaps the best compromise is for the teacher to begin using Latin for everyday communication but then to supplement these efforts with both direct instruction and high-quality Latin reading material reflecting classical Latin usage, as well as with continued study on the teacher's part to improve the modeling of Latinity while decreasing interference from other languages.

REFERENCES

ACTFL (2012), American Council on the Teaching of Foreign Languages. Available online: https://www.actfl.org/publications/guidelines-and-manuals/actfl-proficiency-guidelines-2012/english (accessed 24 January 2020).

Allen, S. (2004), *Vox Latina: A Guide to the Pronunciation of Classical Latin*, Cambridge: Cambridge University Press.

Anchieta, J. (1799), *Epistola quamplurimarum rerum naturalium quae Sancti Vicentii (nunc Sancti Pauli) incolunt sistens descriptionem a Didaco de Toledo Lara Ordonhez adjectis annotationibus edita*, Olisipone: Typis Academiae.

Anderson, M., and J. Jiang (2018), 'Teens, Social Media & Technology 2018'. Available online: http://publicservicesalliance.org/wp-content/uploads/2018/06/Teens-Social-Media-Technology-2018-PEW.pdf (accessed 24 April 2020).

ANDIFES: Associação Nacional dos Dirigentes das Instituições Federais de Ensino Superior (2018), *V Pesquisa Nacional de Perfil Socioeconômico e Cultural dos (as) Graduandos (as) das IFES*. Available online: http://www.andifes.org.br/wp-content/uploads/2019/05/V-Pesquisa-do-Perfil-Socioecon%C3%B4mico-dos-Estudantes-de-Gradua%C3%A7%C3%A3o-das-Universidades-Federais-1.pdf (accessed 26 December 2019).

Apple, M. (2003), 'Competition, Knowledge, and the Loss of Educational Vision', *Philosophy of Music Education Review*, 11 (1), 3–22.

Ash, R. (2019), 'Untextbooking for the CI Latin Class: Why and How to Begin', *Journal of Classics Teaching*, 39: 65–70.

Asher, J. (1977), *Learning Another Language Through Actions*, Los Gatos, CA: Sky Oaks Productions.

Atkinson, D. (1993), 'Teaching in the Target Language: A Problem in the Current Orthodoxy', *Language Learning Journal*, 8 (1): 2–5.

Ávila, M. (2014), *Aléxandros: to Hellenikon Paidion*, Guadix: Cultura Clásica.

Aydogan, H. (2014), 'The Four Basic Language Skills, Whole Language & Integrated Skill Approach in Mainstream University Classrooms in Turkey', *Mediterranean Journal of Social Sciences*, 5 (9), 672–80.

Baddeley, A., M. Eldridge and V. Lewis (1981), 'The Role of Subvocalisation in Reading', *The Quarterly Journal of Experimental Psychology*, 33: 439–54.

Bailey, J. S. (2016), 'The 'Ars' of Latin Questioning: Circling, Personalization, and Beyond', *The Classical Outlook*, 91 (1): 1–5.

Bailey, J. S. (2017), 'The Persistent Perks of Speaking Latin' *Eidolon*. Available online:https://eidolon.pub/the-persistent-perks-of-speaking-latin ba55fd5fe51f#.b9plsyqxr (accessed 26 December 2019).

Bailey, J. S. (2020), 'itinera: ad Balneum Meum . . . et?' *Latin Listening Project*. Available online: https://www.youtube.com/watch?v=SvP4dr5Sk1A (accessed 12 April 2020).

Ball, R., and J. Ellsworth (1996), 'The Emperor's New Clothes: Hyperreality and the Study of Latin', *The Modern Language Journal*, 80 (1): 77–84.

Ball, S. (2017), *The Education Debate*, Bristol: Policy Press.

Balme, M., G. Lawall, L. Miraglia, T. Bórri and G. Guzmán Ramírez (2008), *Athenaze. Introduzione al greco antico. Per il Liceo classico: 1*, Montella (AV): Edizioni Accademia Vivarium Novum.

Balme, M., G. Lawall, L. Miraglia, T. Bórri and G. Guzmán Ramírez (2013), *Athenaze. Introduzione al greco antico. Per il Liceo classico: 20*, Montella (AV): Edizioni Accademia Vivarium Novum.

Banas, J., N. Dunbar, D. Rodriguez and S-J. Liu (2011), 'A Review of Humor in Educational Settings: Four Decades of Research', *Communication Education*, 60 (1): 115–44.

Bate, J. (1993), *Shakespeare and Ovid*, Oxford: Oxford University Press.

Beach, G. (1957), 'The Congress for Living Latin,' *The Classical Journal*, 35 (2): 19–20.

References

Beard, S. (2009), 'Perennial Latin in the Modern World: Where Should We Now Be Heading and Why?', Lecture to the California Classical Association, Southern Section Annual Meeting, 18 April 2009, Los Angeles, CA.

Berra, Y. (2010), *The Yogi Book*, New York: Workman.

Bialik, H. (1935), ''Al 'Umah ve-Lashon', in *Devarim she-be-al Peh*, Tel Aviv: Dvir.

Bobiatyński, L. (2003), 'Wprowadzenie do kultury antyku a nauczanie języków klasycznych', Łódź: *Collectanea Philologica* V: 207–19.

Bracey, J. (2019), 'TPRS, PQA & Circling', *Journal of Classics Teaching*, 39: 60–4.

Brzuska, B. (1990), 'Sytuacja w nauczaniu języków klasycznych w Królestwie Polskim w okresie międzypowstaniowym', *Meander* 2–3: 97–104.

Brzuska, B. (2016), 'Latin and Politics in People's Poland', in E. Olechowska and D. Movrin (eds), *Classics and Class. Greek and Latin Classics and Communism at School*, 229–86, Warsaw-Ljubljana: Wydz. „Artes Liberales" UW: Univ. of Ljubljana.

Brzuska, B. (2019), 'Nim nastanie PRL. Miejsce łaciny w planach reform edukacyjnych czasów okupacji', *Meander LXXIV*: 137–55.

Caius, J., and J. Gable (1968), *De Pronunciatione Graecae et Latinae Linguae Cum Scriptione Nova Libellus (1574)*, Leeds: Leeds Texts and Monographs.

Callahan, C. M., and H. L. Hertberg-Davis (2017), 'Advanced Placement and International Baccalaureate Programs', in C. M. Callahan and H. L. Hertberg-Davis (eds), *Fundamentals of Gifted Education* 333–45, New York: Routledge.

Cambridge School Classics Project (CSCP) (1998), *Cambridge Latin Course Book 1*, Cambridge: Cambridge University Press.

Carlon, J. (2013), 'The Implications of SLA Research for Latin Pedagogy: Modernizing Latin Instruction and Securing Its Place in Curricula', *Teaching Classical Languages*, 4 (2): 106–22.

Carlon, J. (2015), 'Rethinking the Latin Classroom: Changing the Role of Translation in Assessment', *The Classical Outlook*, 96 (4): 138–40.

Carlon, J. (2018), '"Quomodo Dicitur?" The Importance of Memory in Language Learning', *Teaching Classical Languages*, 7 (2): 109–35.

Carr, W. (1930), 'Reading Latin as Latin. Some Difficulties and Some Devices', *The Classical Journal*, 26 (2): 127–40.

Carter, D. (2019), 'Using Translation-Based CI to Read Latin Literature', *Journal of Classics Teaching*, 20 (39): 90–4.

Carpenter, D. (2000), 'Reassessing the Goal of Latin Pedagogy', *The Classical Journal*, 95 (4): 391–5.

Celce-Murcia, M. (1991), *Teaching English as a Second or Foreign Language*, Boston, MA; New York: Heinle & Heinle.

Centre for the Study of the Renaissance (n.d.). Available online: https://warwick.ac.uk/fac/arts/ren/snls/snls_teaching_anthology/ (accessed 9 January 2020).

Chadwick, A. (2019), 'Going Digital: the Principles Behind CyberCaesar', in B. Natoli and S. Hunt (eds), *Teaching Classics with Technology*, 67–80, London: Bloomsbury.

Chambers, G. (1992), 'Teaching in the Target Language', *Language Learning Journal*, 6 (1): 66–7.

Chase, A. (2020), 'Loading up my Little Darlings with Comprehensible Input'. Available online: https://senorachase.com/2019/01/03/write-discuss/ (accessed 35 March 2020).

Chau, C. (2010), 'YouTube as a participatory culture', *New Directions for Youth Development*, 2010: 65–74. Available online: https://onlinelibrary.wiley.com/doi/10.1002/yd.376 (accessed 23 April 2020).

Cheetham, D. (2014), 'The Phonological Loop and Language Acquisition', *English Literature and Language*, 50: 47–64.

Chilingaryan, K., and R. Gorbatenko (2016), 'Motivation in Language Learning,' in SGEM 2016, BK1: Psychology and Psychiatry, Sociology and Healthcare, Education Conference and Proceedings, Vol II.

CKE (2019), Wstępna informacja o wynikach egzaminu maturalnego przeprowadzonego w maju 2019 r. [Introductory information concerning the results of the final highschool exam carried out in May 2019], Warszawa: Centralna Komisja Egzaminacyjna. Available online: www.cke.gov.pl/images/_EGZAMIN_MATURALNY_OD_2015/Informacje_o_wynikach/2019/20190704%20Wst%C4%99pna%20informacja%20o%20wynikach%20matury%202019.pdf (accessed 23 April 2020).

References

Clark, E. V. (2009), *First Language Acquisition*, New York: Cambridge University Press.

Coffee, N. (2012), 'Active Latin: Quo Tendimus?', *The Classical World,* 105 (2): 255–69.

Collins, J. (1988), *A Primer of Ecclesiastical Latin*, Catholic University of America Press: Washington DC.

Common European Framework of Reference for Languages (CEFR) (2011), 'Common European Framework of Reference for Languages: Learning, Teaching, Assessment', Strasbourg: Language Policy Division, Council of Europe. Available online https://www.coe.int/en/web/common-european-framework-reference-languages (accessed 6 April 2020).

Common European Framework of Reference for Languages (CEFR) (2020), 'Global scale – Table 1 (CEFR 3.3): Common Reference levels', Strasbourg: Language Policy Division, Council of Europe. Available online: https://www.coe.int/en/web/common-european-framework-reference-languages/table-1-cefr-3.3-common-reference-levels-global-scale (accessed 11 April 2020).

Conti, A. (2019), *Alexander Veronensis, Carmina Latina per se illustrata*, Madrid: Cultura Clàsica.

Conti, G., and S. Smith (2016), *The Language Teacher Toolkit,* Seattle: CreateSpace Independent Publishing Platform.

Council of University Classics Departments Bulletin (2020), Classics at UK Universities, 2018–19 Statistics. Available online: https://cucd.blogs.sas.ac.uk/files/2020/04/Stats.pdf (accessed 11 April 2020).

Cox, C. (2018), '"The people with burned faces": Greco-Roman anti-black racism and its modern effects', MA diss, Whitman College, Walla Walla, Washington. Available online: http://arminda.whitman.edu/theses/420 (accessed 24 January 2020).

Craft, J. (2019), 'Bridging the Gap Between Students and Antiquity: Language Acquisition Videos with Minecraft and CI/TPRS', in B. Natoli and S. Hunt (eds), *Teaching Classics with Technology,* 181–92, London: Bloomsbury Academic.

Craft, J. (2020), 'Carmen: non longa via est Romam'. Available online: https://www.youtube.com/watch?v=BmMauT_GejA (accessed 23 March 2020).

Craft, J. (2016), 'Domus Romana – Roman House – Latin – Minecraft'. Available online: www.youtube.com/watch?v=evJ7J1eqH2Y (accessed 22 April 2020).

Craft, J. (2017), 'Roman Forum – Latin – Minecraft'. Available online: www.youtube.com/watch?v=evJ7J1eqH2Y (accessed 22 April 2020).

Cramer, J. (1844), *Catenae Graecorum Patrum*, Oxford. Available online: http://patristica.net/cramer/ (accessed 1 May 2020).

Cresswell, L. (2012), 'Personal Responses to Catullus at GCSE', *Journal of Classics Teaching*, 25: 11–13.

Cullen, H. and J. Taylor (2016), *Latin to GCSE, Part 2*, London: Bloomsbury.

Czetwertyńska, G. (2014), 'Komu potrzebna jest łacina w szkole?', *Języki Obce w Szkole* 3: 47–53.

Daily Dose of Latin (n.d.) Available online: https://dailydoseoflatin.com/beginning-daily-dose-of-latin/latin-questions-answers/ (accessed 9 January 2020).

Daugherty, C. (1998), 'Latin Distance Learning and the Electronic Classroom', in R. LaFleur (ed.), *Latin for the 21st Century: From Concept to Classroom*, 251–62, Glenview: Scott Foresman/Addison Wesley.

Davidson, B. (2018), 'Σύνοδος Ελληνικη Day 7'. Available online: https://brianwdavidson.com/2018/07/23/day-7/ (accessed 1 February 2020).

Deacy S., and E. Eidinow (2017), 'Approaches to Teaching Students with Anxiety: Event Report 2017', *Council of University Classics Departments Bulletin*, 46. Available online: https://cucd.blogs.sas.ac.uk/files/2015/01/DEACY-EIDINOW-Students-with-Anxiety.pdf (accessed 9 April 2020).

Deagon, A. (2006), 'Cognitive Style and Learning Strategies in Latin Instruction', in J. Gruber-Miller, *When Dead Tongues Speak: Teaching Beginning Greek and Latin*, 27–49, Oxford: Oxford University Press.

Deci, E., and R. Ryan (1985), *Intrinsic Motivation and Self-Determination in Human Behavior,* New York: Springer.

Demo, D. (2001), 'Discourse Analysis for Language Teachers', *Eric Digest*. Available online: https://eric.ed.gov/?id=ED456672 (accessed 29 April 2020).

Department for Education. (2020), 'Guidance: Teachers' Standards'. Available online: https://assets.publishing.service.gov.uk/government/uploads/system/uploads/attachment_data/file/665520/Teachers__Standards.pdf (accessed 11 April 2020).

References

Dickey, E. (2007), *Ancient Greek Scholarship: A Guide to Finding, Reading, and Understanding Scholia, Commentaries, Lexica, and Grammatical Treatises from Their Beginnings to the Byzantine Period*, New York: Oxford University Press.

Dickey, E. (2016), *Learn Latin from the Romans: A Complete Introductory Course Using Textbooks from the Roman Empire*, Cambridge: Cambridge University Press.

Dinter, M., and A. Khoo (2018), 'Eat Thy Neighbor: What Can Cannibalism Teach Us About Reading Neo-Latin Texts?' *Medium.com*. Available online: https://medium.com/in-medias-res/eat-thy-neighbour-what-can-cannibalism-teach-us-about-reading-neo-latin-texts-7f014b9ba4fd (accessed 26 December 2019).

Dörnyei, Z., and E. Ushoida (2011), *Teaching and Researching Motivation*, Harlow: Longman.

Eisenbeiss, S., N. Bhuvana and V. Maria (2008), 'The Acquisition of Case,' in Malchukov and Spencer (eds), *The Oxford Handbook of Case,* 369–83, Oxford: Oxford University Press.

Emmett, E. (2008), 'A Survey of Student Perceptions of Latin at GCSE,' unpublished report, University of Cambridge, Cambridge.

Eyckmans, J., P. Anckaert and W. Segers (2016), 'Translation and Interpretation Skills', in D. Tsagari and J. Banerjee (eds), *Handbook of Second Language Assessment*, 219–38, Berlin: DeGruyter.

Forrest, M. (1996), *Modernising the Classics. A Study in Curriculum Development*, Exeter: University of Exeter Press.

Forrest, M. (2003), 'The Abolition of Compulsory Latin and its Consequences', in C. Stray (ed.), *The Classical Association. The First Century 1903–2003*, 42–66, Oxford: Oxford University Press.

Fortes, F., and P. Prata (2015), 'A Sobrevivência do Latim', in F. Fortes and P. Prata, *O Latim Hoje*, Campinas, Mercado das Letras.

Foster, P., and A. S. Ohta (2005), 'Negotiation of Meaning and Peer Assistance in Second Language Classrooms'. *Applied Linguistics*, 26 (3): 402–430.

Foster, R., and D. McCarthy (2016), *Ossa Latinitatis Sola Ad Mentem Reginaldi Rationemque*, Washington, DC: The Catholic University of America Press.

Foster, R. (2014), 'Speaking Latin: Understanding the Latin Language', *Latinitatis corpus*. Available online: http://thelatinlanguage.org/featured/speaking-latin/ (accessed 9 December 2019).

Foster, R. (forthcoming), *Ossium Carnes Multae e Marci Tullii Ciceronis epistulis,* Washington, DC: The Catholic University of America Press.

Foxhall, L., J. Story and S. Knight (2012), 'Latin Lives on! Classical and Post-Classical Latin', *Journal for Excellence in Teaching and Learning*, 3, October. Available online: https://www108.lamp.le.ac.uk/ojs1/index.php/jetl/article/view/2342 (accessed 24 April 2020).

Frazer, J, (ed.) (1921), *Apollodorus: The Library, with an English Translation*, Cambridge, MA: Harvard University Press.

Gall, A. (2020), 'A study in the use of embedded readings to improve the accessibility and understanding of Latin literature at A Level', *Journal of Classics Teaching*, 41, forthcoming.

Gambrell, L. (2011), 'Seven Rules of Engagement: What's Most Important to Know About Motivation to Read', *The Reading Teacher*, 65 (3): 172–8.

Gard, A., L. Gilman and J. Gorman (1993), *Speech and Language Development Chart,* Austin: Pro-Ed, Inc.

Gooder, E. (2013), *Latin for Local History: An Introduction*, London: Routledge.

Goodhew, D. (2003), 'Using ICT in Classics. Or How I Stopped Worrying and Love the Computer', in J. Morwood (ed.), *The Teaching of Classics*, 136–44, Cambridge: Cambridge University Press.

Grasha, A. (1984), 'Learning Styles: The Journey from Greenwich Observatory (1796) to the College Classroom (1984)', *Improving College And University Teaching*, 32 (1): 46–53.

Gratius Avitus, A. (2018), 'Spoken Latin: Learning, Teaching, Lecturing and Research', *Journal of Classics Teaching*, 38: 46–52.

Gregg, K. (1984), 'Krashen's Monitor and Occam's Razor', *Applied Linguistics*, 5 (2): 79–100.

Gregorc, A. (1984), 'Style as a Symptom: A Phenomenological Perspective'. *Theory into Practice*, 23 (1): 51–5.

Griffiths, M. (1992), 'Teaching Languages to Adults', *Language Learning Journal*, 5 (1): 63–5.

Griffiths, W. (2008), 'Increasing Access to Latin in Schools', in B. Lister (ed.), *Meeting the Challenge: International Perspectives on the Teaching of Latin,* 71–90, Cambridge: Cambridge University Press.

References

Hall, G., and G. Cook (2012), 'Own-language use in language teaching and learning', *Language Teaching*, 45 (03): 271–08. Available online: https://doi.org/10.1017/S0261444812000067 (accessed 1 May 2020).

Harmar, J. (1969), *Praxis grammatica, 1623. English linguistics, 1500–1800: A Collection of Facsimile Reprints*, Menston (Yorks.): Scolar Publishers.

Hermann, M. (2016), 'Łacina w XXI wieku', *Nowoczesna dydaktyka akademickia języków klasycznych*, Warszawa: 29–38.

Hertberg-Davis, H., and C. M. Callahan (2008) 'A Narrow Escape', *Gifted Child Quarterly*, 52 (3): 199–216.

Herzog, M. (n.d.), 'How did the Language Proficiency Scale get started?' Available online: https://www.govtilr.org/Skills/IRL%20Scale%20History.htm (accessed 1 May 2020).

Hill, R. (forthcoming), 'Task-Based Language Teaching and Ancient Languages', in C. Rico (ed.), *Transmitting a Heritage: The Teaching of Ancient Languages from Antiquity to the 21st Century*, Jerusalem: Polis Institute Press.

Hogrefe, P. (1959), *The Sir Thomas More circle: a program of ideas and their impact on secular drama*, Urbana: University of Illinois Press.

Hood, P. (1994), 'Communicative Grammar: A Practical Problem-Solving Approach?', *Language Learning Journal*, 9 (1): 28–31.

Horowski, J. (1972), 'Lingua Latina secundum naturae rationem explicata', *Języki Obce w Szkole*: 103–07.

Howatt, A. (1984), *A History of English Language Teaching*, Oxford: Oxford University Press.

Hunt, S. (2016), *Starting to Teach Latin*, London: Bloomsbury Academic.

Hunt, S. (2018a), 'Getting Classics into Schools? Classics and the Social Justice Agenda of the UK Coalition Government, 2010–2015', in A. Holmes-Henderson, S. Hunt and M. Musié (eds), *Forward with Classics*, 9–26, London: Bloomsbury Academic.

Hunt, S. (2018b), 'Latin Is Not Dead: The Rise of Communicative Approaches to the Teaching of Latin in the United States', in A. Holmes-Henderson, S. Hunt and M. Musié (eds), *Forward with Classics*, 88–107, London: Bloomsbury Academic.

Hunt, S., C. Letchford, L. Manning, M. Lloyd and R. Plummer (2018), 'The Virtue of Variety. Opening the Doors to Wider Pedagogical Practices in UK Schools and Universities', *Journal of Classics Teaching*, 38: 53–60.

Hunt, S. (2020a), 'School Qualifications in Classical Subjects in the UK. A Brief Overview', *CUCD Bulletin*, 49. Available online: https://cucd.blogs.sas.ac.uk/files/2020/01/HUNT-School-qualifications-in-classical-subjects-in-the-UK-3.pdf (accessed 9 April 2020).

Hunt, S. (2020b). 'Classics Matters. My Double Life', *Classics for All Magazine: Tenth Anniversary Issue*. Available online: https://s3-eu-west-1.amazonaws.com/client-system/classicsforall/2020/03/ClassicsMatters-Spring20.pdf (accessed 9 April 2020).

Hunt, S. (2020c), 'Classics Teaching in the Time of Coronavirus', *ad familiares Magazine*. Available online: https://adfamiliares.classicsforall.org.uk/classics-teaching-in-the-time-of-coronavirus/ (accessed 6 April 2020).

Jenney, C., E. Baade and T. Burgess (1990), *Jenney's First Year Latin*, Needham, MA: Prentice Hall.

Johnson, B. (2010), 'This Lunacy About Latin Makes Me Want To Weep With Rage', *The Daily Telegraph*, 15 March 2010.

Jordan, G. (2004), *Theory Construction in Second Language Acquisition*, Amsterdam: John Benjamins.

Khan-Evans, A. (2018), 'The Appeal of Non-Linguistic Classical Studies Among Sixth-Form Students', in A. Holmes-Henderson, S. Hunt and M. Musié (eds), *Forward with Classics*, 205–14, London: Bloomsbury Academic.

Komorowska, H. (2005), *Metodyka Nauczania Języków Obcych*, Otwock: Fraszka Edukacyjna.

Krashen, S. (1982), *Principles and Practice in Second Language Acquisition*, Oxford: Pergamon Press.

Krashen, S., and T. Terrell (1983), *The Natural Approach. Language Acquisition in the Classroom*, London: Pergamon Press.

Krashen, S. (1985), *The Input Hypothesis: Issues and Implications*, New York: Longman.

Krzyżanowski, J. (1936), 'W liceum mówimy po łacinie i po grecku', *Przegląd Klasyczny* II 7–8: 537–40.

Krzyżanowski, J. (1937a), 'Żywa Łacina (system dr Rouse'a)', *Przegląd Klasyczny* III 9–10: 669–80.

References

Krzyżanowski, J. (1937b), 'Żywa łacina', *Prosto z mostu – tygodnik literacko-artystyczny*, 44 (152): 5.

Kuhn, M., P. Schwanenflugel and E. Meisinger (2010), 'Aligning Theory and Assessment of Reading Fluency: Automaticity, Prosody, and Definitions of Fluency', *Reading Research Quarterly*, 45: 230–51.

Kuhner, J. (2018), 'Global Latinists', *New Criterion*. Available online: https://newcriterion.com/issues/2018/2/global-latinists (accessed 26 December 2019).

Lantolf, J. P., S. L. Thorne and M. E. Poehner (2015), 'Sociocultural Theory and Second Language Development', in B. Van Patten and J. Williams (eds), *Theories in Second Language Acquisition*, 2nd edn, New York: Routledge.

Lanvers, U. (2017), 'Elitism in Language Learning in the UK', in D. Rivers, and K. Kotzmann (eds), *Isms in Language Education*, 50–74, Berlin: Mouton De Guyter.

Latousek, B. (1998), 'Computamus: We Compute!', in R. LaFleur (ed.), *Latin for the 21st Century: From Concept to Classroom*, 263–275, Glenview, Scott Foresman – Addison Wesley.

Lave, J., and E. Wenger (1991), *Situated Learning: Legitimate Peripheral Participation*, Cambridge: Cambridge University Press.

Lenkowski, St. (1937), 'Uwagi o obecnym programie łaciny', *Przegląd Klasyczny* III 9–10: 665–668.

Letchford, C. (2017), 'Living Latin'. Available online: https://warwick.ac.uk/fac/cross_fac/iatl/sharing-practice/staff/all-academic/letchford/ (accessed 8 April 2020).

Letts, M. (2019), 'Oratio de Latine loquendo', unpublished paper given at the Oxford Latinitas Project *Septimana Latina*, Rome, 2019.

Lhomond, C. F. (2009) Carfagni, R. (ed.) *Epitome Historiae Sacrae: brevi Christi vitae narration addita*, USA: Edizioni Accademia Vivarium Novum

Lipsius, J., and J. Moretus (1609), *I. Lipsi[i] De recta pronunciatione Latinæ linguæ dialogus. Editio vltima. De recta pronunciatione Latinæ linguæ dialogus*. Antuerpiae, Ex officina Plantiniana Apud Ioannem Moretum.

Lister, B. (2007), *Changing Classics in Schools*, Cambridge: Cambridge University Press.

Lister, B. (2015), 'Exclusively for Everyone: To What Extent has the Cambridge Latin Course Widened Access to Latin?', in E. Archibald, W. Brockliss and J. Gnoza (eds), *Learning Latin and Greek from Antiquity to the Present*, 184–97, Cambridge: Cambridge University Press.

Llewellyn, N. (2008), 'Wyoming Catholic College: Colloquium Secundum'. Available online: www.youtube.com/watch?v=yNFb0tM9xqE (accessed 24 April 2020).

Lloyd, M. E. (2016), 'Living Latin: An Interview with Professor Terence Tunberg'. *Journal of Classics Teaching* 34: 44–8. Available online: https://doi.org/10.1017/S2058631016000234 (accessed 17 May 2020).

Lloyd, M. E. (2017), 'Living Latin: Exploring a Communicative Approach to Latin Teaching Through a Sociocultural Perspective on Language Learning', PhD thesis, The Open University. Available online: http://oro.open.ac.uk/48886/ (accessed 19 January 2020).

Loch, M. (2013), 'Żywa łacina: między prawdą a mitem. Zarys historii zjawiska oraz próba zdefiniowania terminu żywa łacina', *Literary and Language Studies of Warsaw*, 3: 153–70.

Loch, M. (2015), 'Latine loquor! czyli żywa łacina jako metoda dydaktyczna', *Symbolae Philologorum Posnaniensium* XXV (2): 137–151.

Loch, M. (2018a), 'Jeśli nie tłumaczenie, to co – czyli propozycja zajęć o "Wróbelku" Katullusa'. Available online: www.youtube.com/watch?v=Uv_VUVVr8Yk (accessed 24 April 2020; the introduction is in Polish, but the activity itself is in Latin).

Loch, M. (2018b), 'Martinus docet: Capitulum II Familiae Romanae', Available online: www.youtube.com/watch?v=4obG3dMNupI (accessed 24 April 2020).

Loewen, S. (2007), 'Error Correction in the Second Language Classroom', *Clear News*, 11 (2).

Long, M. (1996), 'The Role of the Linguistic Environment in Second Language Acquisition', in W. Ritchie and T. Bhatia (eds), *Handbook of Second Language Acquisition*, 413–68, San Diego, CA: Academic Press.

Long, M. (2015), *Second Language Acquisition and Task-Based Language Teaching*, Malden, MA: Wiley-Blackwell.

Long, M. (2016), 'In Defense of Tasks and TBLT: Nonissues and Real Issues', *Annual Review of Applied Linguistics*, 36: 5–33.

Long, M., and P. Porter (1985), 'Group Work, Interlanguage Talk, and Second Language Acquisition', *TESOL Quarterly*, 19 (2): 207–28.

Looney, D., and N. Lusin (2018), 'Enrollments in Languages Other than English in United States Institutions of Higher Education, Summer 2016 and Fall 2016: Preliminary Report', *Modern Language Association*. Available online: https://files.eric.ed.gov/fulltext/ED569204.pdf (accessed 24 January 2020).

Macdonald, S. (2011), 'Krashen & Second Language Acquisition (SLA) Theory: A Re-evaluation of How to Teach Classical Languages', *Journal of Classics Teaching*, 22: 3–5.

Malinowski, G. (2016), 'Latin Teaching in Poland: A Historical Outline and the Current Position', *The Journal of Greco-Roman Studies*, 55/3: 65–77.

Manning, L. (2016), 'Duae Orationes Paedagogicae Marci Antonii Mureti De Praestantia Litterarum Humaniorum in Universitate Saeculo Sexto Decimo', MA thesis, University of Kentucky, Lexington.

Manning, L. (forthcoming), 'Toward a Definition of Active Latin: A Mixed-Methods Comparative Case Study', PhD thesis in progress, University of Kentucky, Lexington.

Maranhão, S. (2009), 'Reflexões sobre o ensino de Língua Latina em cursos superiores de Letras Modernas', *Instrumento. Juiz de Fora*, 11, 1: 27–36.

Martindale, C., and R. Thomas (2006), *Classics and the Uses of Reception*, Malden, MA: Blackwell.

Martínez, S. C. (2014), *Diálogos, Prácticas de griego antiguo*. Guadix: Cultura Clásica.

Mason, B., and S. Krashen (2018) 'American Students' Vocabulary Acquisition Rate in Japanese as a Foreign Language from Listening to a Story', *Turkish Online Journal of English Language Teaching (TOJELT)*, 3 (1): 6–9.

Matrix, S. (2014), 'The Netflix Effect: Teens, Binge Watching, and On-Demand Digital Media Trends', *Jeunesse: Young People, Texts, Cultures,* 6 (1): 119–38.

Meisel, J. (2011), *First and Second Language Acquisition: Parallels and Differences*, Cambridge: Cambridge University Press.

Mille Noctes Database (2020), 'Mille Noctes Database'. Available online: http://www.latinteachertoolbox.com/mn-database.html (accessed 25 March 2020).

Miller, D. (2019), *Greek Pedagogy in Crisis: A Pedagogical Analysis and Assessment of New Testament Greek in Twenty-First-Century Theological Education*, Eugene, OR: Wipf and Stock.

Miller, G. (2018), 'Communicative Approaches to Learning Latin: Voice and Tone in Learning Latin Terminations', *Journal of Classics Teaching*, 19: 61–2.

Minkova, M., and T. Tunberg (2004), *Readings and Exercises in Latin Prose Composition, from Antiquity to the Renaissance*, Newburyport, MA: Focus Publishing.

Minkova, M., and T. Tunberg (2012), 'Active Latin: Speaking, Writing, Hearing the Language', *New England Classical Journal*, 39 (2):113–28.

Miotti, C. (2006), *O Ensino do Latim nas Universidades Públicas do Estado de São Paulo e o Método Inglês Reading Latin: um Estudo de Caso. Dissertação.* Instituto de Estudos da Linguagem: UNICAMP.

Miraglia, L. (2009), *Nova via Latine doceo*, Montella: Edizioni Accademia Vivarium Novum.

Miraglia, L. (2009), *Lingua Latina per se illustrata. Nova via. Latine doceo. Guida per gl'insegnanti. Parte I: Familia Romana*, Montella.

Miraglia, L. (2010), *Fabulae Syrae. Graecorum Romanorumque fabulae ad usum discipulorum Latine narratae, Romae*, Montella.

Mitchell, R., F. Myles and E. Marsden, (eds) (2013), *Second Language Learning Theories*, 3rd edn, New York: Routledge.

Mitchell, R., F. Myles and E. Marsden, (eds) (2019), *Second Language Learning Theories*, 4th edn, New York: Routledge.

Modern Language Centre (MLC) Kings College London (2016) *Syllabus for Post Graduate non-assessed module Italian Beginners*, London: KCL MLC.

Morgan, C. (2001), 'The effects of negative managerial feedback on student motivation: Implications for gender differences in teacher-student relations', *Sex Roles*, 44, (9–10) (05): 513–35. Available online: https://link.springer.com/article/10.1023/A:1012286907894 (accessed 24 January 2020).

Morris, S. (1966), *Viae Novae: New Techniques in Latin Teaching*, London: Hulton Educational Publications.

References

Mulroy, D. (2013), *The War Against Grammar,* Portsmouth, NH: Heinemann.

Murray, T. and Dimock, G. ([1919]1998) *Homer. Odyssey. Vol. 1: Books 1–12*, Cambridge, MA: Harvard University Press.

Nation, I. (2001), *Learning Vocabulary in Another Language,* Cambridge: Cambridge University Press.

Navarro, E. (n.d.), *Vida e obra de José de Anchieta*. Cursos de Tupi Antigo e Língua Geral (Nheengatu). Available online: http://tupi.fflch.usp.br/node/36 (accessed 26 December 2019).

Norlin, G. (1929), Isocrates. Vol. 2: *On the Peace*; *Areopagiticus*; *Against the Sophists*; *Antidosis*; *Panathenaicus*, Cambridge, MA: Harvard University Press.

Nunan, D. (1989), *Designing Tasks for the Communicative Classroom*, Cambridge: Cambridge University Press.

Nuttall, C. (2005), *Teaching Reading Skills in a Foreign Language*, London: Heinemann Educational.

Ochman, K. (2014), 'Nauczanie łaciny. Immersja czy gramatyka?', *Języki Obce w Szkole*, 3: 54–8.

Olimpi, A. (2019), 'Legere Discitur Legendo: Extensive Reading in the Latin Classroom', *Journal of Classics Teaching*, 39: 83–9.

Ørberg, H. (2006), *Lingua Latina per se Illustrata: Colloquia Personarum*, London: Hackett Publishing Company.

Ørberg, H. (2011), *Lingua Latina per se Illustrata: Familia Romana*, London: Hackett Publishing Company.

Ørberg, H. (2017), *Lingua Latina per se Illustrata: Roma Aeterna*. London: Hackett Publishing Company.

Osipowicz, A. (2003), 'Jak rozumiem pojęcie LATINITAS VIVA – na podstawie praktyki szkolnej w liceum i pracy nad podręcznikiem ROMA LATINE DICTA', *Collectanea Philologica* V, Łódź, 221–29.

Ostrowski S. (1981), *Metodyka nauczania języka łacińskiego*, Warszawa: WSiP.

Owens, P. (2016), 'Barbarians at the Gate: An Analysis of Some Perils in Active Latin Pedagogy', *Classical World*, 109 (4): 507–23.

Paton, W. ([1918, 1971] 1979) *The Greek Anthology. Vol. 4: Books x–xii*, Cambridge: Harvard University Press.

Patrick, B. (2011), 'TPRS & Latin in the Classroom. Experiences of a US Latin Teacher', *Journal of Classics Teaching*, 22: 8–10.

Patrick, B. (2015), 'Making Sense of Comprehensible Input in the Latin Classroom', *Teaching Classical Languages*, Spring: 108–36.

Patrick, B. (2019), 'Comprehensible Input and Krashen's theory', *Journal of Classics Teaching*, 39: 37–44.

Paul, J. (2013), 'The Democratic Turn in (and through) Pedagogy: A Case Study of the Cambridge Latin Course', in L. Hardwick and S. Harrison (eds), *Classics in the Modern World. A 'Democratic' Turn*, 143–56, Oxford: Oxford University Press.

Perrone-Bertolotti, M., J. Kujala, J. Vidal, C. Hamame, T. Ossandon, O. Bertrand, L. Minotti, P. Kahane, K. Jerbi and J-P. Lachaux (2012), 'How Silent Is Silent Reading? Intracerebral Evidence for Top-Down Activation of Temporal Voice Areas during Reading', *Journal of Neuroscience* 32: 17554–62.

Petrovic, A. (2015), '"Sacred Law"', in E. Eidinow and J. Kindt (eds), *The Oxford Handbook of Ancient Greek Religion*, 339–52, Oxford: Oxford University Press.

Piantaggini, L. (2019) 'Input-Based Activities', *Journal of Classics Teaching*, 39: 51–6.

Piazza, J. (2019), 'Structuring CI-Based Practices for Success' *Journal of Classics Teaching*, 39: 57–9.

Pinto, N, (2015), 'Nossa herança, nosso trabalho', in F. Fortes and P. Prata (eds), *O Latim Hoje,* Campinas: Mercado das Letras.

Popiak, W. (2005), *Łacina i greka w polskiej szkole w latach 1919–1939*, Warszawa.

Pope, A. (1711), 'An Essay on Criticism'. Available online: https://www.poetryfoundation.org/articles/69379/an-essay-on-criticism (accessed 1 May 2020).

Posselius, J. (1589), *Johannis Posselii Orationes Octo, Habitae In Publicis Congressibus Academiae Rostochiensis. Francofurdi Ad Moenum*, Spessius.

Poznański, A. (2009), 'Review of H.H. Orberg, Lingua Latina per se illustrata', *Classica Wratislaviensia* 29: 145–147.

PTF (2017), 'Szkoła przyjazna łacinie'. Available online: www.ptf.edu.pl/szkola-przyjazna-lacinie (accessed 24 April 2020).

References

Quigley, A. (2018), *Closing the Vocabulary Gap*, London: Routledge.
Ramahlo, M. (2019), 'On Starting to Teach Using CI', *Journal of Classics Teaching*, 39: 45–50.
Rasmussen, S. (2015), 'Why Oral Latin?', *Teaching Classical Languages*, 6 (1): 37–45.
Reynolds, L. (1998), *M. Tulli Ciceronis de Finibus Bonorum et Malorum Libri Quinque*, Oxford: Clarendon Press.
Ribeiro Leite, L. (2016), *Latine Loqui: Curso Básico de Latim*. Goiabeiras, Vitória: EDUFES, Press of the Federal University of Espírito Santo Press. Available online: http://edufes.ufes.br/items/show/394 (accessed 28 March 2020).
Richards, J., and T. Rodgers (2001), *Approaches and Methods in Language Teaching*, Cambridge: Cambridge University Press.
Richards, J., and T. Rodgers (2009), *Approaches and Methods in Language Teaching*, 2nd edn, Cambridge: Cambridge University Press.
Richards, J., and T. Rodgers (2014), *Approaches and Methods in Language Teaching*, 3rd edn, Cambridge: Cambridge University Press.
Rico, C. (2015), *Polis*, Jerusalem, Israel: Polis Institute Press.
Ristoff, D. (2014), 'O novo perfil do campus brasileiro: uma análise do perfil socioeconômico do estudante de graduação', *Avaliação* (Campinas), 19, 3 Sorocaba Available online: http://www.scielo.br/scielo.php?script=sci_arttext&pid=S1414-40772014000300010&lng=pt&tlng=pt (accessed 26 December 2019).
Rivers, W. (1987), *Interactive Language Teaching,* Cambridge: Cambridge University Press.
Rogers, K. (2019), 'Comprehensible Input FAQs', *Journal of Classics Teaching*, 39: 33–6.
Rogers, K. (2011), 'Editorial'. *Journal of Classics Teaching*, 22: 1.
Rosenthal, G. (1924), *Lebendiges Latein. Neue Wege im Lateinunterricht*, Leipzig: Ernst Oldenburg.
Rouse, W. (1909), *A Greek Boy at Home: A Story Written in Greek*, London: Blackie and Son.
Russell, K. (2018), 'Read Like a Roman: Teaching Students to Read in Latin Word Order', *Journal of Classics Teaching*, 37: 17–29.
Ryan, C. (2017), 'Review of Speaking Ancient Greek as a Living Language: Level One, Student's Volume, Polis Institute Press, *Journal of Classics Teaching*, 36: 40–50.
Ryan, R., and M. Deci (2000), 'Intrinsic and Extrinsic Motivations: Classic Definitions and New Directions', *Contemporary Educational Psychology*, 25: 54–67.
Ryba, J. (2015), 'Nauczanie języków klasycznych w Polsce w latach 1945–2008 (The teaching of classical languages in Poland 1945–2008)', PhD thesis, Jagiellonian University, Cracow.
Ryba, J. (2019), *Języki klasyczne i kultura antyczna w zreformowanym liceum ogólnokształcącym*, Eos CVI (forthcoming).
Ryba, J., E. Wolanin and A. Klęczar (2017), *Homo Romanus 1. Podręcznik do języka łacińskiego i kultury antycznej*, Kraków: Draco.
Ryba, J., E. Wolanin and A. Klęczar (2019), *Homo Romanus 2. Podręcznik do języka łacińskiego i kultury antycznej*, Kraków: Draco.
Sawyer, B. (2016), 'Latin for All Identities', *Journal of Classics Teaching*, 33: 35–9.
Schmitt, N. (2000), *Vocabulary in Language Teaching*, Cambridge: Cambridge University Press.
Schwamm, J. (2019), 'Auream Quisquis Medocritatem Diligit: The Joyful Learning Community Model for Learning Latin Online', in B. Natoli, and S. Hunt (eds), *Teaching Classics with Technology*, 19–28, London: Bloomsbury Academic.
Schwarcz, L., and F. Gomes, (eds) (2018), *Dicionário da Escravidão e Liberdade*, São Paulo: Companhia das Letras.
Sears, L., and K. Ballestrini (2019), 'Adapting Antiquity: Using Tiered Texts to Increase Latin Reading Proficiency', *Journal of Classics Teaching*, 39: 71–7.
Seebohm, F. (1867), *The Oxford Reformers: John Colet, Erasmus and Thomas More*, London: Longmans Green.
Sidwell, K. (1995), *Reading Medieval Latin*, Cambridge: Cambridge University Press.
Sidwell, K., and P. Jones (1998), *Reading Latin*, Cambridge: Cambridge University Press.
Sinclair, J. (2018), '"Not so Much Learning to Speak Latin, but Speaking to Learn It": Action Research on the Use of Conversational, Spoken Latin in the UK Secondary School Classroom', *Journal of Classics Teaching,* 38: 63–4.

References

Sokolowski, F. (1962), *Lois sacrées des cités grecques*. Supplément, Paris: E. de Boccard.
Sokolowski, F. (1969), *Lois sacrées des cités grecques*, Paris: E. de Boccard.
Stern, H. (1983), *Fundamental Concepts of Language Teaching*, Oxford: Oxford University Press.
Stray, C. (1992), *The Living Word: W.H.D. Rouse and the Crisis of Classics in Edwardian England*, London: Bristol Classical Press.
Stray, C. (2003), 'Classics in the Curriculum up to the 1960s', in J. Morwood (ed.), *The Teaching of Classics*, 1–5, Cambridge: Cambridge University Press.
Stray, C. (2018), *Classics in Britain. Scholarship, Education, and Publishing*, Oxford: Oxford University Press.
Streett, D. (2010), 'Is Biblical Greek Oral-Aural Pedagogy Worthwhile?'. Available online: http://www.academia.edu/2997032/Is_Biblical_Greek_Oral-Aural_Pedagogy_Worthwhile (accessed May 2020).
Streett, D. (n.d.), 'καὶ τὰ λοιπά'. Available online: https://danielstreett.com/category/greek-pedagogy/ (accessed 1 May 2020).
Strycharczyk, B. (2014), 'Do czego dzisiaj potrzebna jest łacina?', *Języki Obce w Szkole*, 3: 62–5.
Swain, M. (1985), 'Communicative Competence: Some Roles of Comprehensible Input and Comprehensible Output in Its Development', in S. Gass and C. Madden (eds), *Input in Second Language Acquisition*, 235–53, Rowley, MA: Newbury House.
Swain, M. (1993), 'The Output Hypothesis: Just Speaking and Writing Aren't Enough', *The Canadian Modern Language Review*, 50 (1): 158–64.
Tacke, O. (1923), *Der Sprachunterricht muss umkehren!*, Leipzig: Ernst Oldenburg.
Tanca, E. (2018), 'Linee guida per l'insegnamento delle lingue latina e greca al liceo classico'. [Available online: www.academia.edu/36284018/LINEE_GUIDA_PER_LINSEGNAMENTO_DELLE_LINGUE_LATINA_E_GRECA_AL_LICEO_CLASSICO (accessed 24 April 2020).
Teaching Latin for Acquisition (2020). Teaching Latin for Acquisition Facebook Group. Facebook. Available online: https://www.facebook.com/groups/AcquireLatin/ (accessed 24 April 2020).
Toczko, R. (2014), 'Polska w Europie: łacina w szkole', *Języki Obce w Szkole* 3: 66–71.
Torchia, W. (1973), 'Teaching Latinly', *The Classical Outlook*, 51 (1): 5.
Traupman, J. (2007), *Conversational Latin for Oral Proficiency*, Mudelein, IL: Bolchazy Carducci Publishers.
Tres Columnae Project (n.d.), *Tres Columnae* Project. Available online:http://trescolumnae.com/gamma/ (accessed 6 April 2020.
Truscott, J (2016) 'The effectiveness of error correction: Why do meta-analytic reviews produce such different answers?', in Y. Leung (ed.) *Epoch making in English Teaching and Learning: Evolution, Innovation, Revolution,* Taipei: Crane.
Tunberg, T. (2012), 'De rationibus quibus homines docti artem Latine colloquendi et ex tempore dicendi saeculis XVI et XVII coluerunt,' *Supplementa Humanistica Lovaniensia*, 31, Leuven: University Press.
Tyrtarion (2010), 'Lugete, o Veneres (Catulli Carmen III)'. Available online: www.youtube.com/watch?v=wKLDQLjCLG4 (accessed 24 April 2020).
Tyrtarion (2011), 'Tristia (ex Ovidii Tristibus, I,3; versus 1–24)'. Available online: www.youtube.com/watch?v=44LjyjnVHQU (accessed 24 April 2020).
US Department of State (n.d.), 'Foreign Language Training'. Available online: https://www.state.gov/foreign-language-training/ (accessed 1 May 2020).
Van den Arend, A. (2018), 'Something Old, Something New: Marrying Early Modern Latin Pedagogy and Second Language Acquisition (SLA) Theory', *Teaching Classical Languages,* 10 (1): 1–32.
VanPatten, B., and J. Williams (2015), 'Early Theories in SLA', in B. VanPatten and J. Williams (eds), *Theories in Second Language Acquisition: An Introduction*, 17–33, New York: Routledge.
Verbaal, W, Y. Maes, Y. and J. Papy (2007), *Latinitas Perennis, Volume I: The Continuity of Latin Literature*, Leiden: Brill.
Viëtor, W. (1882), *Der Sprachunterricht muss umkehren!*, Heilbronn: Henninger.
Vygotsky, L. S. (1978), *Mind in Society: the development of higher psychological processes*, Cambridge, MA; London: Harvard University Press.
Waddell, H. (1932), *A Book of Medieval Latin for Schools*, London: Constable.

References

Walden, V. (2019), 'Distance learning and Technology: Teaching Latin, Greek and Classical Civilization at a Distance from the UK', in B. Natoli and S. Hunt (eds), *Teaching Classics with Technology*, 29–38, London: Bloomsbury Academic.

Walker, R. (2019), 'Education at Bat: Seven Principles for Educators'. Available online: https://www.gse.harvard.edu/news/uk/09/01/education-bat-seven-principles-educators (accessed 6 April 2020).

Waugh, E. (1945), *Brideshead Revisited: The Sacred and Profane Memories of Captain Charles Ryder*, London: Chapman and Hall.

Wegenhart, T. (2015), 'Better Reading Through Science: Using Research-Based Models to Help Students Read Latin Better', *Journal of Classics Teaching*, 31: 8–13.

Wheelock, F. and LaFleur, R. (2011), *Wheelock's Latin*, 7th ed., New York: Harper Collins.

White, J. (2015), 'Blitz Latin Revisited', *Journal of Classics Teaching*, 32, 43–9.

Whyte, S. (2019a), 'Learner Motivation, Teacher Competence and Indigenous Assessment Criteria in ESP', *Teaching Languages with Technology Second Language Resources, Teacher Education, and Research (blog)*, 11 November 2019. Available online: https://shonawhyte.wordpress.com/2019/11/11/learner-motivation-teacher-competence-and-indigenous-assessment-criteria-in-esp/ (accessed 24 April 2020).

Whyte, S. (2019b), 'Widdowson Plenary: New Starts and Different Kinds of Failure'. *On Teaching Languages with Technology Second Language Resources, Teacher Education, and Research (blog)*, 13 November 2019. Available online: https://shonawhyte.wordpress.com/2019/11/13/widdowson-plenary-new-starts-and-different-kinds-of-failure/ (accessed 24 April 2020).

Wikipedia (2020). Wikepedia notes. Available online: https://en.wikipedia.org/wiki/Rorschach_test (accessed 25 March 2020).

Wilding, L. (1995), *Latin Course for Schools*, Bristol: Bristol Classical Press.

Wilkins, J. (1969). 'Teaching the Classical Languages: towards a theory I'. *Didaskalos*, 3 (1).

Wills, J. (1998), 'Speaking Latin in Schools and Colleges', *The Classical World*, 92 (1): 27–34.

Wolanin, H. (1991), 'Kształtowanie i kontrola sprawności rozumienia tekstu łacińskiego', *Języki obce w szkole*, rok XXXV, maj–czerwiec, 3 (173): 195–8.

Wolanin, H. (1992), 'Techniki bezpośrednie w nauczaniu łaciny', *Języki obce w szkole*, rok XXXVI, maj–czerwiec, 3 (178): 205–07.

Wringe, C. (2016), *Understanding Educational Aims*, London: Routledge.

Yonge, C. (1856), *The Orations of Marcus Tullius Cicero (trans)*. London: Henry G. Bohn. Available online: https://www.perseus.tufts.edu/hopper/text?doc=Perseus:text:1999.02.0019:text=Catil.:speech=1:chapter=1 (accessed 20 March 2020).

ABBREVIATIONS

A level	Advanced level examination.
ACTFL	American Council on the Teaching of Foreign Languages.
ANDIFES	Associação Nacional dos Dirigentes das Instituições Federais de Ensino Superior: National Association of the Deans of Federal Higher Education Institutions.
AS level	Advanced Subsidiary level.
CD	Compact disc.
CEFR	Common European Framework of Reference for Language.
CI	Comprehensible input.
CLC	Cambridge Latin Course (Latin coursebook).
CLC	*Circulus Latinus Cantabrigiensis.*
CLT	Communicative Language Teaching.
CSCP	Cambridge School Classics Project. The authors of the Cambridge Latin Course.
DfE	Department for Education (UK).
EDUQAS	A UK examination board which is part of WJEC (see below). Sets Latin GCSEs (see below).
EFL	English as a Foreign Language.
ESP	English for Specific Purposes.
FSI	Foreign Service Institute, a training organization for American diplomats.
FVR	Free Voluntary Reading.
GCSE	General Certificate of Secondary Education.
GT	Grammar-Translation.
IB	International Baccalaureate is an international qualification set by the IB programme in Geneva. Taken by students aged seventeen to eighteen. Consists of a range of subject-specific assessments.
INEP	Instituto Nacional de Estudos e Pesquisas Educacionais Anísio Teixeira: Anísio Teixeira National Institute of Educational Studies and Research.
K-12	Kindergarten–Year 12 (ages four to eighteen) in the US school system.
KCL	King's College London.
L1	First language.
L2	Second language.

Abbreviations

LLPSI	*Lingua Latina per se Illustrata*. Latin course book by Øberg.
LSE	Living Sequential Expression.
MFL	Modern Foreign Languages.
MLC	Modern Language Centre (at King's College, London).
O level	UK examination series taken at age sixteen. Replaced by GCSE examinations in 1988.
OCR	Oxford and Cambridge and RSA examinations board. Sets Latin GCSEs (see above).
OLP	Oxford Latinitas Project.
PGCE	Postgraduate Certificate in Education. Academic qualification for teaching in the UK schools.
PTF	Polskie Towarzystwo Filologiczne: Societas Philologa Polonorum / Polish Philological Association.
SI	Societas Iesu, a Roman Catholic religious order, also known as the Jesuits.
Sixth form	Two-year period when students aged sixteen to eighteen in the UK follow specialized courses leading to A level examinations (see above). Also known as Years 12–13.
SLA	Second Language Acquisition.
TENOR	Teaching English for No Other Reason.
TBLT	Task-Based Language Teaching.
TPR	Total Physical Response.
TPRS	Teaching Proficiency through Reading and Storytelling.
UK	United Kingdom.
US	United States.
USSR	Union of Soviet Socialist Republics.
WJEC	Welsh Joint Education Committee. Sets Latin qualifications at Certificate Levels 1 and 2.

INDEX

A Primer of Ecclesiastical Latin, *see* publications
A level examination, *see* examinations
Accademia Vivarium Novum 26–7, 28, 30–1, 81–2, 83, 86, 179–82, 183
accuracy
　of forms, moving away from 2, 85
　of reading 27, 30, 56, 136
ad Alpes, *see* publications
affective filter, importance of 17, 63, 67, 70, 93, 135
　see also Krashen
Alexandros, *see* publications
American Classical League (ACL) 9, 16
American Council on the Teaching of Foreign Languages (ACTFL) 14, 47–8, 51, 53
de Anchieta, Joseph (scholar) 94–9
antonyms 85–6, 149
　see also synonyms
Aquinas, Thomas (philosopher) 190, 192
Archaeological Institute of America 16
armadillo 94–8
Association for the Reform of Latin Teaching (ARLT) 162
Asterix, *see* publications
Athenaze, *see* publications
audience
　global 132, 197
　new types of 113
　performing to 193
　writing for 48, 52–4, 60, 130
audiobooks 198–200
audio-visual learning 94, 102, 104, 111, 135, 154, 173, 189, 196–201
Augustine (Roman author) 184, 203
autodidact 196, 199, 202

Bacon, Francis (scholar) 131
Baker, Kenneth (politician) 55
The Bible 11, 119, 130, 133, 139, 152, 154–9
Bingo, *see* games
Blair, Tony (politician) 55
Boccaccio, Giovanni (scholar) 88
Boethius, Anicius (philosopher) 181
de Busbecq, Ogier (scholar) 131
Butterfield, David (academic) 185–6

Caesar (Roman author) 99, 105, 111, 127–8
Cambridge Latin Course, *see* publications
Capelle, Jean (scholar) 129
Catiline Conspiracy 34–44, 193
Cato (Roman author) 11–12, 198

Cattus Petasatus, *see* publications
Catullus (Roman author) 93, 95, 131, 166–8, 182, 184–5
Cereta, Laura (scholar) 181
Cicero (Roman author)
　declaiming 193
　as model 11–12, 127–8
　using extracts from 102, 105–7, 131, 181, 184, 191, 197–8, 200
Circulus Latine Loquentium Wratislaviensis 163
Circulus Latinus Cantabrigiensis 183–6
Classics for All (charity) xi, 57
cognates, use of 20, 69
Colet, John (scholar) 179
colloquia 11, 102, 131, 165
Colloquia Personarum, *see* publications
Common European Framework of Reference (CERF) 47, 67, 213
Communicative Language Teaching (CLT) 2, 115, 121, 162–3 173–4
composition
　creative 28, 44, 51, 98, 111, 127–8, 130–1, 149, 155, 184–5, 190
　traditional 'prose composition', *see also* Translation into Latin or Greek
Comprehensible Input (CI) 3, 20, 23, 48, 56, 69, 115, 119, 135–6, 144, 154
　see also Krashen
Conti, Alessandro (musician) 168
Conti, Gianfranco (educationalist) 120
conventicula 14, 16, 17, 20, 68, 77, 107, 125–31, 133–40, 204
Conversational Latin for Oral Proficiency, *see* publications
Copernicus, Nicolaus (scholar) 129
Corderius (scholar) 131
corrections
　demotivating effect of 72–3
　receiving 204
　self-correcting 12, 74, 120
Covid-19 177
culture
　ancient 9, 15–16, 33, 47–9, 58, 60, 75–6, 80, 97, 145, 173–7, 181
　cultural exchange 161
　cultural references 143
　modern 90–1, 93, 96–7, 177
Curious George, *see* publications

Daily Dose of Latin, *see* Social Media
Descartes, René (philosopher) 190

Index

Dialogos, see publications
dictation 113, 118–20, 189
dictionary, use of 86, 103, 125, 139, 164, 176–7, 195–7, 200
Direct Method 1, 26, 117, 121, 162, 184
diversity
    of curriculum 125, 161, 174
    of student body 13, 57, 82, 179
drawings, use of 15, 39–40, 58–9, 94, 118, 208
    see also pictures

Ecce Romani, see publications
eclectic approach 56, 76
Education Reform Act 1932 (Poland) 162
Education Reform Act 1988 (England) 55
enarratio 88, 127, 131
engagement, improvement of 9, 10, 11, 14, 16, 38, 52, 55, 86, 88, 93, 115, 179
English as a Foreign Language (EFL) 2, 68, 130, 163
enjoyment, student
    lacking 116, 174
    through collaboration 137
    through drama 128
    through playing games 191
    through reading 28, 107, 154–6, 208
    through singing 83, 86–8
    through speaking 16, 33, 51, 58, 79, 93–4, 99, 177, 179, 195
    through us of technology 197
    through writing 49
Ennius (Roman author) 198
enrolment, student 9–10, 14, 16, 69, 91, 125, 140, 202
Epitome Historiae Sacrae, see publications
Erasmus, Desiderius (scholar) 10, 88, 102, 116, 129, 131, 179, 181, 184, 190, 200
etymology 142, 149
examinations, types of
    A Level 25, 27, 29, 88, 114
    GCSE 25, 27–30, 55–6, 80–1
    International Baccalaureate 10
exegesis 151–9
extemporization 3, 59, 60, 68–78, 83, 97, 125, 127, 190
extra-mural learning 189–93

Facebook, *see* social media
Familia Romana, see publications
fan fiction 48
feedback
    peer 136
    speed of 30
    student 83–8
    teacher 103
    usage 197–9
    see also corrections
flipped classroom 85
fluency
    expectations of 159, 179–80, 184, 191
    feelings of inadequacy about 23

pursuit of 17–18, 182–4
reading 82, 85, 88, 111–12, 117, 119, 153–6, 173, 179–80
speaking 101–2, 107–9, 111–12, 126, 143, 152–6, 168, 184
Foster, Reginald (scholar) 103, 111, 190–2
Free Voluntary Reading (FVR) 118
Fux, Johann (composer) 131

Galileo (astronomer) 190
games
    engagement with 83
    lack of commercial availability of 173
    purpose of 15, 146, 176, 183
    types of
        'Bingo' 192
        gladiator games 192
        'Latin Speed Dating' 192
        'ludi domestici' 102–3
        'Mafia' 171
        'Messenger' 169
        'Taboo' 171
        'Twenty Questions' 191
        word games 127
GCSE examinations, *see* examinations
gesture, using 60–1, 63, 70, 85, 142, 197
gladiator games, *see* games
Gouin, François (academic) 143–4
Gove, Michael (politician) 55
grammar teaching
    acquisition of 28, 49, 51–3, 83, 87, 99, 133, 185
    English grammar 87
    grammar books 86, 102, 114–15, 127, 176–7, 196–7, 199–201
    grammar knowledge
        development in young children 201–19
        instruction 3, 11–12, 13, 18, 19, 21, 29–30, 36, 44, 48–9, 56–8, 69, 84, 104, 109, 114, 117, 121, 127, 135, 137, 141, 145–7, 149, 170, 179, 180
        instruction in ancient language 109, 141, 158, 176, 180, 191
    grammar testing 88, 107–8, 109–10
    grammar-translation method 2, 9, 11–12, 19, 48, 51–2, 55, 82, 115, 139, 151, 153, 156–8, 162–3, 174–6, 192, 195–6, 202
    necessity for 23, 173
    pop-up grammar 121
    simplified 92
    Universal Grammar 203
Greek Anthology, The 147

Hadrian (Roman author) 181
Héloïse and Abélard 181
Herodotus (Greek author) 138
Holberg, Ludvig (scholar) 129, 131
Homer (Greek author) 147
Homo Romanus, see publications

Index

Horace (Roman author) 93, 95, 99, 131, 192
Horowski, Jan (academic) 162
Hrosvitha (poet) 190
Huxley, Aldous (author) 131

imitatio 49–53
immersion events 2–4, 14–5, 17, 22–3, 67–8, 79, 119, 125–31, 141–9, 159, 181, 183–5, 191–2
interaction hypothesis 136
interactive approaches 2–3, 20, 28, 33, 37–9, 40, 42, 45, 50, 59, 67–8, 72–9, 87, 97, 101, 104, 125–7, 135–6, 140, 142, 174, 194, 196, 204
International Baccalaureate, *see* examinations
intersex character 53

Jenney Latin Programme, *see* publications
Johnson, Boris (politician) 55, 64
Josephus (Greek author) 159
Juvenal (Roman author) 131

Kepler, Johannes (mathematician) 129, 131
koine Greek 134–5, 147, 151
Krashen, Stephen (academic) 3, 17, 20, 35, 40, 56–7, 69–70, 76, 93, 116, 135–6, 154
Krżyzanowski, Juliusz (academic) 162

Latin Course for Schools, *see* publications
Latin to GCSE, *see* publications
Latin for Local History, *see* publications
'Latin Speed Dating', *see* games
Linacre, Thomas (scholar) 191
von Linné, Carl (botanist) 190
listening
    assessment of 63, 94, 97, 108, 143, 154, 170–1
    to each other 28, 30, 42, 45, 59, 76, 78, 97, 100, 120, 142–3, 164, 176
    lack of 139, 155
    to lecture 185
    to music 168
    repeated 197–9, 202
    to self 71
    skill of 2, 9, 11–15, 17, 20, 45, 47, 91, 94, 115, 130, 152, 154, 174–5
    to a story 20–1, 40, 60–1, 71, 93
    tasks 35–9
Livy (Roman author) 105, 127, 128, 191
ludi domestici, *see* games

'Mafia', *see* games
Memes, *see* social media
memorization
    of grammar 9, 12, 83, 175, 179, 195, 209
    of lexical phrases 106
    of lines from a play 28
    using music or drama 84, 181, 191–3
    of vocabulary 30, 77, 151, 153–5
    without understanding 205
mentor, teacher as 74–6

'Messenger', *see* games
metalanguage 153–8
Mille Noctes Database, *see* social media
Minecraft, *see* technology
mini-whiteboards 63
mnemonics 58
Modern Foreign Languages xi, 1–4, 10, 56, 67–8, 104, 114, 119, 121, 156
monitor hypothesis 75, 135
    see also Krashen
More, Thomas (philosopher) 10, 116, 129, 179
Morphology 33, 42, 136, 142, 144–9, 175, 195, 200, 205–6, 209
Mosselanus (scholar) 131
Motherese ('baby language') 204
motivation 9, 11, 15, 55, 57–8, 60, 67, 106, 115–18, 120, 139
Muretus, Marcus Antonius (scholar) 10, 131
mythocosm 48
mythology 53, 82, 136, 169, 197–8, 208

native competence in language 2, 23, 26, 67, 152, 155, 208
neo-Latin 59, 91–9, 112, 129–32, 184
New Testament, *see* The Bible
Newton, Isaac (scholar) 129, 190
nursery rhymes 147, 185
    see also singing

Old Testament, *see* The Bible
online teaching and learning 42, 47–53, 85, 103, 127, 132–3, 140, 156, 163, 167, 173, 177–9, 190, 195–200
    see also technology
Ørberg, Hans (academic) 27–8, 60, 68–79, 83–4, 87–9, 113, 162–6, 168, 180, 183
Orff, Carl (composer) 93
Orwell, George (author) 131
Ovid (Roman author) 111, 131, 168, 181, 191
Oxford Latinitas Project (OLP) 114, 118, 179–82
Ożóg, Jan (priest) 163

paraphrase 12, 127, 131, 148–9, 157–8, 171, 177
parsing 19, 21, 48, 151, 156, 173–4
Pascoli, Giovanni (poet) 190
Petrarch (scholar) 129, 181
Petronius (Roman author) 197
Phaedrus (Roman author) 112, 134
Philostratus (Greek author) 134
phonological loop 153–4
pictures, use of 13, 15, 27, 30, 40–1, 43–4, 49–60, 63, 78, 84, 94–5, 108, 138, 153, 157, 166–70, 173, 180, 204
Platina, Bartolomeo (scholar) 183–4
Plato (Greek author) 131, 134, 138
Plautus (Roman author) 27–8, 30–1, 105, 193
Plutarch (Greek author) 134
Polis, *see* publications

Index

Polis Institute 114, 140, 141–9
Polish Philosophical Society, The 172
Pope, Alexander (poet) 151, 159, 184
pop-up grammar, *see* grammar
Posselius, Johannes (scholar) 11–15
pronunciation
    as aid to understanding 21
    choice 25, 119, 134–5, 171, 209
    modelling 84, 148, 176, 204
Propertius (Roman author) 131
props, use of 28, 85, 87, 143, 147
publications
    A Primer of Ecclesiastical Latin 114
    ad Alpes 198
    Alexandros 171, 175
    Asterix 208
    Athenaze 171, 175
    Cambridge Latin Course 29, 51, 54, 61, 68, 71
    Cattus Petasatus 208
    Colloquia Personarum 68
    Conversational Latin for Oral Proficiency 102
    Curious George 22
    Dialogos 171, 175
    Ecce Romani 19, 21, 51, 118
    Eptiome Historiae Sacrae 68
    Familia Romana 27–30, 60, 68–74, 83–8, 113, 162–5, 180–3
    Homo Romanus 173
    Jenney Latin Programme 12
    Latin Course for Schools 81
    Latin to GCSE 28
    Latin for Local History 114
    Polis 114, 171–5
    pugio Bruti 198–202
    Reading Latin 82
    Reading Medieval Latin 114
    Roma Aeterna 28
    Wheelock's Latin 12, 82
pugio Bruti, *see* publications

questions
    asking 36–8
    designing 35–6
Quintilian (Roman author) 104, 203

reading
    extensive 48, 113, 116, 118, 121, 196
    intensive 48
    post-reading activities 149
    pre-reading activities 121, 147–8
    reading-comprehension method 41, 47–8, 51, 55, 59–60, 75, 113, 128, 154, 164, 1902
    skill of 2, 9, 11–12, 14–15, 17, 21, 23, 29, 33, 35, 39–45, 47–54, 55–63, 67–71, 75–9, 80, 84–8, 91–100, 101–3, 106–11, 113–17, 125, 128, 130–1, 133, 137–9, 144, 147–9, 152–5, 157–9, 164–8, 173–5, 179–81, 183–5, 189, 192–4, 195–9, 202, 208–10

Reading Latin, *see* publications
Reading Medieval Latin, *see* publications
The Renaissance 10–12, 88, 114, 128, 174, 179, 181
role-play 15, 28–9, 48, 53, 56, 62, 85–7, 115, 157, 168–9, 177, 193
Roma Aeterna, *see* publications
Rouse, W. H. D. (educationalist) 1, 26, 57, 116, 121, 133, 162, 184

Sallust (Roman author) 198
scaffolding, use of 27, 42, 56, 65, 70, 74–80, 137
schools
    names of
        Brookfield Academy 18
        Eton College 26
        Harrow School 26
        King Edward VI Grammar School 25
        Magdalen College School, Oxford 117
        The Perse School 184
    types of
        elementary 9
        grammar 25, 56
        high 9, 13, 51, 139, 161–3, 165, 171, 172–4, 196, 200, 202
        middle school 9, 52, 196
Schottenius (scholar) 131
seminary, teaching in 13, 151, 154–9, 163
Seneca (Roman author) 102, 182, 184, 192
Shakespeare, William (playwright) 25, 27
singing 26, 84, 84, 168, 181, 191
    see also nursery rhymes
slaves and slavery 10, 27, 28, 92, 117, 165
smartphone, *see* technology
social media
    Daily Dose of Latin 119
    Facebook 57, 58, 59
    memes 51
    Mille Noctes Database 42
    Twitter 118–19
    YouTube 94, 165–6, 168, 196
Society for Classical Studies, The 16
Star Trek 131
STEM (Science, Technology, Engineering and Maths) 55
Stevens, William (scholar) 113
story-listening 40
subvocalization 154
Suetonius (Greek author) 105, 192, 198
Swain, Meryl (academic) 135–6
Swift, Johnathan (poet) 131, 184
synonyms 30, 60, 63, 85, 86, 127, 131, 148–9, 191
    see also antonyms

'Taboo', *see* games
Tacitus (Roman author) 131
Task-based Language Learning (TBLT) 138–40
Teaching Proficiency through Reading and Storytelling (TPRS) 170

228

technology, using
    Minecraft 27, 166
    smartphone 85, 197
Terence (Roman author) 197
textbooks, *see* publications
Tibullus (Roman author) 131
Tiresias (mythical character) 53
tone of voice 22, 62
Total Physical Response (TPR) 143, 144, 170, 189
transcripts 41, 57, 70–6, 78–9, 198
translation
    as assessment 56, 58–9, 83, 88
    'fifth skill' of 91
    from Latin or Greek 2, 9, 1, 15, 18, 22, 33, 48, 59, 60, 103, 105, 107, 119, 153–9, 163–4, 173–6, 186, 191, 195–6
    into Latin 12, 43, 48, 51–2, 81, 83, 189–90
    understanding without 21, 27–8, 30, 88, 94, 97, 102, 111, 120, 125, 127, 130, 141, 147–8, 152, 168, 179, 184
Tres Columnae Project 48, 52–3
Tunberg, Terence (academic) 68, 113, 119, 129, 133, 140, 208
'Twenty Questions', *see* games
Twitter, *see* social media
Tyrtarion (music group) 168

University
    Adam Mickiewicz University 164
    Cambridge xi, 4, 183–6
    Cornell 101–2, 104–6
    Edinburgh xi
    Jagiellonian University 164
    Kentucky 128–33
    King's College London xi, xii, 67
    Leeds xii
    Leicester xi, xii, 113
    Manchester 187
    Notre Dame 102
    Open xi
    Oxford 4, 25, 27, 113, 120, 179–86
    Sussex xii
    University College Cork 185
    Warwick 81–3, 87–9
    Wrocław 162–3

Valerius Maximus (Roman author) 131
Valla, Lorenzo (scholar) 131
Vatican, The 13, 190
Virgil (Roman author) 29, 103–5, 107–9, 191, 197
Vives, Juan Luis (philosopher) 131
vocabulary
    acquisition of 21, 28, 30, 40, 69–73, 75–8, 82–8, 117, 144, 166, 168, 174, 176, 180, 182, 192, 197, 204, 209
    for conversation 138, 147, 169
    flashcards 19, 21
    games 127
    general 9, 21, 27, 30, 42, 43, 51, 59, 60, 61, 63, 69–73, 93, 103, 104–5, 108, 127, 136–7
    learning 11, 29, 30, 48, 61, 75–6, 84, 86, 87–9, 93, 97, 99, 102, 109–10, 146, 151, 173–4, 176, 190, 198
    lists 18, 29, 33, 35, 40, 49, 59, 68, 82–6, 117, 144, 151, 185, 198–9
    repetition 39, 59, 61, 93–4, 144
    testing 30, 151, 153
    for writing 134

Waterhouse, John William (artist) 136–8
Waugh, Evelyn (author) 26
Weltwissen 143
Wheelock's Latin, *see* publications
writing
    dictation 120, 127
    essays in English 58
    in imitation of ancient authors 179
    letters 200–2
    poetry 171
    rewriting 130–1
    skill of 2, 9, 11–12, 14–15, 20, 29, 35, 42, 47–9, 91, 115, 130, 154, 174
    stories in Latin 44–5, 51–4, 91–4, 97–100, 109–10, 149, 183–5, 208–9

Xenophon (Greek author) 134

YouTube, *see* social media

Zamyati, Yevgeny (author) 131
Zone of Proximal Development (ZPD) 76